Analysis and Ev
2007–2008

The Chartered
Institute of Marketing

Analysis and Evaluation
2007–2008

Wendy Lomax and Adam Raman

ELSEVIER

AMSTERDAM • BOSTON • HEIDELBERG • LONDON • NEW YORK • OXFORD
PARIS • SAN DIEGO • SAN FRANCISCO • SINGAPORE • SYDNEY • TOKYO

Butterworth-Heinemann is an imprint of Elsevier

Butterworth-Heinemann is an imprint of Elsevier
Linacre House, Jordan Hill, Oxford OX2 8DP, UK
30 Corporate Drive, Suite 400, Burlington, MA 01803, USA

First edition 2007

British Library Cataloguing in Publication Data
A catalogue record for this book is available from the British Library

Library of Congress Cataloging-in-Publication Data
A catalogue record for this book is available from the Library of Congress

ISBN: 978-0-7506-8501-6

For information on all Butterworth-Heinemann publications
visit our website at http://books.elsevier.com

Printed and bound in Italy

07 08 09 10 11   10 9 8 7 6 5 4 3 2 1

Working together to grow
libraries in developing countries

www.elsevier.com | www.bookaid.org | www.sabre.org

ELSEVIER   BOOK AID International   Sabre Foundation

Contents

Preface	**Welcome to the CIM coursebooks**	**vii**
Unit 1	**Introduction to analysis and evaluation**	**1**
	Introduction	3
	Statements of related marketing practice	6
	Introduction	8
	Marketing philosophy	12
	Market orientation	12
	Marketing stakeholders	19
	Marketing and value	20
	The role of marketing in corporate strategy	20
	The role of A&E in marketing planning	21
	The strategic market management process	23
Unit 2	**Evaluating performance: marketing metrics**	**38**
	How will this unit help you and how does it fit within the A&E course structure?	39
	Statements of related marketing practice	41
	Introduction	42
	The balanced scorecard	51
Unit 3	**Brand valuation**	**58**
	How will this unit help you and what can you expect to achieve after completing this unit?	60
	Statements of related marketing practice	62
	Introduction	62
	Brands as assets	63
	Branding exercise	71
Unit 4	**Auditing marketing activities**	**75**
	How will this unit help you and what can you expect to achieve after completing this unit?	76
	Marketing audits and market research	77
	Statements of related marketing practice	77
	Historical perspective of marketing audits	78
	Audit of marketing activities	78
	Further considerations for developing a distribution audit	97
	Other important audits	98
Unit 5	**Evaluating performance: financial measures**	**103**
	Statements of related marketing practice	105
	How will this unit help you and what can you expect to achieve after completing this unit?	105
	Introduction	110
	Financial statements	111

Management accounts		114
Shareholder value analysis		121
Economic value added		122
Outsourcing		124

Unit 6 — Analysing the external environment — **131**
Statements of related marketing practice — 133
How will this unit help you and what can you expect to achieve after completing this unit? — 134
Introduction — 135
Environmental monitoring — 135
The macro- and micro-environments — 137
Porter's five forces — 152

Unit 7 — Analysing the internal environment — **157**
Statements of related marketing practice — 159
How will this unit help you and what can you expect to achieve after completing this unit? — 159
Resource-based view of the firm — 161
Models to assess attractiveness of products and markets — 161
Portfolio analysis models — 161
Value chain analysis — 172
The innovation audit — 173

Unit 8 — Characteristics of the global marketplace — **178**
Statements of related marketing practice — 179
Introduction — 179
International market intelligence gathering — 181
Assessing the attractiveness of markets — 188
The International marketing intelligence system — 189
Market entry methods — 192
Culture — 195
Role of IT — 196

Unit 9 — Defining competitive advantage — **201**
What is competitive advantage? — 202
How to use generic strategies — 209

Appendices
1 Guidance on examination preparation — 218
2 Answers and debriefings — 230
3 Past examination papers and examiners' reports — 240
4 Curriculum information and reading list — 260

Index — **267**

Preface

welcome to the CIM coursebooks

A message from the authors

This coursebook is designed to meet the needs of students studying for the Chartered Institute of Marketing's Analysis and Evaluation examination. The structure of the coursebook mirrors the Analysis and Evaluation syllabus and reflects the relative weighting given to each subject. The Analysis and Evaluation module acts as a foundation on which the other Postgraduate Professional Diploma subjects are based. This module builds on the operational aspects that have already been covered at Professional Diploma and Professional Certificate level. However, this module is designed to look at the strategic implications of the analysis and to evaluate them, rather than merely cover the mechanics of the process.

The module is designed to be valuable to those who plan or aspire to work at a strategic level in an organization.

The Analysis and Evaluation syllabus is one of the four modules which comprise the Professional Postgraduate Diploma in Marketing. It is strongly recommended that this module is taken first since the other three modules are built upon it. The four modules are:

1. *Analysis and Evaluation* – Covers the concepts, techniques and models involved in developing a detailed understanding of the market, customers and competitive environment internally and externally, the organization, its capabilities and assets, the opportunities available to it and its current performance.
2. *Strategic Marketing Decisions* – Covers the concepts, techniques and models involved in formulating a customer-focused competitive business or corporate strategy and developing a specific and differentiated competitive position. It includes investment decisions affecting marketing assets.
3. *Managing Marketing Performance* – Covers the implementation stage of the strategy. This encompasses managing marketing teams, managing change, implementing strategy through marketing activities and working with other departments, and using measurement as a basis for improvement.
4. *Strategic Marketing in Practice* – Provides the opportunity to explore strategic marketing in a practical setting. It also incorporates the latest trends and innovations in marketing.

This module has been developed to provide the knowledge and skills for analysis and evaluation of performance required by strategic marketers. It is designed to prepare you for practice at a strategic marketing level. Assuming you have appropriate experience, you should be able to apply the knowledge that you have learned immediately within your organization and add value quickly to yourself and your employer.

The coursebook reflects the syllabus and the relative weighting of the different elements:

Element 1: Strategic management and the role of marketing (10 per cent)

- ○ The role of marketing within different organizations
- ○ Degrees of market orientation
- ○ How marketing creates value customers, shareholders and other stakeholders
- ○ Criteria for success.

Element 2: Evaluation of business performance (30 per cent)

- ○ Processes and techniques used to evaluate past and current performance to allow informed decisions about future activity
- ○ Financial and marketing measures of performance, including evaluation of brand equity.

Element 3: Analysis of the internal environment (20 per cent)

- ○ Objective analysis of an organization's internal capabilities and environment
- ○ Identification of core competencies
- ○ Frameworks for evaluation such as value chain and portfolio analysis.

Element 4: Analysis of the external environment (20 per cent)

- ○ Objective analysis of the organization's position in the external environment
- ○ Analysis of micro and macro environments using PEST or similar and Five Forces
- ○ Synthesis of results from internal and external analyses to give objective summary of competitive position and performance.

Element 5: Characteristics of the global marketplace (20 per cent)

- ○ Differences in foreign markets
- ○ Entry evaluation and modes of entry
- ○ Role of the Internet.

At the end of each unit there is Further study. Try not to be overwhelmed by this and pace yourself. It is important that you do some additional reading as this text is designed to complement additional texts rather than replace them.

We, as examiners, are always looking for breadth of knowledge as well as depth. We need to see that you have the ability to apply the concepts, techniques and frameworks to practical situations. It is a good idea to develop a portfolio of examples which you can use to illustrate your answers. Make sure that you read the business press and the marketing trade magazines so that you can build a portfolio of examples to impress the examiners with your ability to apply what you have learned.

The authors would like to thank all the copyright holders who have given permission for their work to be reproduced here. Particular thanks are due to Kingdom Business School and the Chartered Institute of Marketing for their generous waiving of copyright. Every attempt has been made to contact the owners of copyright but should any omission have occurred please contact us to resolve the matter.

An introduction from the academic development advisor

The authoring team, Elsevier Butterworth-Heinemann and Lomax, and Raman have all aimed to rigorously revise and update the coursebook series to make sure that every title is the best possible study aid and accurately reflects the latest CIM syllabus. This has been further enhanced through independent reviews carried out by CIM.

We have aimed to develop the assessment support to include some additional support for the assignment route as well as the examination, so we hope you will find this helpful.

The authors and indeed senior examiners in the series have been commissioned for their CIM course teaching and examining experience, as well as their research into specific curriculum-related areas and their wide general knowledge of the latest thinking in marketing.

We are certain that you will find these coursebooks highly beneficial in terms of the content and assessment opportunities and a study tool that will prepare you for both CIM examinations and continuous/integrative assessment opportunities. They will guide you in a logical and structured way through the detail of the syllabus, providing you with the required underpinning knowledge, understanding and application of theory.

The editorial team and authors wish you every success as you embark upon your studies.

Karen Beamish

Academic Development Advisor

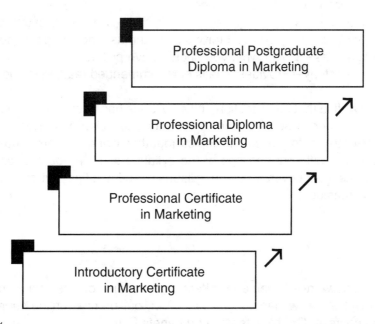

Study note © 2006

How to use these coursebooks

Everyone who has contributed to this series has been careful to structure the books with the exams in mind. Each unit, therefore, covers an essential part of the syllabus. You need to work through the complete coursebook systematically to ensure that you have covered everything you need to know.

This coursebook is divided into units each containing a selection of the following standard elements:

- o *Learning objectives* – Tell you what you will be expected to know, having read the unit.
- o *Syllabus references* – Outline what part of the syllabus is covered in the module.
- o *Study guides* – Tell you how long the unit is and how long its activities take to do.
- o *Questions* – Are designed to give you practice – they will be similar to those you get in the exam.
- o *Answers* – (at the end of the book) Give you a suggested format for answering exam questions. *Remember* there is no such thing as a model answer – you should use these examples only as guidelines.
- o *Activities* – Give you a chance to put what you have learned into practice.
- o *Debriefings* – (at the end of the book) Shed light on the methodologies involved in the activities.
- o *Hints and tips* – Are tips from the senior examiner, examiner or author and are designed to help you avoid common mistakes made by previous candidates and give you guidance on improving your knowledge base.
- o *Insights* – Encourage you to contextualize your academic knowledge by providing reference to real-life experience.
- o *Key definitions* – Highlight and explain the key points relevant to that module.
- o *Definitions* – May be used for words you must know to pass the exam.
- o *Summaries* – Cover what you should have picked up from reading the unit.
- o *Further study* – Provides details of recommended reading in addition to the coursebook.

While you will find that each section of the syllabus has been covered within this text, you might find that the order of some of the topics has been changed. This is because it sometimes makes more sense to put certain topics together when you are studying, even though they might appear in different sections of the syllabus itself. If you are following the reading and other activities, your coverage of the syllabus will be just fine, but do not forget to follow up with trade press reading!

About MarketingOnline

Elsevier Butterworth-Heinemann offers purchasers of the coursebooks free access to MarketingOnline (www.marketingonline.co.uk), our premier online support engine for the CIM marketing courses. On this site you can benefit from:

- o Fully customizable electronic versions of the coursebooks enabling you to annotate, cut and paste sections of text to create your own tailored learning notes.
- o The capacity to search the coursebook online for instant access to definitions and key concepts.
- o Useful links to e-marketing articles, provided by Dave Chaffey, director of Marketing Insights Ltd and a leading UK e-marketing consultant, trainer and author.
- o A glossary providing a comprehensive dictionary of marketing terms.
- o A Frequently Asked Questions (FAQs) section providing guidance and advice on common problems or queries.

Using MarketingOnline

Logging on

Before you can access MaketingOnline you will first need to get a password. Please go to www.marketingonline.co.uk and click on the registration button where you will then find registration instructions for coursebook purchasers. Once you have got your password, you will need to log on using the onscreen instructions. This will give you access to the various functions of the site.

If you have specific queries about using MarketingOnline then you should consult our fully searchable FAQs section, accessible through the appropriate link in the top right-hand corner of any page of the site. Please also note that a *full user guide* can be downloaded by clicking on the link on the opening page of the website.

unit 1
introduction to analysis and evaluation

Learning objectives

The Analysis and Evaluation (A&E) module of the Professional Postgraduate Diploma covers the foundations of strategic marketing within a global context. It will provide you with the knowledge and skills required to undertake strategic analysis and will enable you to evaluate an organization's (probably your own) current situation. Once you can do this effectively you are in a strong position to make sound strategic marketing decisions. Understanding this unit will form the foundation for the Strategic Marketing Decisions module. Those decisions allow you to create stakeholder value and give strategic insights into the organization, its customers and the challenges it faces. In this unit you will:

- ○ Appreciate the role of marketing in adding value to an organization, whether that organization is driven by profit or not-for-profit motives (see syllabus 1.1, 1.2)

- ○ Understand the importance of market orientation in determining the success of an organization (see syllabus 1.3, 1.4)

- ○ Understand the range of tasks involved in undertaking rigorous evaluation and analysis

- ○ Review the strategic process and understand the importance of A&E within it

- ○ Understand the motivation behind the Professional Postgraduate Diploma Analysis and Evaluation syllabus

- ○ Gain an overview of the main approaches to situational A&E

- ○ Appreciate the role of marketing within the strategic planning process (see syllabus 1.5).

Once you have completed this unit you will be able to:

- ○ Appreciate the role of different stakeholders in the success of an organization

- ○ Develop a broad definition of value which includes all stakeholder groups

- ○ Understand the importance of developing rigorous marketing metrics to allow for hard-edged marketing.

Sections of the syllabus being covered in this unit:

Element 1: Strategic management and the role of marketing (10 per cent).

1.1 Demonstrate an understanding of the role of marketing in creating exceptional value for customers and shareholders.

1.2 Demonstrate an understanding of the role of marketing in organizations that are driven by performance measures other than shareholder value, for example not-for-profit organizations.

1.3 Critically evaluate the characteristics of the marketing models and criteria for success used in organizations with a strong market orientation.

1.4 Critically evaluate the characteristics of marketing models used by, and the challenges facing marketing in, organizations with a weak market orientation.

1.5 Give examples of the strategic planning process used in organizations and evaluate marketing's role within it.

Exam Hint 1.1

In terms of the Analysis and Evaluation examination you need to gain a good understanding of the expectation of the examiners at an early stage. The majority of the marks are not given for remembering and reciting theory; at this level you are expected to apply the theory directly to the question in hand and through application one can clearly see whether or not you have understood the concepts.

Exam Hint 1.2: Marketing contexts

Students need to appreciate the different industry types that they will be expected to apply strategic marketing techniques. The following extract is from the Syllabus-Professional PG Diploma Issue 2 Page 4 © The Chartered Institute of Marketing March 2004 (students ought to familarize themselves with this syllabus which is available on the CIM website):

Organizations operating in a variety of contexts use different marketing activities. There is no 'one size fits all' approach. Organizations and their marketers have to select and use techniques appropriate to their specific context. The typical context characteristics in marketing are summarized as below.

Key definitions

Fast-Moving Consumer Goods (FMCG) – Used in organizations with a strong market orientation, the 'Standard' model of marketing is based on identification of customers' needs and techniques of segmentation, targeting and positioning supported by branding and customer communications.

B2B – The model of marketing adopted depends on factors such as the importance of face-to-face selling, the dominant orientation and power of buyers. Markets are often less information-rich than FMCG markets, which constrains marketing decisions.

Capital projects – A variant of the B2B model where opportunities for positioning are few and the value of any single order constitutes a significant proportion of turnover in a period.

Not-for-profit – The organization is not driven by shareholder value and competition may not be a significant factor in strategy.

Small businesses can operate in any of the above sectors, SMEs are characterized by their limited marketing resources and the limited use of marketing techniques. Not-for-profit organizations are driven not by shareholders but by other stakeholders, such as government (public sector), beneficiaries (charities) and volunteers (voluntary sector). The concept of shareholder value may not be relevant in these organizations where instead concepts such as 'best value' (public sector) and the level of disbursements to beneficiaries operate. The element of competition may not be explicit in the strategy of these organizations, whose strategies may be more collaborative. Such organizations may use a narrower and more tactical repertoire of marketing techniques than larger commercial organizations with a strong market orientation and driven by shareholder value. This syllabus does not define specific recipes or sets of techniques for each context. Instead students will be required to explore the application of marketing in a range of different contexts.

You ought to expect that questions set within the exams could relate to companies in any one of the above-mentioned marketing contexts and students should familiarize themselves with the strategic issues relating to the different environments through wider reading and application in classroom or wherever they have the opportunity.

Introduction

It is important for you to appreciate that the A&E unit is fully integrated with the other units of the Professional Postgraduate Diploma in Marketing (PPDIPM) course units, namely Strategic Marketing Decisions (SMD), Managing Marketing Performance (MMP) and Strategic Marketing in Practice (SMiP). It is important to have this holistic outlook which means you ought to appreciate where each unit fits with respect to each other, even before studying them in detail, as it will improve your performance in the exam because you will have a better understanding of the relevance that each unit will help potential senior managers like you in formulating effective marketing strategies that satisfy a whole range of stakeholders which in turn will increase long-term shareholder value for the owners of an organization.

As this is the unit of the new PPDIPM, an attempt will be made to show you the main objective of the overall course and to give you a perspective of how the different units interact with each other.

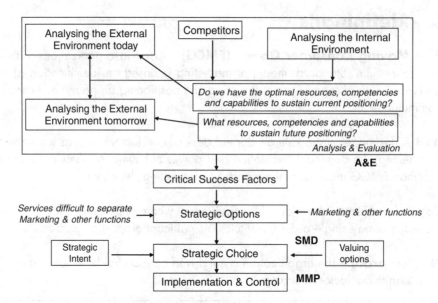

Figure 1.1 Formulating Strategy – Remember what we are trying to achieve?

Referring to Figure 1.1, one can appreciate that the whole purpose of the course is to be able to get you to handle commercial situations and to formulate and select an appropriate range of strategic options that can be effectively and realistically implemented over an approved time frame. This means whenever you are exposed to a commercial/marketing problem, whether it is in real life or within the safe confines of a case study, you will be expected to make decisions. The main issue is what decisions are open to you and which ones would be the most appropriate for all stakeholders concerned; this is the remit of the SMD course. It would be silly to make decisions on the best likely course without considering whether it can be implemented, which means that you should think ahead before choosing your optimal strategy in order to check whether you have the right people with the right skill set as well as competencies and capabilities such as appropriate organizational culture, processes and management styles as well as having the ability to raise adequate finances (a good reason for why you should be able to interpret financial statements). These capabilities are represented in the 7S Framework developed by Peters and Waterman (Figure 1.2) and could be used to develop an audit to identify the necessary resources and capabilities required to implement a differential competitive strategy.

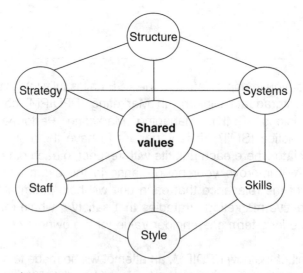

Figure 1.2 The 7S Framework
Source: Peters and Waterman (1982) and Pascale and Athos (1982)

Having an implementation plan in place and deciding on how to best manage it is the purpose of the MMP course.

Exam Hint 1.3

In conclusion whenever you face an Analysis and Evaluation question in the exams you should ask yourself what decisions are likely to be warranted by the issues raised in the question followed by what tools and frameworks are required to identify the issues as possible measures and scales required to define their importance. You also need an appreciation at this stage of some of the analytical tools and frameworks required to evaluate implementation issues. Basically, the Analysis and Evaluation part of the syllabus provides the theoretical basis for the other units which will enable senior managers to make and successfully implement strategic marketing decisions.

 ## Activity 1.1

Please read the short scenario and attempt to answer the question at the end.

A major pharmaceutical company was developing an innovative drug to treat cancer. The drug was originally discovered from research undertaken by a smaller biotechnology company and was licensed in by the bigger company who did not have a history of competing in the international cancer markets and did not have a cancer portfolio. Having gone through a merger with another pharmaceutical company who did possess a large innovative cancer treatment pipeline, the country's equivalent of the 'Competition Commission' decided that the new company would stifle competition in the world cancer markets and recommended that the new drug be divested. The drug was returned to its original discoverer. The drug was later out-licensed to another major company who did possess a large cancer portfolio of older treatments.

Question 1.1

What are the major strategic marketing issues facing each of the companies relating to their resources and capabilities in relation to the innovative cancer treatment?

Now you may be asking yourself why we are considering A&E as the penultimate course unit and it is being taught as the first unit. This would be a good question for you to ask and it is the first example of critical evaluation – a very important skill to possess for passing all units in the new PPDIPM. Critical evaluation will be sought after by all the examiners reading your exam scripts, so it is a good idea for you to get into the habit of practising this skill regularly. You should appreciate the need that marketers have to formulate strategic options and develop plans but you should also appreciate their need to distinguish between appropriate and inappropriate options.

So how would you or any marketer know which strategies are potentially available let alone formulating and evaluating implementation initiatives? Well, I suppose you could utilize guess-work or use your gut feeling which would amount to nothing more than gambling, or alternatively you could consult the astrology charts. In reality it would be wiser to use a selection of tools and knowledge techniques (theory) derived from either researching actual practice or representing the preferred captured wisdom of the experts of the day to assist you to frame the marketing/commercial issues and to identify potential opportunities open to the organization. This is the whole purpose of the first unit and it provides you with the basis for critically evaluating the different tools and processes available to senior executives which would help them to identify the relevant issues and discard irrelevant ones as well as help them identify potential opportunities and threats which would lead to more appropriate less risky decisions being made.

Statements of related marketing practice

The Chartered Institute of Marketing have developed statements of related marketing practice (CIM Documentation) which clearly specify the key skill areas or business competencies that a marketing executive needs to develop and highlight the specific units and sections of the syllabus that are intended to assist the student to develop these skills.

It is very important for you as a student to be aware of the skill areas expected to be developed within the course units as well as being familiar with the syllabus of each course unit as these are the areas that examiners will expect you to demonstrate within the examinations. Therefore, when answering any assignment it would be wise to ensure that your answers have met the learning objectives of the syllabus as well as demonstrating the relevant marketing skill set.

The following are the main skill or business competency areas which are being developed in this section:

- To develop appropriate structures and frameworks to identify appropriate information requirements to define and structure marketing-related business problems.
- To be able to critically evaluate different analytical perspectives which will lead executives to gain a better understanding of their external and internal environment within the specific context of their industries, thus setting and placing them in a better position to make better informed decisions potentially leading to minimize risks and uncertainty.

Exam Hint 1.4

Key skills for marketers – why are they needed? (Extract from the Syllabus – Professional PG Diploma In Marketing p. 13)

There is only so much that a syllabus can include. The syllabus itself is designed to cover the knowledge and skills highlighted by research as core to professional marketers in organizations. However, marketing is performed in an organizational context so there are other broader business and organizational skills that marketing professionals should also possess. The 'key skills for marketers' are therefore an essential part of armoury of the 'complete marketer' in today's organizations.

What are they?

'Key skills' are areas of knowledge and competency common to business professionals. They fall outside the CIM's syllabus, providing underpinning knowledge and skills. As such they will be treated as systemic to all marketing activities, rather than subjects treated independently in their turn. A single key skill is applicable at this level: 'Personal skills development.' This consists of communication, problem solving and working with others.

How do they relate to the syllabus?

Key skills relate to the stages of the syllabus as follows:

- Level 3 key skills. The Professional Certificate syllabus
- Level 4 key skills. The Professional Diploma syllabus
- Level 5 key skills. The Professional PG Diploma syllabus

The relevance of the key skills to each unit of the syllabus is illustrated in the table below. Study centres will be encouraged to incorporate these key skills in their programmes.

Key Skill unit: Personal skills development	Analysis & Evaluation	Strategic Marketing Decisions	Managing Marketing Performance	Strategic Marketing in Practice
Communication				
Interpret and evaluate information	✓	✓		✓
Synthesise and structure information	✓	✓		✓
Present information	✓	✓		✓
Problem solving				
Select and use strategies to solve problems		✓		✓
Establish what is needed to get results		✓		✓
Monitor progress		✓	✓	✓
Working with others				
Gain commitment			✓	✓
Brief others			✓	✓
Lead implementation			✓	✓

It is important for students to bear in mind that in answering the exam they need to demonstrate the relevant marketing skills required of the course unit.

Key definitions

Market orientation – is the sum of the specific activities which translate the philosophy of marketing into reality.

Customer orientation – involves understanding customers well enough to create superior value for them continuously.

Competitor orientation – is the awareness of the capabilities of competitors.

Interfunctional co-ordination – involves the company using all its resources and departments to create value for its target customers.

Study guide

This coursebook is critical to an overall understanding of the A&E process. This process forms the foundations for the strategic marketing process. And as any builder will tell you, unless you have the foundations right, the building is doomed.

As you work through this unit remember that:

1. Time spent on analysis is not wasted but the benefits may not always be immediately obvious.
2. There is always a temptation to rush into action without considering the implications of those actions. Action is only the tip of the iceberg, what is underneath (i.e. the analysis) is far more impressive.
3. You cannot decide where you are going until you know where you are now and how you got there.
4. Fools rush in where angels fear to tread. You will be an angel at the end of this unit!

Introduction

The A&E unit of the Professional Postgraduate Diploma on Marketing covers the first part of strategic marketing in a global context. It is important to distinguish between analysis and evaluation; the title of this unit was very carefully chosen. Analysis represents a structure and method for gaining information relating to external markets and internal assets. Evaluation is the study of options in the light of company capabilities and attitude to risk. This unit has three concise objectives:

1. To provide you with the knowledge and skills required to undertake strategic A&E of the organization's current position as a foundation to formulating marketing strategy.
2. To allow you to develop strategic insights into the company and the problems and opportunities it faces.
3. To provide you with the foundation on which to make sound strategic marketing decisions.

The Professional Postgraduate Diploma is targeted at aspiring marketers – those who are already in a senior marketing position and want to consolidate their knowledge to move onto the next stage, or those who want to be promoted to a senior marketing position.

This unit has been developed to allow you to:

- Explain the concept of business orientation and critically appraise the different orientations in management and planning and the roles of marketing used by organizations.
- Identify the business intelligence required to inform the organization's strategy-making activities in domestic and international markets.
- Assess the impact of the major trends in the strategic and global context on the strategy-making process.
- Conduct and synthesize a detailed strategic audit of the organization's internal and external environment, including an evaluation of business performance, using appropriate tools and models and analysis of numerical data and management information to support decisions on key strategic issues.
- Appraise the nature of culture within organizations and the importance of its fit with strategy and operations across different cultures.
- Synthesize a coherent and concise assessment of the situation facing an organization, and develop alternative scenarios.

These learning outcomes in the list above are very important. They are the outcomes against which the examiners will be assessing you in the examination!

On completion of this unit you should be able to define marketing intelligence requirements and lead the intelligence-gathering process within an organization. You will also benefit from having a detailed understanding of the organization and its environment.

This will be achieved by working through the main models, frameworks and techniques used in strategic analysis, both marketing and financial. It examines the internal and external environments to allow for effective evaluation of strategic alternatives.

At the same time the contents of this module have been designed to complement the other three Professional Postgraduate Diploma papers of SMD, MMP and SMiP and to build on the materials from the Professional Certificate and Professional Diploma (Table 1.1).

Table 1.1 Chartered Institute of Marketing Syllabus

	Entry modules	Research & Analysis	Planning	Implementation	Management of Marketing
Professional Postgraduate Diploma	Entry module – Stage 3	Analysis & Evaluation	Strategic Marketing Decisions	Managing Marketing Performance	Strategic Marketing in Practice
Professional Diploma	Entry module – Stage 2	Marketing Research & Information	Marketing Planning	Marketing Communications	Marketing Management in Practice
Professional Certificate		Marketing Environment	Marketing Fundamentals	Customer Communications	Marketing in Practice
Introductory Certificate	Supporting marketing processes (Research & Analysis, Planning & Implementation)				

Source: Chartered Institute of Marketing

This coursebook has been designed to provide you with a clear insight into analytical and evaluation processes and the ways in which these can be applied to the commercial world as well as, of course, to the CIM Professional Postgraduate Diploma examination paper.

In each of these units, relevant concepts are outlined and discussed to help increase your knowledge and understanding. Then exercises are given which help you to apply your newly found understanding. This should allow you to:

○ Make the right decisions faster
○ Focus resources and creativity effectively
○ Identify ways to create value for all stakeholders
○ Be able to make a convincing business case to senior and board level managers.

The syllabus for this unit is divided into five elements (Figure 1.3). Each of these has a weighting attached. You will not be assessed on all of these. As we have already said, your assessment will be on whether or not you have achieved the learning outcomes. The weightings are there only to give you an idea of the importance that should be placed on each subject and to give you an indication of the proportion of your time to spend on each.

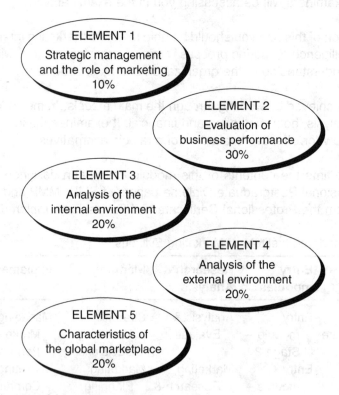

Figure 1.3 The five elements of the A&E unit

Although this coursebook is designed to give you a good grounding in the A&E unit, you may find it helpful to refer to other books to supplement and consolidate your knowledge.

The texts you may find useful are:

○ *Marketing Strategy and Competitive Positioning*, G.J. Hooley, J.A. Saunders and N.F. Piercy, 2nd edition, Prentice-Hall, 1998.
○ *Value Based Marketing: Marketing Strategies for Corporate Growth and Shareholder Value*, P. Doyle, Wiley, 2000.
○ *Global Marketing: Foreign Entry, Local Marketing and Global Management*, J.K. Johansson and Irwin, McGraw-Hill, 2000.

If you want to read further, the following texts may help:

- o *Marketing Management and Strategy*, P. Doyle, 3rd edition, Pearson Education.
- o *Strategic Marketing Management*, C. Gilligan and R. Wilson, 3rd edition, Butterworth-Heinemann.

Other resources that you may wish to use are websites. Below is a summary of some of the most useful ones. However, such is the nature of the Internet that websites are constantly being added and deleted, so you may need to update this list. Websites are obviously an extremely valuable resource as they have the ability to be far more up to date than other resources and can provide you with contemporary relevant examples.

www.ipa.co.uk	Institute of Practitioners in Advertising
www.legislation.org.uk	Online guide to the Data Protection Act with access to a downloadable DPA guide to help companies comply
www.keynote.co.uk	Market research reports
www.verdict.co.uk	Retail research reports
www.mintel.com	Consumer market research
www.datamonitor.com	Global market research
www.ft.com	Online newspaper and archives
www.royalmail.co.uk	Direct marketing advice and information
www.statistics.gov.uk	Demographic information on the United Kingdom
www.new-marketing.org	Updates on new marketing issues
www.cbi.org.uk/innovation/ index.html	Information on innovation in UK industry
www.ipa.co.uk	Advertising and media trade body and professional institute
www.asa.org.uk	Advertising Standards Authority which administers the CAP code (www.cap.org.uk) which ensures that ads are legal, honest, decent and truthful
www.connectedinmarketing.com	E-marketing
www.wnim.com	Focus on new and innovative themes in marketing, with an emphasis on new technology
www.CreativeShowcase.net	Online creative site
www.AllAboutCookies.org	Information on data protection on the Internet
www.IABuk.net	UK trade association and think-tank for the commercial interactive industry
www.IABEurope.ws	As above but for other European countries
www.InteractiveJargonGuide.org	Guide to web jargon
www.marketing.haynet.com/ keynote/index.html	Access to research data
www.cim.co.uk	Chartered Institute of Marketing
www.shapetheagenda.com	Updates on contemporary marketing issues

Marketing philosophy

Markets are becoming increasingly competitive and dynamic. The main drive behind the marketing concept is the belief that organizations are more likely to succeed if they are focused on the customer. If organizations spend time understanding the customer's expectations and needs, the customers are more likely to want to buy from them than from competing organizations that have a lesser understanding. This is likely to be true regardless of the nature of the business. Charities, for example, benefit from understanding their donor base and what triggers people to make donations. Whether the organization exists for profit or not-for-profit reasons, the key to success comes from making the exchange process mutually beneficial, so that both participants walk away from the encounter feeling satisfied. When you buy a magazine and enjoy reading it, you feel as if you are getting value for money for its entertainment value and the publisher is also happy with the resulting profit. The benefits coming from the exchange can be even more intangible. If you give to a charity you feel rewarded; you feel that you are a better person, more benevolent and caring. The charity benefits from increased revenue, and you feel good about yourself.

Question 1.2

Think about the following transactions or exchanges. What are the benefits to the parties involved?

1. A grocery retailer
2. Local government
3. A management consultancy
4. A professional qualification.

Market orientation

Exam Hint 1.5

Knowing whether a company is market-orientated or not is possibly one of the most important concepts you will need to know as a strategic marketing executive and it will help you solve real strategic marketing problems as those you will come across in later units. If an organization is not marketing-orientated it does not have a marketing culture and therefore the senior marketing executive is likely to face considerable resistance getting the necessary 'buy-in' from other functional senior managers to adopt and implement the marketing strategy. The marketing executive will need to develop internal marketing communication strategies to effectuate the necessary change amongst other board members to adopt the relevant strategies (this is the scope of the third unit Managing Marketing Performance but the theoretical concept to define and evaluate marketing orientation is developed within the Analysis and Evaluation coursebook).

The important thing in marketing is to transfer this laudable aim of mutual benefit into reality. This is what we call market orientation, that is, the specific activities which an organization undertakes to achieve this objective.

There are a number of ways to define market orientation. Let us look at two of them here.

Two important studies were published in 1990 and offer different perspectives.

Kohli and Jaworski (1990) see market orientation as the generation and dissemination of, and responsiveness to, marketing intelligence throughout the organization. Specifically that:

o One or more departments are engaged in activities geared towards developing an understanding of customers' current and future needs and the factors affecting them
o This is shared across departments
o Departments act to meet select customer needs.

Narver and Slater (1990) approach the subject from a different perspective. They see organizational culture as the key. Market orientation emphasizes a culture which encourages behaviour that creates value for the customer, leading to superior performance for the business. They see five components of market orientation.

At the core is a focus on long-term profits. The business needs to be sustainable and have a strategic perspective rather than a tactical one. This should be supported by an organizational culture that encourages employees at every level to promote customer satisfaction. This should be underpinned by customer orientation, competitor orientation and inter-functional co-ordination.

Although it seems that a strong market orientation leads to superior performance and can increase employee commitment, there are barriers to achieving it.

The extent of an organization's marketing orientation is probably the most important question you could ask yourself, as any strategy involving a marketing solution that is likely to be adopted by other functional executives within the firm will be strongly determined by the type of business culture currently in place. This issue is exemplified in the following two mini cases.

Mini Case 1 – MAHATSA SWEETS

MAHATSA SWEETS is a small chocolate and sweet manufacturer and was formed in 1997 by a dessert chef in response to the several requests he had for his sweets from other restaurants. He decided there was sufficient demand to make sweets for other establishments and created MAHATSA SWEETS. The company was formed with three chefs and consisted of design, production and finance expertise. The company was now looking to maximize its production capacity and was looking to expand its activities and find new opportunities for its sweets. As part of a government initiative they recruited young marketing executives to help identify new market opportunities nationally and internationally.

Unfortunately, the marketing executives failed as the company had no appreciation of what marketing was all about and decided to stay product focused. Individual customer needs were not seen as important and the creations of the owner chef was seen as more important than trying to understand what customers really wanted. No investment in information systems were undertaken and were perceived as a waste of time. The owner's gut feeling was seen as the most important. Marketing in this organization was seen as a sales lead generator with purpose of pushing the company's standardized offering.

Mini Case 2 – BIG JAKE SOLICITORS

Adamski Romanov is a marketing consultant and was asked by a friend, a practising lawyer, to help a senior partner in the firm with advising him on marketing issues. This was a favour for a friend and Adamski agreed for the mere sum of a 'free lunch' to listen to the legal partner. Apparently the partner was appointed as the marketing partner in the lawyer's absence and was given the task of building the marketing practice for this large legal practice. He was completely clueless about marketing and wanted to know where to start. Having discussed the concepts of customer needs and satisfaction it transpired during the conversation that a lot of customers were confused and concerned about what they were being charged for. One idea being discussed over lunch was the opportunity that transparent billing systems could offer in differentiating the firm from other legal firms in the area. The partner was slightly amused at one point and when asked why, he replied that appreciating customer needs was a completely new philosophy for the firm and that any customer query about quality or costs usually resulted in the senior partners phoning the customers and reprimanding them for not being appreciative of the fact that it was their privilege for the firm to want to work on their case. What the partner wanted from marketing was to employ a part-time administrator who would develop mailings.

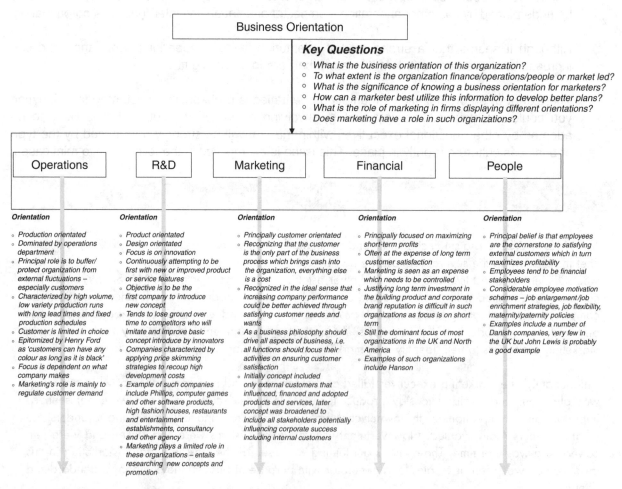

Figure 1.4

The different types of business cultures are represented in Figure 1.4 and should provide you with a framework to analyse and evaluate companies so as to help you decide the extent of the marketing orientation of any organization that you may come across. There are several possible types of business orientations, each one having evolved over different periods to suit the new forms of external environments as they changed over time.

Practising a marketing philosophy for many organizations was not an automatic process and many organizations even today have not selected marketing as the best form of business practice through choice; many organizations were forced to listen to their customers as the economic changes to their external environment, primarily after the Second World War, with several companies beginning to improve their cost structure through large-scale mass production which provided them with greater economies of scale. They also benefited through large-scale manufacturing from the positive effects of the experience/learning curves which were the strategic concepts of the day. Having created greater choice for customers through reducing supply issues, customers were now able to discriminate between companies. Organizations that were not taking customer needs into account were likely to significantly reduce their chances of surviving.

The extent to which organizations have embraced the marketing philosophy and applied it across several functions is varied. It is important for you to appreciate the interrelationship between marketing and the other business functions as well as appreciating that it is likely to involve considerable effort in the shape of change management communication programmes to instil a marketing orientation within many companies. This does not necessarily happen overnight and you will need to be appreciative of the intensive resources required to achieve it and include them within your marketing strategic plans.

Activity 1.2

Use the framework in Figure 1.5 to analyse and evaluate how customers are likely to be treated by different car suppliers adopting different business philosophies?

Discussion – the framework in Figure 1.4 should allow you to consider the possible customer insights of different suppliers who have different business outlooks.

A supplier focused on operations and R&D is likely to perceive the creation of their products as their pride and joy. Although they need to make money to survive, this is not their primary goal, it is designing and crafting cars. They often see themselves as doing the customer a favour. As Jeremy Clarkson, the famous car journalist, once said in an interview on television talking about a new Aston Martin: 'Car enthusiasts should get on their hands and knees and thank God that a car manufacturer has been brave enough to make a car like this in this day and age.' These companies are characterized by very long production lead times and extensive waiting lists. A number of car manufacturers fit this profile.

Car suppliers who are operations-focused see the need to protect the organization from customers who need to organize themselves around the suppliers' schedule. The customer will only be able to choose cars from a limited selection with very little optional extras. Delivery times will be long and after-sales service will also be slow with very little customer support, for example, providing courtesy cars when customer cars are being serviced. Sales promotions will probably be utilized as a tool to influence demand in the short term but again will be seen as a way to buffer the operations function. Very little will be done in the way of personal selling to differentiate customer needs such as business users or particular needs of female drivers where the sales people will always address the male partner even though it is the woman buying the car.

Finance-driven car suppliers are those who see only the profit of the firms as being important and will have every mechanism in place to ensure that they collect all the money from the customers at the earliest opportunity. Again these companies are characterized by limited choice and service.

Marketing-led car suppliers will embrace customer orientation as an integral part of their organizations. All aspects of the marketing mix will be taken into account from product design right through operations, sales and after-sales service. These companies do not see themselves as car suppliers but as solution providers for their customers. The car is only one constituent in the solution package with other services such as extended warranties, financing packages also being sought after. The operations, finance and HRM functions within these organizations will be structured in a manner to ensure they are capable of maintaining a differential competitive advantage relative to the competition in the long term.

The extent to which an organization is marketing-orientated is also dependent on culture. A study by Doyle, Wong and Saunders (1993) demonstrated that Anglo-Saxon companies such as those operating in North America and the United Kingdom were short term in outlook by being more profit-orientated, whereas Japanese companies had a balanced orientation, taking each business function into consideration and taking a longer-term business perspective (Figure 1.5). The study also indicated that adopting a purely marketing approach was not likely to improve performance as much as applying a balanced approached as depicted in Figure 1.5. Therefore, by adapting Doyle *et al.*'s result one could interpret that a successful company should not develop strategies within a single function but should ensure that all functions operate together to meet the needs of not only the customers but a whole range of internal as well as external stakeholders.

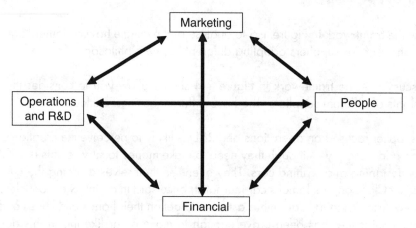

Figure 1.5 Balanced orientation
Source: Adapted from Doyle, Wong and Saunders (1993)

According to Whittington (1993), it is also important to appreciate that different cultural contexts exist towards profit-maximizing strategies and will therefore impact upon business orientation. Organizations such as those operating in different countries, charities and other non-profit organizations as well as SMEs may have purposes other than just making profit. It does not mean profit is not important to them as they do need it to survive, but profit is seen by them as a means to achieve other objectives. This is important to consider when developing marketing strategies as different organizational cultures are likely to adopt certain strategies more than others.

In many high-contact service organizations, there exists significant interaction between customers and operations functions. In these types of organizations, it is very difficult for marketing issues to be separated from either operations or human resource issues. According to Lovelock (1992), it is important for service organizations to integrate all three functions to achieve customer satisfaction, otherwise a deterioration of competitive positioning as well as long-term shareholder value is likely to result. Therefore, evaluating services organizations emphasizes the importance of having a balanced orientation.

Many professional service organizations such as law firms, advertising agencies and other consultancies have had major issues with their new business teams for defining customer needs, scoping and selling in a project followed by moving on leaving the operations team to deliver it. For such a project to be successfully implemented, it is important that marketing issues are not separated from the operational issues, otherwise major HRM conflict management issues are likely to surface. Therefore the organization ought to ensure an appropriate culture by recruiting and training their staff across functions to ensure that appropriate sensitivities are being taken into account.

Maison Blanc (MB)

Maison Blanc is a premium priced French Patisserie located in prosperous towns across the United Kingdom. The store in Kingston is similar to the ones in other locations. The store frontage is characterized by a complete glass front with the company logo printed in big letters on the windows and glass door. The purpose of this is to enable passers-by to see inside the store where three display cabinets are located, two on the left-hand side as you walk in and one against the back wall opposite the door. Between the third cabinet and the front of the store there are four tables each with four chairs.

The first cabinet displays a selection of handmade cakes, the second displays pastries and a coffee-making machine and a basket of different types of French breads are displayed behind the counter. The second cabinet displays handmade chocolates and has a space dedicated to making specialized cakes for weddings and birthdays. Behind this cabinet is a door which leads to the kitchen and store rooms. The door is always left open and the kitchen staff can always be seen.

The store is always manned with two full-time workers at the front and atleast one person in the kitchen.

Maison Blanc perceives itself as a designer and creator of exceptional cakes and the stores provide the opportunity for so-called 'cake worshippers' to come together either to purchase their cake for consumption outside the store – 'takeaways' – or to facilitate the consumption of the cakes in store with coffee being provided to 'wash the cake down'. They are by no means a coffee shop and do not wish to be considered as one. The other items in the store are there as support items so people having consumed their cakes can then either purchase chocolates or order a specialized cake or buy some French bread before going home.

Alan Wakehurst was planning a last minute picnic near Hampton Court with his new girlfriend and was going round the stores to purchase different savoury items. He went to several stores and the only item that he could not find on this day was a French baguette. He then remembered that MB had a good selection of French bread and decided that the *Pain aux olives* would be an ideal choice with the selection of Greek dips that he had purchased.

The two staff were occupied when he walked into MB. One was serving a couple who wanted to order some French pastries and coffee, they were certainly taking their time. The other was helping select a cake for a birthday party. After 20 minutes Alan was getting impatient, the store was gradually filling up and he decided to walk across and pick up the bread and leave the money on the counter. In response to this, one of the staff serving the couple looked into the kitchen and beckoned one of the kitchen staff to come out and help which he did and served the customer behind Alan. Alan was so disgusted that he stormed out the store in such a bad mood that it completely ruined his date.

Questions for consideration

1. What problem is MB potentially facing?
2. How can MB effectively analyse and evaluate the situation?
3. What should they do?

Comments: (This commentary constitutes only one possible analysis for the situation – other possibilities potentially exist.)

The main problem that MB may be facing is the possibility that they have a disgruntled customer who is likely to be giving the company a bad reputation through 'word of mouth' which in turn may affect their future competitive positioning as their customers migrate to the competition. So MB should consider many of the service recovery strategies available to recover the situation. Unfortunately, this is too late for Alan but MB should ensure that this occurrence is only 'a one-off' and does not occur regularly.

The next question is how MB can stop the same thing happening to another customer. As a closer analysis of the situation demonstrates, it is actually difficult to avoid because:

1. In service organizations it is difficult to match capacity with demand. One can try and forecast the demand fluctuations but this is very difficult to achieve in reality. In running an operation like MB, one is always either over-stretched by being understaffed or alternatively being under stretched by having too much staff and no customers. Both situations are not ideal as the first leads to dissatisfied customers and the second you have dissatisfied shareholders who are losing money, through poor utilization of assets. The second problem appears to be alleviated by MB by offering a portfolio of other products which potentially increases the selling opportunities and increases the utilization of staff. This suggests that MB's senior management has a strong finance orientation.
2. There are too few staff serving and MB should increase the number of staff. Again this is not ideal as we have a constrained amount of space and due to the laws of diminishing returns there is only a limited capacity for increasing the staff numbers. We are also in the same situation of not being able to predict what customers will want at any one time so one may be experiencing bottlenecks at one counter and none at the other. One could utilize kitchen staff but it is important to distinguish between back room staff who may be more reserved and shy compared to front office staff who are more outgoing and quickly establish customer relationships. This is exemplified by the fact that the kitchen staff did not serve Alan and served somebody else.
3. Other issues such as reducing or separating out the product portfolio could be investigated to improve customer satisfaction but it is likely to impact on the financial and risk needs of other stakeholders.
4. Finally, using relationship management theory one could argue that Alan is not a high value customer and MB was not first on the list. He rarely visits them anyway. In addition, one could also identify why customers are in fact purchasing MB products. You may find it as a product-orientated company with few or no competitors and their cakes are so highly sought after that it does not really matter if their service levels are poor. However, this situation should be carefully monitored as competitive environments usually change and MB should minimize its chances of being caught out.

In conclusion, the case really exemplifies the issues of having to integrate marketing with operations and HRM in service-type organizations and highlights the practical issues of managing customer satisfaction as well as other stakeholders.

Marketing stakeholders

So far we have talked about three groups of stakeholders in the process of creating value: customers, competitors and employees. But other groups are also affected by and can influence the success of an organization. The seven markets model is shown in Figure 1.6.

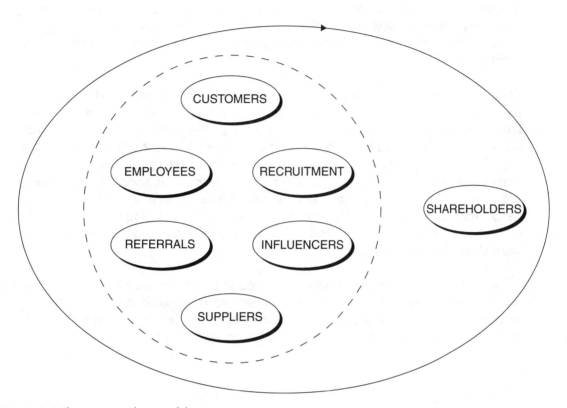

Figure 1.6 The seven markets model

Effective marketing involves the realization that all stakeholders matter. Imagine a business without employees, for example (or without customers). Even competitors and publics have their uses! And referral groups are very important as word-of-mouth recommendation becomes increasingly valued by consumers.

But pragmatically shareholders matter most of all. They invest in the company and allow the business to invest in itself. But shareholders do not exist in a vacuum. There is overlap between the different groups. Employees may become shareholders, for example. Many companies have share schemes specifically to encourage this crossover. Shareholders may be encouraged by reference groups.

 Activity 1.3

Profile the stakeholders in your organization. How can you add value to each of them?

Marketing and value

We can see from the above activity that the definition of value can differ depending on perspective. Marketing has been criticized in the past for focusing solely on customer value, largely ignoring the other stakeholder groups. Marketing needs to define value more broadly in terms of economic value. Economic value is based on the idea that every activity should create a surplus, that is outputs should have a higher value than inputs. Obviously every organization needs this sort of surplus (economic profit) to remain in business. For marketing to be seen as relevant inside the business, we need to demonstrate that marketing activities contribute to that profit by creating value, not destroying it.

Although the importance of marketing is generally acknowledged in the business world, it has been (unfairly, of course!) criticized. Marketing can be viewed from outside as being 'pink and fluffy', not being accountable and adding to cost. We need to meet these challenges and develop marketing into a hard-edged subject. We need to change perceptions of our functional area by becoming more disciplined and applying that discipline to the marketing decision-making process. It is important that we can objectively demonstrate how marketing adds value to business by using rigorous business metrics for all marketing activities. We need to have a robust process which allows us to allocate scarce marketing resources to deliver optimal return. This unit, A&E, is the first stage for you to become a hard-edged marketer (see www.shapetheagenda.com).

To show how our activities add value we need to be able to measure their contribution. This whole area is discussed in more depth when we move onto marketing metrics in Unit 2. A metric is a performance measure that matters to the whole business. Ideally it should be high level, necessary, sufficient, unambiguous and predictive.

The role of marketing in corporate strategy

We have talked about the importance of a market orientation to the success of an organization. To implement this marketing needs to be at the core of corporate strategy. There are three important roles for marketing to be fulfilled in the planning process.

Identification of customer requirements

If we are to adopt a customer-orientated approach, we need to know everything we can about the people who are buying our product. This will involve market research, probably from both primary and secondary sources. We need to understand who these people or organizations are. How many of them are there? What is their profile? How do they make their buying decisions? Who else is involved in decision-making? The answers to the questions are not always obvious. For example, a parent may purchase breakfast cereal but their child may influence that decision and may well end up consuming the product. Who is the customer in this case? The parent with the money? The child with the pester power? And what are their requirements? The parent could want a high quality, good value nutritious breakfast meal, the child could want a cereal packet with a toy in it and a cereal which tastes sweet. The task for marketing is to keep both these groups happy – a balance of satisfying one without alienating the other.

Exam Hint 1.6

Identifying the extent to which an organization is marketing-orientated requires an understanding of the extent to which they have necessary internal capabilities to understanding customer needs and requirements. This means they need a Knowledge Management capability supported by an intensive market research capability. Basic market research is not taught at this level but it is essential that you have an understanding of how to conduct basic primary and secondary research which you need to revise from a general text if you have forgotten the basic principles. This forms the basis of finding information for the various marketing audits discussed in later sections as well as providing the basis of non-financial performance measures to measure the extent of marketing orientation within organizations discussed later.

Determining competitive positioning

Markets tend to be heterogeneous, that is they are made of groups of people (or organizations) who are similar to each other but differ from other groups. We call these groups as segments and we aim to cluster these around the same need. Once we have done this and decided which groups we want to target, we need to decide how we would like our target to perceive us. In other words, what will our competitive positioning be? Before we can do this we need to find out how attractive the potential targets are, what are the requirements of that target and what are our competencies to meet that requirement.

Implementing the marketing strategy

Once we have the relevant information we can move to implementing the strategy. It is particularly important for organizations aiming to have a strong market orientation that emphasis is given to co-ordination between functions. It has been argued that marketing is too important to be left to the marketing department! Communication across the functions is critical to smooth implementation. This is even more important in service companies where the customer may have contact with several front-line employees. Each must give a consistent message of what the company is about. These 'boundary spanners' (so-called because they span the boundary between the customer and the company) are critical to the success or otherwise of any service organization. Imagine going to your local supermarket. The man operating the car park is rude to you. The staff stacking the shelves are very helpful. The person on the checkout is disinterested and is wearing a dirty and torn uniform. What do you think of the supermarket? Probably mixed feelings. But imagine if all the staff were courteous and professional. Your impression is likely to be far more positive and consistent. This is what an organization needs to aim for.

The role of A&E in marketing planning

Managing the marketing planning process needs to begin with a thorough analysis of the company's situation. The company needs to analyse its markets and the marketing environment to evaluate potential opportunities and threats. We need to answer the question 'Where are we now?' before we can move on to decide where we want to be and how we are going to get there. The fields of strategy and marketing are intimately linked, and there is a considerable amount of theory overlap in the literature of both fields. Certain strategy texts divide strategy formulation in companies into three distinct areas (Figure 1.7).

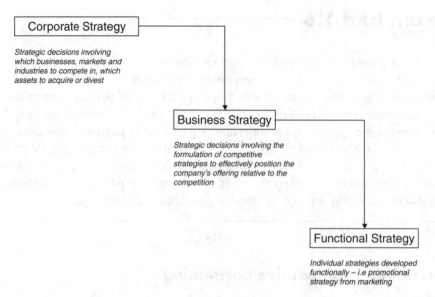

Figure 1.7 Strategy formulation at different levels within an organization

Traditionally marketing in organizations is perceived as the marketing department developing and implementing a promotional plan. This would be a rather narrow definition of marketing as a managerial functional activity. The marketing concept adopted in this course at this level is one of a business philosophy where customer satisfaction is pervasive throughout the whole organization. As the acquisition of assets and decisions of where to compete at the corporate level potentially affects marketing decisions further down the line, it is imperative a marketer is taken into account at this level. This means that either a senior marketer needs to address the board or that the chief executive or managing director takes into account the impact on marketing whilst deciding upon corporate issues.

This unit covers five main elements:

1. Strategic management and the role of marketing (Unit 1)
2. Evaluation of business performance (Units 2, 3–5)
3. Analysis of the external environment (Unit 6)
4. Analysis of the internal environment (Unit 7)
5. Characteristics of the global marketplace (Unit 8).

In addition it is important to appreciate that there is an underlying assumption within the new syllabus to include a number of contemporary issues within the analyses. These include: globalization, corporate social responsibility, technology – the Internet and Customer Relationship Management (CRM) – see Figure 1.8.

Figure 1.8 Contemporary issues requiring consideration in the analytical portions of the new syllabus in additions formulating marketing strategies

The final unit (Unit 9) consolidates the above elements by focusing on the definition of competitive advantage. This draws the previous units together to review their implications for the organization's future.

The strategic market management process

This A&E unit forms the basis of the strategic market management process. Figure 1.9 outlines the strategic market management process. The dashed line delineates the remit of this unit. The cut-off point is in the selection of strategy which leads us into the Strategic Marketing Decisions unit.

To summarize we need to undertake analysis of the external and internal environments.

External analysis covers customers, competitors, market and macro-environment. Specifically:

- ○ *Customer* – segments, motivations, unmet needs
- ○ *Competitors* – identification, strategic groups, cost structures, strengths, weaknesses, competencies
- ○ *Market* – size, growth, profitability, entry barriers, cost structure, distribution networks, entry barriers, attractiveness
- ○ *Macro-environment* – political, economic, social, demographic, cultural, environmental, legal.

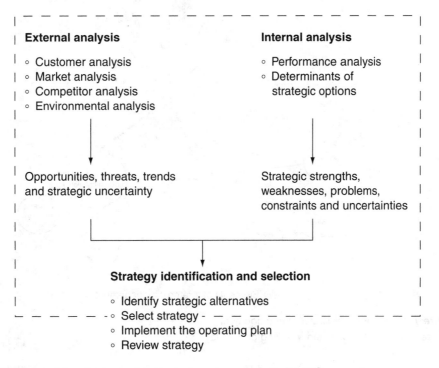

Figure 1.9 Overview of the strategic market management process
Source: Adapted from Aaker (1998)

Internal analysis covers performance analysis and determinants of strategic options. Specifically:

- ○ *Performance* – Financial and marketing measures of past and current performance, for example ratio analysis, profitability, shareholder value analysis (SVA), economic value, sales, market share, brand equity, effectiveness of marketing activities, portfolio analysis, customer satisfaction, complaining rates and so on.

o *Determinants of strategic options* – Past and current strategies, strategic problems, organizational capabilities and constraints, financial resources and constraints, strengths and weaknesses.

These two strands of external and internal analyses need to be pulled together in some sort of consolidated summary. A common format for this is a SWOT (strengths, weaknesses, opportunities and threats) analysis, but it is also possible to use a more general issue analysis.

This synthesis is used to identify strategic options, in terms of product-market, modes of entry and so on. These options are evaluated in the light of the analysis, potential, risk and so on and a decision made on the most appropriate strategy.

In the old days of strategic planning clear divisions existed within the strategic thinking process and the implementation process of the strategic plan. Traditional ways of representing strategic plans tended to misrepresent the focus between the importance of planning and implementation. Strategic planning over the decades has failed to deliver shareholder expectations in terms of performance and for this reason there has been a shift from strategic planning to strategic management as represented by the framework depicted by Johnson, Scholes and Whittington (Figure 1.10). This framework, according to the authors, captures the essence of strategic marketing formulation across all four units of the Post Graduate Professional Diploma.

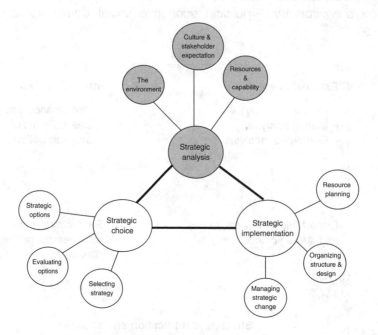

Elements of strategic management

Figure 1.10 Elements of strategic management
Source: Johnson, Scholes and Whittington (2005)

Within the Johnson, Scholes and Whittington framework analysis of strategy issues, formulation of strategy decisions and its implementation need to be considered in parallel and share equal importance. One can think of strategic analysis part as corresponding to the A&E and strategic choice and implementation as corresponding to strategic marketing decisions and managing marketing performance. This means that when we analyse opportunities and threats we need to appreciate the context of the likely decisions and one cannot make a decision without thinking through whether the organization can in fact implement it. Therefore overlaps exist within the individual units but students are expected to appreciate this facet and not to delve deeply into the other subject areas.

Summary

In this introductory unit we have considered the format and the approach that this book will take in addressing the A&E syllabus and the importance of using this book in conjunction with the recommended supplementary reading. We have also considered the detailed analysis of the syllabus as well as the all-important learning objectives and the outcomes required for a successful attempt at the examination itself. Finally we have considered the nature of this module and how it fits within the processes of an organization with a market orientation. We have concluded that:

o Market orientation is strategic and concentrates on long-term performance.
o It emphasizes customer focus. Organizations need to understand their customers and competitors but as a means to deliver shareholder value rather than an end in itself.
o The marketing process should be inter-functional.

In this unit we have seen why A&E are the essential foundation stones of an effective marketing strategy. Detailed market research and analysis are essential to ensure that an organization makes the most of any opportunities. In addition A&E helps companies avoid potential risks or as a minimum ensures that they are prepared. A range of models exists to help you structure your analysis which are covered in later units. An emphasis is placed on understanding the strategic implications of your analysis.

Perhaps most importantly we have seen how marketing needs to adopt a broad definition of value which embraces all stakeholder groups but emphasizes the importance of shareholders. The importance of hard-wiring marketing metrics in the organization is discussed to ensure that marketing is seen as accountable. We will return to this issue in later units.

Finally we looked at how the contents of the unit fit within the strategic market management process. Rigorous analysis should be undertaken and synthesized. This is followed by generation of strategic alternatives and evaluation of these options.

Further study

Hard-Edged Marketing, www.shapetheagenda.com

Hints and tips

The examination questions will often ask you to demonstrate your knowledge by your use of relevant and up-to-date examples. The focus of the Professional Postgraduate Diploma is on the application of knowledge; it is not sufficient to be able to describe a model, you also need to apply it to a particular context. So at the end of a unit, or any activity, try to think of examples and commit them to memory. This will save you from exam panic and try to come up with examples 'on the spot'. Your answers should therefore be more thoughtful and informed.

Another useful tip is to allocate your time in accordance with the number of marks allocated to a question. So even if you have a question that you could spend the whole three hours on, don't! It is always easier to get the first few marks rather than the last few. Even knowledgeable students can fail if they do not manage their time properly.

It is also very important to answer the question that is set. There is a danger, particularly in Section B, that students spend time telling the examiner all they know about a subject rather than focusing their answer on a particular context. Marks are to be gained by application rather than mere regurgitation of knowledge. It is worth spending a few minutes planning your answer before you start to write so that the answer shows a logical train of thought rather than a brain dump.

After each examination the senior examiners write a report for the Chartered Institute of Marketing in which they discuss how the students coped with the examination and highlight any particular problems that have been experienced.

Mini Case 3 – Marks & Spencer – (Source CIM June 2001 Part A Exam for Planning and Control)

Question

Please read the following case study regarding Marks & Spencer

The following case, although written in 2001, is highly relevant and demonstrates the dynamic nature of strategic marketing. The Strategic Marketing Process requires students to answer the following questions relating to their organizations:

- ○ Where are we now? – Main remit of the Analysis & Evaluation (A&E) Module

    – Current situation analysis of the organization in terms of its:

- ○ Customers (Markets)/Competitors (Industries)/Resources & Capabilities

    – How did we get here? – Mix remit of all modules

- ○ Review of past decisions and strategies, operating values and beliefs

    – Where do we want to be? – Main remit of Strategic Marketing Decisions (SMD) Module
    – How do we get there and what do we need? – Main remit of Managing Marketing Performance (MMP) Module
    – How will we know when we have arrived? – Remit of A&E and MMP Modules

The M&S case is a good exemplar of how shareholder value is affected by consumer actions and students should benefit from this by evaluating the links between revenue, profitability, consumer actions and impact upon share price and therefore shareholder value. This case based upon the strategic marketing process involves how did the company end up at its current situation today.

There are several strategic options recommended in the case. How can an understanding of marketing orientation help evaluate the appropriateness of the recommended strategies?

Marks & Spencer

Over the last three decades Marks & Spencer (M&S) has been seen as the leading clothing retailer in the United Kingdom, operating around 300 stores. The quality and range of its functional and fashionable clothes combined with good customer service had proved to be unbeatable in the past. The retailer's position was so strong in the UK market that it could even refuse to take payments by credit cards from customers. The company also did not see the need to undertake any advertising.

Marks & Spencer's recent performance

Marks & Spencer's fortunes, however, have recently been in decline. This started initially with a poor year in the Southeast Asian market, which in itself should not have been too damaging. However, in the last few years, there has been increasing competition in UK clothing from more aggressive middle-market, high-street retailers such as Next and Gap, as well as revitalized departmental stores such as Debenhams and discount outlets such as Matalan. The result has been a sharp decline in annual profitability for M&S since 1998 with a consequent fall in the company's share price, dropping 70 per cent from its peak in 1997 (Table 1.2). In fact the share price fell as low as £1.70 (£5 billion from its 1998 value of £17 billion).

Table 1.2 Marks & Spencer's profits and share price 1996–2000

Year	Profit (£m)	Share price £ (High)
1996	996	5.31
1997	1102	6.65
1998	1115	6.20
1999	546	4.61
2000	418	3.32

Competition

- *Gap* – This middle market company has taken market share by creating a high profile lifestyle brand, based on attitude and meaning.
- *Next* – Is another middle market competitor. It demonstrated its increasing ability to attract consumers by reporting a 19 per cent increase in sales. Next bases its business on giving 25- to 45-year-old customers fashionable clothing at a reasonable price.
- *Matalan* – Is a discount clothing and homeware retailer operating 111 stores, mostly out of town. Garment sales make up 82 per cent of group profits. Matalan forecasts that it can continue to grow at 30 per cent a year compound for the next 3 years. Matalan plans include entering the financial services market with its own credit card and personal loans and, potentially, insurance products.
- *Debenhams* – Has also been attempting to take market share away from mid-market retailers such as Marks & Spencer by focusing on the needs of working women. In the financial year 1999–2000, Debenhams increased its share of the UK lingerie market, previously an M&S staple, from 3.75 to 4.8 per cent.

Marks & Spencer's responses

M&S has taken a number of measures over the last decade to regain its market position, in particular, introducing more fashionable lines of clothing. These, however, have not been an overwhelming success. They were widely seen as alienating the company's traditional customers, mainly ABC1 house-wives. At the same time younger, more fashion-oriented customers did not associate fashion with the M&S brand.

M&S has also been undertaking a severe round of cost cutting measures. As part of this process the company has started to shift production of its clothing from the United Kingdom to cheaper factories internationally. This has led to large-scale redundancies in the UK clothing industry. The move to international production has also meant that M&S is no longer so able to place late orders for particular items or colours that are proving popular.

October 2000 saw a new management team announcing a range of new initiatives. To accompany the women's designer collection, which features clothes designed by Betty Jackson, Julien Macdonald and Katherine Hamnett, M&S then also launched its first ever designer menswear collection in five stores in the United Kingdom.

Marks & Spencer's financial services are to open in around 30 of the company's stores, offering customers confidential consultations on their personal finances. M&S's financial services are also planning to launch a range of new products. Both these moves are likely to lead to greater competition with the traditional banks. The company aims to launch a poster advertising campaign involving placing advertisements in areas near traditional banks stating 'Unhappy with your bank? Come to M&S.'

The company has taken a stake in the Confetti Network, a website business specializing in products bought for weddings. The aim is that M&S will become the leading retailer in the online retail site developed by Confetti.

Marks & Spencer has also unveiled plans to open a chain of new lingerie boutiques in continental Europe, starting in Paris, Hamburg and Dusseldorf. The stores will operate under the brand name of 'msl'. Twenty-five per cent of the lingerie range will be exclusively designed for the new stores, the rest will come from M&S's current range. There are no plans to open msl boutiques in the United Kingdom.

Finally M&S has also launched a £20 million advertising campaign, emphasizing quality and wide range of products, under the slogan 'Exclusively for everyone'.

Commentary: There are several approaches one could take with this case but whichever one you take you should appreciate the following:

1. The symptoms of M&S is that they are losing profitability which is likely being caused by changing customer-buyer behaviour needs resulting from either changing tastes or that their needs are being better served by a competitor. It, therefore, needs to improve its marketing information systems to identify the problems followed by developing strategies which will win customers back.
2. Another problem is that the share price is also being affected showing that shareholders are also unhappy. M&S needs to address their needs.

Marks & Spencer's management has suggested several options within the case; however the organization is in a real dilemma as it needs to undertake activities that will gain investor confidence and they are likely to be looking to the company's management to increase efficiencies through operational re-engineering. This is likely to have the effect of improving short-term profitability. In addition, the management may also have the problem of convincing current shareholders to suffer short-term profit losses while it invests in longer-term marketing initiatives to booster long-term shareholder value. In the longer term it is customer purchases that will determine the longevity of an organization and this will not happen if the company stops satisfying their needs. The extent to which shareholders will allow the management to select their customer driven or operational efficiency strategies will be dependent on their business orientation.

Source: This mini case study has been prepared from secondary sources.

Additional activities relating to M&S

Using various search engines and bibliographic databases, search for information relating to the current situation of M&S, using this information:

- Analyse and evaluate to what extent did the strategies mentioned in the above case impact upon shareholder value.
- What further actions did the company undertake in light of your findings in Question 1?
- Evaluate the extent to which the current situation of M&S is sustainable into the future.

Mini Case 4 – Kodak

Analysing the macro-environment

Background

Josh Maguire was reviewing the latest press clippings from his PR department regarding the recent news about the re-organization plans of Kodak, the camera and processed film manufacturer (Appendices I and II, below).

Kodak, an organization with a long heritage, was perceived as being firmly established and everybody including Josh believed that a company with resources could 'ride the waves in choppy waters'.

Josh, a recent CIM graduate, was asked to compile a presentation for an investment bank to help identify whether Kodak had been a victim of its own success or whether the situation was the fault of external factors beyond the company's control.

The task

Please read the press clippings in Appendices I and II below and answer the following questions:

1. What can John do to answer the question being posed by the investment bank?
2. What tools and frameworks can be utilized to answer the question?
3. How can the tools be utilized to answer the question?
4. What conclusions can be reached having undertaken the analysis?
5. What are the implications of the conclusions?

Prepare a 20-minute presentation outlining your answers to the above questions.

APPENDIX I

Kodak cuts 15 000 jobs worldwide

Last Updated: Thursday, 22 January 2004, 15:46 GMT

Photography giant Eastman Kodak is to slash up to 15 000 jobs worldwide over the next 3 years.

The news comes after the US firm announced a sharp fall in profits for the last 3 months of 2003.

Kodak said the job cuts – which represent around 20 per cent of its global workforce – would save the company up to $1 billion (£546 million) a year by 2007.

The firm said last week that it would stop selling traditional film cameras in the United States, Canada and Western Europe.

It plans to cut product lines with declining appeal in favour of fast-growing digital products.

The latest staff cuts come on top of 6000 job losses announced by the firm last year.

Kodak said it would also take $1.3 billion to $1.7 billion in charges over the next 3 years, as it moves to reposition itself to keep pace with the development of digital products.

Antonio Perez, the company's president and chief operating officer, said the job cuts were 'absolutely required for Kodak to succeed in traditional markets as well as the digital markets to which our businesses are rapidly shifting'.

The cuts were 'the consequence of market realities' and would help fund future growth, he said.

New York-based Kodak reported fourth quarter net profits of $19 million, compared with $113 million for the same period in 2002.

However, the firm said sales in the quarter totalled $3.78 billion, up 10 per cent from a year ago.

Separately, Kodak said it would launch a $35 million offer to buy the remaining shares of Japanese digital camera supplier Chinon Industries which it does not already own.

Kodak said the move would enable it to increase its global design and manufacturing capability for consumer digital cameras and accessories.

Unions vow fight over Kodak jobs

Last Updated: Wednesday, 6 October 2004, 08:30 GMT 09:30 UK

The union representing 350 workers who are facing the axe at Nottingham's Kodak factory says it will fight to keep the site open.

On Tuesday bosses announced a total of 600 job losses at plants in Annesley, Nottinghamshire and Harrow in north London.

The Transport and General Workers' Union (TGWU) says managers could have done more to prepare for the consumer shift to the digital market.

The union says the 12-month notice gives them time to form a rescue plan.

Digital revolution

Jim Mowatt, the national secretary of the TGWU, insisted the loss of the factory was not a foregone conclusion.

He said: 'The members are very angry and shocked – after the surprise came the anger.'

'We have a number of options; occupying the plant, industrial action, negotiation, going to the government to see if there is regional development funding available.'

'If it comes to pass that the factory is going to close we will not sit back, we will see if we can find a purchaser for the site, which is a world-class site, highly maintained with a highly skilled work force.'

Kodak currently employs about 3000 people in the United Kingdom.

The company announced in January that it planned to shed up to 15 000 jobs worldwide over the next 3 years as it sought to reposition its business in the digital age.

Source: Tuesday, 13 January 2004, 20:25 GMT

Kodak embraces digital revolution

Photography giant Eastman Kodak has announced plans to stop selling traditional film cameras in North America and Europe.

The firm said it would concentrate instead on digital models.

The move marks a milestone in the history of Kodak, which brought photography to the masses through cheap, easy-to-use film cameras.

It reflects a recent surge in demand for filmless digital cameras, which now outsell traditional models.

Industry figures show that 12.5 million digital cameras were sold in the United States last year, compared with 12.1 million film cameras.

Kodak said it would continue selling its range of popular disposable cameras, as well as film and other accessories in North America and Europe.

Changing times

It will also continue to sell traditional cameras in Asia, Latin America and Eastern Europe.

The decision is in line with the firm's strategy of moving away from traditional products in favour of high-growth digital technologies.

Bernard Mason, the head of Kodak's digital and film imaging division, said the firm remained 'committed to manufacturing and marketing the world's highest quality film'.

'We will focus our film investments on opportunities that provide faster and attractive returns, while reducing investments where we see unsatisfactory returns.'

Last year, Kodak controversially slashed its payout to shareholders in an effort to raise $3 billion needed to expand its presence in the market for digital cameras and imaging technologies.

The change in strategy prompted warnings from analysts that the company may struggle to catch up with rivals such as Canon, Dell and Hewlett Packard, which made the switch to digital products sooner.

But Wall Street investors welcomed the latest news, market Kodak shares 1.3 per cent higher at $26.70 in mid-morning trade in New York on Tuesday.

Kodak to shed 600 UK jobs

Last Updated: Tuesday, 5 October 2004, 12:25 GMT 13:25 UK

Photography equipment maker Kodak is to cut 600 jobs in the United Kingdom and close a factory in Nottinghamshire.

About 350 jobs will be lost following the closure of the factory at Annesley, Nottinghamshire, while 250 posts will go at its site in Harrow, north London.

The layoffs are part of a global restructuring plan that the US-based firm unveiled in January this year.

Kodak has been hit hard by the shift away from traditional camera film to the use of digital cameras.

Kodak currently employs about 3000 people in the United Kingdom.

New trends

Kodak announced in January that it planned to shed up to 15 000 jobs worldwide over the next 3 years as it sought to reposition its business in the digital age.

The closure of the Annesley film plant will take place in a year's time, while the Harrow job cuts are set to be made by March 2005.

However, the Harrow site will gain 300 jobs which are being moved from the company's head office in Hemel Hempstead, Hertfordshire. The Harrow site will also become Kodak's UK headquarters.

'Today's announcements are driven by fundamental, structural change in the imaging industry world-wide and Kodak's intent to transform the company and remain the leader in imaging', said Peter Blackwell, managing director of Kodak in the United Kingdom.

'The simple fact is that customer and consumer preferences are changing and demand for traditional products such as film and paper has fallen with the rising popularity of digital photography.'

Disappointment

Trade unions T&G and Amicus said they were 'deeply disappointed' at Kodak's plans and were surprised at the scale of the job losses.

The redundancy proposals, they said, went against Kodak's policy of moving production out of the United States.

Union leaders said they did not accept the company's rationale for closing the Nottinghamshire site nor for the jettisoning of jobs in Harrow.

'Both unions and shop stewards are fully committed to supporting every single one of our members in Harrow and Annesley', said Joe McGowan, a full-time official of Amicus.

Meanwhile, the T&G vowed to make sure job losses at Harrow would only be on a voluntary basis.

'Not one union member in Kodak will be forced to "walk the plank" because of the company's proposals', said Peter Allsopp, the T&G branch secretary.

APPENDIX II

Kodak pulls down factory shutters [NORTH WALES Edition]

Daily Post. Liverpool (UK): Oct 6, 2004. p. 5

(Copyright © 2004 Liverpool Daily Post and Echo Ltd.)

PHOTOGRAPHIC equipment manufacturer Kodak is to cut 600 jobs in the United Kingdom and close a factory in Nottingham.

The group plans to shut its photo film finishing plant at Annesley with the loss of 350 jobs. Kodak also said it was closing part of its operations at a site in Harrow, Middlesex, reducing the 1350-strong workforce there by 250 people. The cuts are part of a global restructuring programme announced by Kodak in January. The US-based company is being forced to reshape its operations in the face of declining demand for traditional photographic film and the rising popularity of digital cameras.

Kodak to cut 600 jobs in United Kingdom; Kirkby plant not affected [NORTHWEST & MERSEYSIDE Edition]

TONY McDONOUGH. Daily Post. Liverpool (UK): Oct 6, 2004. p. 4

(Copyright © 2004 Liverpool Daily Post and Echo Ltd.)

PHOTOGRAPHIC equipment manufacturer Kodak yesterday announced the loss of 600 jobs across the United Kingdom.

However, 100 workers at the company's plant at Kirkby in Merseyside will not be affected by the cuts.

The group plans to shut its photo film finishing plant at Annesley in Nottingham with the loss of 350 jobs.

Kodak also said it was closing part of its operations at a site in Harrow, Middlesex, reducing the 1350-strong workforce there by 250.

Workers at the Kirkby factory make chemicals for both conventional and digital photo printing and is seen as one of the group's most productive sites.

Plant manager Tony Field said yesterday: 'This announcement does not impact on Kirkby.'

'The facility here remains an important part of the business and has recently seen a transfer of volume from the US.'

The cuts are part of a global restructuring programme announced by Kodak in January.

The US-based company is being forced to reshape its operations in the face of declining demand for traditional photographic film and the rising popularity of digital cameras.

The Annesley factory is due to close in a year's time while the cuts at Harrow will take place by March. Kodak employs 3000 people in the United Kingdom.

Kodak said Harrow eventually would become the headquarters for its UK operations.

The company said it planned to move more than 300 jobs to Harrow from its present UK head office in Hemel Hempstead, Hertfordshire. The remaining staff of 350 would stay in Hemel Hempstead, it said.

Kodak is looking to reduce its global facilities by about one third over 3 years.

It said there was a 'fundamental shift in customer and consumer behaviour' taking place in the face of the rising popularity of digital photography.

Demand for digital cameras brings cuts at Kodak [LONDON 1ST EDITION]

JONATHAN GUTHRIE. Financial Times. London (UK): Oct 6, 2004. p. 3

The growing popularity of digital photography added to the woes of manufacturing yesterday when Kodak United Kingdom announced it would cut 600 jobs in Nottinghamshire and north-west London.

The news has coincided with a TV advertising campaign by Kodak encouraging customers to use the digital photo printing units it is installing in stores across the country as a substitute to having old-fashioned rolls of film processed.

Demand has been falling for photographic film, which is cut, pierced with sprocket holes and put into cassettes at Kodak's factory in Annesley, Nottinghamshire. Kodak plans to close the plant with 350 job losses next year and will cut another 250 jobs in an operation making film for graphics applications at its Harrow base, where it has 1300 staff.

Falling prices and increasing memory means digital cameras are no longer the preserve of early adopters and have become an everyday consumer item. Eastman Kodak, the US parent, has responded by launching a restructuring involving 12 000–15 000 job cuts worldwide, announced in outline earlier this year.

Peter Blackwell, chairman and managing director of Kodak in the United Kingdom, said: 'The market for traditional film has fallen 10 per cent a year over the last couple of years, although it has been offset for us by rising sales of digital cameras. Unfortunately this does not support so many jobs.' Kodak UK's turnover in digital products was roughly £70 million last year, he said. Growth was running at 40 per cent a year, which meant digital sales would shortly overtake those of traditional products.

Kodak manufactures digital cameras in the Far East. The US plants make in-store digital printing kiosks, which produce higher quality prints than many home computers. About 1500 have been installed in the United Kingdom.

Jim Mowatt, national secretary of the T&G union, complained that 'colour film has been the milch cow nurturing the production of digital cameras in the Far East'. However, he praised Kodak for giving a year's notice of the closure of the plant, which he hoped would be sold as a going concern.

Mr Mowatt said the planned closure was bad news for Annesley, a former coalfields community so rundown 'it looks as if it has been napalmed'.

Digital rise costs 600 jobs at Kodak [01A Edition]

Journal. Newcastle-upon-Tyne (UK): Oct 6, 2004. p. 23

Photographic equipment manufacturer Kodak yesterday blamed the rise of digital photography for 600 job losses and a factory closure.

The company said declining demand for traditional camera film had forced it to close a film finishing and packing plant at Annesley in Nottingham, with 350 redundancies.

The group also said it was closing part of its operations at a site in Harrow, Middlesex, and reducing the 1350-strong workforce there by 250 people.

Trade unions said they were 'deeply disappointed by the shock announcement' and pledged to fight the job cuts.

But Kodak said there had been a 'fundamental shift in customer and consumer behaviour' due to the rising popularity of digital cameras. It said it expected sales of digital products to increase 36 per cent a year between 2003 and 2007.

The US group's UK managing director, Peter Blackwell, said: 'The simple fact is that customer and consumer preferences are changing and demand for traditional products such as film and paper has fallen.'

'These have been difficult decisions to take.'

Eastman Kodak Co.: United Kingdom, France Film Operations To Close, Affecting 870 Jobs

(Copyright © 2004, Dow Jones & Company Inc. Reproduced with permission of copyright owner. Further reproduction or distribution is prohibited without permission.)

Eastman Kodak Co., as part of its plan to focus on its digital businesses, said it will trim its film operations in the United Kingdom and France and cut about 870 jobs. The Rochester, N.Y., maker of cameras and film said the move is part of a 3-year programme, announced in January, to reduce its global work force by 12 000–15 000 and to cut the total square footage of its facilities by a third. Eastman Kodak said it will consolidate its UK operations with its UK headquarters in Harrow, England. The company will close a facility that sensitizes film for the graphics industry by the end of March, with the loss of 250 jobs. The company also will shut down its Annesley, England, plant, which mainly produces consumer photographic film, because of declining demand. The plant is scheduled to close by September 2005, with the loss of about 350 jobs. In France, Eastman Kodak will halt its production of consumer films and colour photographic paper by the end of September 2005.

Possible solutions – (Do not read the following until you have attempted the question by yourself)

A whole range of solutions are possible but a good answer would highlight the main issues of whether Kodak was left behind in the sense of there being a change in the socio-cultural aspects of the external environment (PEST analysis) due to a threat from a substitute technology (Porter's Five Forces/PEST) being introduced. To what extent were these changes in the macro-environment in fact an irreversible process or could Kodak have taken the lead in adapting to the change by extending its capability to the digital segment? How was Kodak defining itself (strategic intent)? Was it a photography solutions company or did it define itself as a film processing company therefore making itself a product rather than a marketing-orientated company? In order to survive Kodak would have to maximize shareholder value through increased long-term cash flows effectuated by satisfied customers' repeat purchases. Having not invested in promoting its brand image in photography rather than film, the company is at risk of losing revenue as customers do not associate Kodak with digital but with the older technology of film. Kodak therefore needs to re-position itself in the digital market, which according to its latest advertising campaign is what the company is doing.

Bibliography

Doyle, P., Wong, V., Saunders, J. (1993) 'Business orientation and corporate success', *Journal of Strategic Marketing*, **1**, pp. 20–40.

Johnson, G., Scholes, K. and Whittington, R. (2005) *Exploring Corporate Strategy*, 7th edition, Prentice-Hall Europe.

Kohli, A.K., Jaworski, B.J. (1990) 'Market orientation: the construct, research propositions and managerial implications', *Journal of Marketing*, **54** (2), pp. 1–18.

Lovelock, C.H. (1992) *Managing Services*, 2nd edition, Prentice-Hall International, New Jersey.

Narver, J.C., Slater, S.F. (1990) 'The effect of a market orientation on business profitability', *Journal of Marketing*, **54** (4), pp. 20–35.

Pascale, R.T., Athos, A.G. (1982) *The Art of Japanese Management*, Penguin.

Peters, T.J., Waterman, R.H. (1982) *In Search of Excellence*, Harper & Row.

Whittington, R. (1993) *What is Strategy and Does it Matter?* International Thompson Press.

unit 2
evaluating performance: marketing metrics

To analyse an organization thoroughly it needs to be viewed from several perspectives. The next two units examine measures of marketing performance. This unit focuses on marketing measures, the next one looks at more financially orientated measures. In this unit you will:

o Understand the quantitative techniques which can be used to evaluate business performance (see syllabus 2.1)

o Examine customer measures (see syllabus 2.1)

o Consider how to evaluate marketing activities (see syllabus 2.1).

Having completed this unit you will be able to:

o Use the various marketing measures of performance appropriately

o Use the balanced scorecard

o Evaluate performance over current and historic business cycles.

It is important for one to appreciate that the syllabus is non-linear which means that you will be using components and theory discussed in other syllabus sections to solve problems prior to covering in any real depth. In the exams you will find that this is the approach which is undertaken and one should get used to it as early as possible. You will also find that familiarizing yourself with the theory will make solving A&E problems easier once you have completed the unit.

Sections of the syllabus being covered in this unit:

Element 2: Evaluation of business and marketing performance (30 per cent).

2.1 Critically evaluate and use quantitative techniques for evaluating business and marketing performance over current and historic business cycles. Techniques to be covered should include:

o Balanced scorecard, with an emphasis on customer and innovation measures.

o Evaluation of marketing performance including the audit of marketing activities and valuation of marketing assets, such as brands.

o Financial techniques such as SVA (using total shareholder return and economic profit), financial ratio analysis, trend analysis, benchmarketing and evaluation of historical financial decisions.

Exam Hint 2.1

When answering a question on business performance it is important to mention the importance of measuring performance within the context of the specific company as well as linking the issues of business performance to different stakeholder needs as well as financial stakeholders through shareholder value.

Although the concept of shareholder value is a financial measure it is important to appreciate that other non-financial parameters such as promotional activity can influence it through building stronger relationships with customers therefore building brand equity which is discussed further in a different unit.

Exam Hint 2.2

It is therefore important to write a plan for questions in this examination and failing to do so will not enable you to link different parts of the syllabus to the question in hand. Questions are not likely to draw from only one part of the syllabus which is the same as in real life where marketing problems are likely to be multifaceted incorporating many elements listed in the theory. Students should be aware of this when structuring their answers and therefore writing a plan to structure their answers is essential. It is surprising to see the high number of students who do not write a plan for their questions in the examination.

How will this unit help you and how does it fit within the A&E course structure

The new syllabus of the PPDIPM is intended to develop your skills as a professional marketing executive to make and implement effective marketing decisions within a range of different types of organizations. Therefore, your skills will need to include being able to utilize a range of theoretical frameworks to identify a host of external and internal organizational issues that will give rise to opportunities and threats. Your next task will be to formulate marketing strategies intended to exploit these opportunities and minimize the threats. Now think about how you would proceed to identify what the issues are:

- o What descriptions would you use to identify as well as communicate them to other stakeholders?
- o How would you ensure that all stakeholders were talking about the same thing, therefore seeing and thinking about the issues in a similar way?

In most situations you cannot make decisions in isolation of other internal organizational stakeholders – this is unless you run a small business which you completely own and even then you will be pushed not to communicate with other stakeholders. Each stakeholder will have their own culture and language for communicating and it is imperative for marketers to be able to understand the thinking and language used by the other stakeholders, otherwise they are unlikely to be able to get their strategy proposals accepted and the shareholders are likely to lose their confidence by selling their shares indicating that they too have an expectation of what needs to be communicated.

Therefore in order for marketers to communicate their plans to address the opportunities and threats they need to define the parameters which give rise to the opportunity or threat as well as provide some idea to its magnitude. *Developing measures and scales are, therefore, imperative otherwise you are unlikely to be able to effectively define the issue as well as gain agreement of what to do about it*. Therefore, before you can proceed to analyse and evaluate followed by formulating strategies you will need to appreciate how to develop metrics in marketing and business, which is the subject of this unit, as well as consider some particular issues to developing metrics for certain marketing activities such as branding.

The common language in business tends to be finance and it is used across a number of functions in order to measure viability of different strategy options proposed. This is not difficult to appreciate as at the end of the day a business will not be viable unless it makes a reasonable return within the expectation of their shareholders. This is also true for non-profit organizations. So shareholders are expecting us as marketers to invest their money wisely in projects that will provide financial expected returns. Customers, on the other hand, are also looking for value and want companies to either be more financially efficient through continuously improving their perceived offering over time or through improving their features and performance. So finance is a very important language for all of us to learn to effectively communicate in business and will be covered in Unit 3. Unfortunately due to historical reasons finance has tended to dominate the business decision-making landscape within organizations even though it is in fact limited in providing appropriate measures for the performance of a number of business areas. Finance-dominated organizational cultures came about at the end of the 1950s and 1960s when the multidivisional organization structure, commonly known as the M-Form organization, originated by General Motors in the United States, was perceived to be the most efficient structure run by the organizations. One of the characteristics of the M-Form organization was that pyramids of financial ratios were utilized to access any financial problem within any division as well as any function within the divisions. Financial quantification was, therefore, seen as paramount for making decisions as well as controlling activities within firms through budgeting. Therefore any business or marketing activity that was proposed tended to be rejected unless it could demonstrate adequate financial returns. This was very difficult for many marketing activities such as advertising, public relations and, more recently, corporate social responsibility as the performance link into actual financial performance is sometimes very difficult to establish, let alone measure.

Over time even the accountants began to question whether financial performance measures were everything that they were cracked up to be. Researchers such as Kaplan and Norton began to see financial performance as only one element of a host of other performance measures which all needed to be achieved to maintain long-term financial viability. The concept of a balanced performance approach where executives must show linkages between proposed activities and long-term financial viability, and how by measuring the performance of the proposed activities as a surrogate is likely to improve financial performance, is becoming more widely accepted. This is the basis of the balance scorecard.

So ultimately what we are trying to achieve is to identify marketing activities that are likely to impact on financial performance including demonstrating how the activities are linked. This will then be followed by identifying metrics to measure the activity which we can assume will also impact on financial viability.

Exam Hint 2.3

The above points provide you with the unique opportunity of gaining considerable marks in the examination by allowing you to demonstrate the marketing skills discussed in Unit 1. It is highly likely that there will be questions relating to business performance and you can therefore show why performance measurement is important for the company mentioned in the question and what the problems are relating to performance measurement, as well as its implications for senior executives within the company.

Statements of related marketing practice

The main skill or business competency areas being developed in this section and are likely to be examined are:

- To develop appropriate structures and frameworks to identify appropriate information requirements to define and structure marketing-related business problems.
- To be able to critically evaluate different analytical perspectives which will lead executives to gain a better understanding of their external and internal environment within the specific context of their industries, thus setting and placing them in a better position to make better informed decisions potentially leading to minimize risks and uncertainties.

Key definitions

Objectives – are the specific intended outcomes of a strategy.

The balanced scorecard – is an analytical approach which links setting objectives and setting performance measures.

ROCE – is Return on Capital Employed.

Marketing metrics – are agreed units of marketing measurement and their application.

SMEs – are small- to medium-sized enterprises, that is, companies which employ fewer than 250 employees.

Introduction

Evaluating performance is a very important area. If we view the contribution of marketing as worthwhile within the organization, then we need to be able to justify it. There are quantitative measures available which allow us to assess how:

- o the company is performing in marketing terms (Unit 2)
- o how we can value our marketing assets, in particular our brands (Unit 3)
- o how we can audit our marketing activities (Unit 4).

The first part of this century has seen much activity in the development of marketing metrics for two main reasons. First, it was felt that marketing has never really been made accountable. Secondly, technology now allows us to measure and evaluate performance in ways that was previously impossible or at least impractical. The rule of marketing metrics is that:

If you can't measure it, think carefully about whether you should do it.

These measures become particularly significant when we appreciate that many organizations are operating internationally. With companies operating in a great variety of marketplaces, it is invaluable to have a common set of measures which allow us to make comparisons across international boundaries. These can help us to make informed investment decisions and to assess performance objectively. Even if your organization is not an international one, its customers will be. Virtually every consumer is an international shopper, the advent of the World Wide Web has assured that. Growth in Internet shopping continues with Christmas 2003 being the highest yet.

Objectives

To make an assessment of how an organization is performing, we need to look first at what it was aiming to achieve. Objectives tend to be set in a hierarchy, that is corporate objectives precede functional objectives which develop into operational objectives. So a corporate objective might be to increase operating profit by 10 per cent. One of the resultant marketing objectives could be to increase market share to 15 per cent. This marketing objective needs to be broken down into marketing mix objectives such as implementing a price increase of 6 per cent by June, adding two new distributors and so on.

Performance outcomes

Easily the most commonly used measures of performance are sales, usually in the form of market share, and profitability. They appear to be fairly simple, though that is misleading. We know that market definition is complicated and subjective. The relationship between share and profit is not at all clear-cut. Other measures have also become more popular such as customer retention and acquisition rates as companies appreciate the value of loyalty. The next few sections examine each of these in turn.

Market share

Market share is one of the basic measures of market performance. It allows us to evaluate how we are performing against the competition without the confounding factor of changes in the market size and growth rates. Valuable though this measure is, there are a number of issues we need to take into account before we can generate a meaningful analysis which allows us to move forward towards strategic implications. We need to define our market (not always as easy as it sounds!), define the appropriate timescale on which to evaluate market share and examine the relationship between value and volume.

Market definition

A complicating factor is, how do we define our market? If we start with the traditional marketing view of defining our market by the needs met, this may be too broad.

For example, take the crisps market. What is the need met here? Nutrition possibly. But that would mean that our market would comprise all food products. So our market share might be 0.000003 per cent. Not very helpful when it comes to measuring trends. What would we make of our movement from 0.0000030 to 0.0000034 per cent? It could be a major shift or merely noise in collecting the data.

Maybe the need met is for a snack. Then we are competing against a smaller subset of the food market, items like fruit, confectionery, bagged snacks made from ingredients such as maize and so on. But our overall share is still very small so again we face the same problems. How do we know whether a change is important or not? Although a market definition based on needs met may be useful for some purposes, for example competitor definition and understanding macro-trends, it is not always appropriate.

The question of properly defining your market has also been covered in your earlier marketing studies with identifying appropriate market segments. Segmenting the market and correctly identifying the segments in which the company is deliberately positioning their offering through choice (targeting) or undeliberately where customers are *'pigeon holing'* a product through their own perceptions rather than being encouraged by the company. Segmentation, targeting and positioning is the basis of strategic marketing and the important factor in defining market segments is that they are measurable. There are many examples of where the proper market segments have not been identified, for example the international position strategy for Parker Pens in the 1980s and 1990s was against Schaeffer another brand of premium pens, whereas in fact the biggest competitor to Parker was the Ronson lighter which was being offered as an alternative to a pen in the gifts market. Mercedes and BMW jeeps are not competing in the segments as Ford and General Motor jeeps as they represent different lifestyle segments. Some time ago at the international tennis tournament at Wimbledon someone reading the *Financial Times* mentioned the performance of Swatch watches to an executive of Rolex who appeared disinterested; on being asked why he was not interested in the watch market he mentioned that Rolex did not compete in the watch market. Ensuring that an organization has a marketing orientation through being able to better utilize information to appropriately segment, target and offer a differential positioning of their relative to the competition is a prerequisite to competitive success.

For market share purposes, we need to define our market at a level that is useful for us whilst viewing it within the wider context of market definition. So for the crisps market we may choose other crisps brands. This may be an oversimplification as we know that realistically consumers may be choosing between a bag of crisps, an apple or a chocolate bar. But we can handle that complexity by looking at micro- and macro-environmental trends since it is not helpful to introduce them now.

So market definition is a balance between the extended market (e.g. food, snacks) and micro-markets (e.g. salt and vinegar flavoured crinkle cut crisps in 25 gram packets sold at bars in Berlin). Neither definition is valuable in the context of market share analysis; at one extreme our share might be infinitesimally small and at the other we may command 100 per cent share. But how does that help us? We cannot make judgements and strategic decisions on the basis of this type of information.

The important issue to remember about market definition is to define it at the appropriate level for the task in hand. And to bear in mind that the definition of the market is a moveable feast. It is likely that you will find that one level is useful for market share analysis, another for macro-environmental analysis and possibly another for competitor analysis. So to continue with the crisps example, the crisps market might be appropriate at a market share level, the snacks market would certainly be useful at the macro-level and possibly other bagged snacks manu-facturers at a competitor level.

Once the market has been defined, we need to determine the most useful timescale over which to evaluate the share shifts.

Timescale

The timescale over which to evaluate share is critical. It is important not to over-react to short-term fluctuations and yet to be responsive if there is a problem. Not an easy balancing act!

The choice of timescale will be largely dependent on your product category. There are few product categories where a daily analysis of share would be appropriate, but probably none where a five yearly review of share would be helpful. In many markets some sort of smoothing of the data may be appropriate such as using a Moving Annual Total.

If your product is a FMCG then quarterly reviews, that is every 13 weeks, tend to be the norm. The heaven (and the hell) of working in this type of market is that there tends to be a lot of data available. The challenge here is to reduce this data down to a manageable form and to translate it into information. The issue here is normally data overload.

Other types of market are less (or more) fortunate. In these, managers may have their own revenue figures but have to make estimates of market size and competitor revenues. Here objectivity needs to be enforced. Estimates should be made separately by several managers, and ideally also by independent observers, for example analysts.

Volume and value

When examining market share we need to make a clear distinction between volume (units) and value (revenue). Both are important, separately and in relation to each other. Each tells a different story and their interaction is very important.

Another critical factor is trends over time. Is our brand on an upward surge or a downward spiral? Let us look at the following scenario to see how these factors can affect our evaluation of the situation.

Question 2.1

There are three main competitors operating in catering for large corporations within a limited geographic area. They win their business by contract and then go to supply those organizations with meals, drinks and so on for their employees for a fixed term.

Table 2.1 shows how the Big Three in this market (Stokes Services, Edwards Enterprises and Woods for Work) are performing.

Table 2.1 Market information for the contract catering industry

		2000	2001	2002	2003	2004
Stokes services	Revenue in Euros (m)	10	12	13	14	14
	Number of contracts	5	6	7	7	7
Woods for work	Revenue in Euros (m)	8	12	13	16	20
	Number of contracts	4	5	4	5	4
Edwards enterprises	Revenue in Euros (m)	5	4	4	4	4
	Number of contracts	10	10	11	12	14
Total market	Revenue in Euros (m)	25	30	32	38	45
	Number of contracts	20	21	22	24	25

Using this information, assess the following:

1. The relative market share positions of the three competitors in 2004 in volume and value terms
2. Volume and value market trends over time
3. Market size trends and structure
4. The strategies which appear to have been employed over the period 2000–2004
5. Which appears to have been the most successful?

We normally assume that a high market share reflects superior positional advantages in the past. It may, on the other hand, be the result of luck, or chance. There is an argument that, if share changes each period are distributed randomly, some firms will gain at the expense of others. The superior profits they earn from this short-term gain may support the development of superior resources, which will deliver superior positional advantage and so on. High market share will become self-reinforcing. This will be discussed in Unit 7 when we look at sources of competitive advantage.

Of more concern to us here is whether current share is a good predictor of future share, as it must be if it is to be classified as an advantage. Here we can turn to the Profit Impact in Market Strategy (PIMS) database. This database began as a corporate appraisal technique in GE (the American General Electric Company) in the late 1960s but has subsequently been developed into a major longitudinal research and evaluation programme based at Harvard University. Thousands of businesses give details to the Harvard researchers who examine the links between strategy and performance, strategy and profit, market share and profit, market share and key ratios and so on. Since the study has been running for some 40 years its results do have credibility.

Their results suggest a significant regression towards the mean, that is high initial shares tend to decline and low shares tend to increase over time (Buzzell and Gale, 1987). Thus pioneers (the first into a market) gain an early share advantage of 17 percentage points over followers in industrial markets, and 23 percentage points in consumer industries. After 20 years, this lead is reduced on an average to 13 points for both industrial and consumer markets (Robinson, 1988).

The probable explanation is that, as a market matures, product quality advantages deteriorate. Unless the leader can innovate continuously, the other competitors will catch up gradually. High profits earned by the leader also attract entrants, so the market is likely to become more competitive. High shares can be defended, but some erosion seems to be inevitable.

Market share and profitability

The causal direction of the relationship between share and profit is unclear. Early share gains may be due to luck, or initially superior resources. First-mover advantages may or may not exist. What then happens over time depends on how well managers defend their positions and keep up to date with technology and the market. The current share may be the result of past profits, or may deliver future profits, or both (or, in some highly contested strategic groups, neither).

To be useful to us in the present context, market share must:

- Have been gained in a way that competitors will find hard to copy
- Refer to a market with fairly stable boundaries. In dynamic markets, which are being redefined by new competitors, market share will be a less reliable advantage.

Profitability

Some of the problems with market share also apply here. It is complicated by the uncertainties surrounding the term 'profit' itself. It may seem simple and unambiguous, but it is not.

As with market share, we need to decide at what level we examine profit. Again we need to decide what our objective is in determining profitability. Do we want to make a comparison between lines? Brands? Divisions? Countries? Companies? Once we have made this decision, the process is broadly similar, only the level of aggregation varies.

We need to compare like with like, apples with apples rather than with pears. So the level of profit needs to be consistent so that we can make comparisons. Are we going to look at gross profit, that is, before costs, or net, that is, after costs? Or somewhere in between, that is, after fixed costs but before marketing costs? Or before tax? Or before tax and interest? Again the key here is to think about the issue we want to address.

If, for example, we want to evaluate the relative profitability of brands, we might want to examine their margins twice. First, we could look at profit after all costs including marketing expenditure, and then again at profits excluding marketing expenditure. In this way we might attempt to discover which brands are successful because of their marketing support.

Differences in the allocation of overheads may change the apparent profitability of products or firms. It is always important that you understand how figures are derived before undertaking analysis. This allows you to understand potential weaknesses and biases in the data. Then you can either compensate for them or run the data in a different form so that the data more accurately reflects your research problem.

Taking profitability alone, it may be the result of positional advantage. If we genuinely have lower costs than competitors for equivalent quality, or can charge a premium price because of superior customer benefits (and our extra costs are less than the additional margin), then we ought to expect superior profit. We will return to this in Unit 9 when we discuss competitive advantage.

Loyalty

Recent interest in loyalty was triggered and has been developed by Reichheld (1996). He refers to loyalty as 'the litmus test of corporate performance'.

An increasingly important marketing measure is the degree of 'churn' in the customer base.

We can measure our sales by revenue. And sometimes we can measure our sales by customer base. But one of the basic tenets of marketing is the idea of mutually beneficial exchange, that is, we want the customer to be satisfied, to come back wanting more, to talk positively about our product. So we need to know about the extent to which our business comes from new customers and from existing ones. Of course, in an ideal world all our existing customers would remain with us buying vast amounts from our organization into eternity, whilst simultaneously encouraging new customers in their droves to join them in their loyalty to us, their only supplier. But if we come down to earth, this is probably not the case.

Why are loyal customers more profitable?
The generic figure below summarizes the potential sources of additional profit for a retained customer. Bear in mind that industries will differ. Acquisition costs may be high for a mortgage company but low for FMCG, for example. Referral rates may diminish over time as novelty wears off and so on.

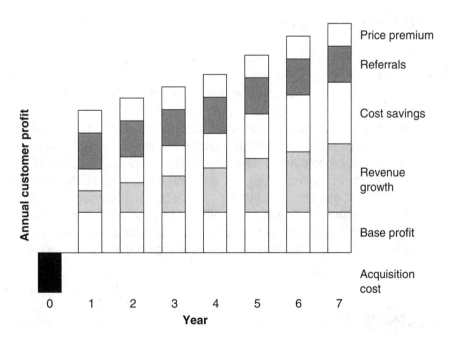

Figure 2.1 Why are loyal customers more profitable?
Source: Reichheld (1996)

Let us examine each of these factors in turn.

1. *Acquisition cost* – This refers to the cost of getting a new customer or donor. This may be by advertising, personal selling, direct mail, expense of opening a new store, time invested in writing a proposal or making a pitch and so on. Some of these are obvious and some are hidden. The important thing is to make sure that all costs are taken into account to ensure that an objective and realistic figure is gained of the cost of gaining a new customer.

2. *Base profit* – Our customers pay a price for our product which is in excess of the costs of producing it (normally). The longer a customer stays with your organization, the longer you can continue to earn the base profit, which you can trade off against your initial acquisition costs.

3. *Revenue growth* – In most industry sectors, customer spending tends to accelerate with time as customer familiarity grows with the brand. As the customer appreciates the range on offer from a retailer, for example, they tend to extend their purchasing across categories. Some sectors have a built-in accelerator effect, for example home and contents insurance where the premiums automatically increase each year.

But Reichheld warns that although this concept is easy to understand, it can be difficult to get an accurate measure.

If you just take a snapshot of the current customer base, this could be misleading. It is tempting to divide the present customers by tenure and measure the revenue from each group. There are three problems with this. First, it ignores the fact that different customer cohorts may have different characteristics, perhaps in terms of demography or lifestyle. Secondly, that cohorts become smaller as they age; attrition over time reduces the sample size. And finally, it is likely that defectors are different in some way to those that are retained. This means that any projection based on the current base is likely to be over-optimistic.

The behaviour of defectors needs to be analysed as well as that of retained customers.

4. *Operating costs* – As customers become more familiar with the company and its portfolio, they become more efficient as buyers. They become less reliant on the organization as they become knowledgeable. They understand the extent of the portfolio and the processes of the organization.

5. *Referrals* – Referrals occur when customers recommend your product to potential clients. A benefit of long-term customer retention is that satisfied customers tend to refer more, according to Reichheld. The evidence on this is actually quite mixed depending on product category. In some categories customers tend to refer more in the early stages of custom when the novelty encourages word of mouth.

6. *Price premium* – Old customers effectively pay higher prices than new ones. They do not benefit from introductory offers or discounts, or also tend not to be as price sensitive. Their increased product knowledge creates their own personal barrier to exit.

 Activity 2.1

For each of the factors listed above, that is acquisition cost, base profit, revenue growth, cost savings, referrals and price premium, give an example of an industry where you might expect the value to be high and one where it might be low.

Reichheld suggests a loyalty strategy which has eight elements:

1. Building a superior customer value proposition
2. Finding the right customers
3. Earning customer loyalty
4. Finding the right employees
5. Earning employee loyalty
6. Gaining cost advantage through superior productivity
7. Finding the right investors
8. Earning investor loyalty.

You can see from this list that there is a focus on three stakeholder groups – customers, employees and investors. He suggests different strategies to encourage loyalty in each. Since this unit is concerned with A&E, we will focus on the analytical side of this process and its implications rather than the implementation aspects.

Reichheld suggests seven question areas that a company needs to answer before applying the eight stages above.

Area	Specific questions	Measures
Agreement on purpose	Do you want to enter into a long-term partnership with each other? Can you commit to value creation for customers as a primary mission?	
Economic quantification	Does the shift make economic sense to the company?	Specific elements of customer and employee loyalty which improve the economics of your business
Ownership strategy	Will the investors endorse your strategy and accept a long-term orientation?	
Partnership incentives	Do you have an adequate system of partnership incentives for the senior management team and other parts of the supply chain, for example suppliers, employees and distributors?	
Getting the facts	Why do customers join and why do they defect? Why do employees join and why do they defect?	
System failures	What is the nature and scope of your business's system failures?	Defection rates, acquisition rates, yield rates
Measures, tools and targets	How will you measure your progress?	Rates of value flow, employee turnover

Case study

William Hill

Betting firm William Hill has a thriving online arm, which has brought in 10 per cent of the 70-year-old company's worldwide bets, totalling £3.9 billion, in 2002, and is outperforming other parts of the group. Its aim was simple: to build on this success by acquiring 200 000 or more new online customers at a cost of £50 per account.

'Online gamblers are only a small subset of the UK population so precision marketing is important', says Peter Nolan, Group Marketing Director at William Hill.

William Hill brought in eCRM company RedEye to help it increase online revenue. 'Some 50 per cent of people don't place money in their online accounts straightaway when they register and a significant number never do so', explains Jonathan Kay, chief operating officer at RedEye. It decided to follow up these people with follow-up e-mails after they had registered. It tested three different e-mail executions using different creative, language and timing against a control group that did not receive an e-mail.

In all cases, those who received an e-mail were five times more likely to convert to being an actual user than those who did not. RedEye is reluctant to say which of the three e-mails tested worked the best, but the follow-up e-mail that has been adopted by William Hill now drives 1.2 per cent of all new accounts, and for every pound spent, the firm gets back £1.25.

RedEye also focused on increasing the number and spend of high-value customers. The William Hill website contains some editorial content that is not highly used and is expensive to maintain. RedEye wanted to track whether this content had any effect on high-value customers before trying to get rid of it. It selected two segments of visitors, those who had not seen the content but had placed a bet and those who had seen the content and placed a bet. It found that the group that had seen the content were betting twice as frequently and spending five times as much.

Although only 6 per cent of the site's visitors used the content, they brought in 30 per cent of the revenue. The result of these findings was that, rather than binning the content section, William Hill decided to drive people to it with targeted e-mails. 'You can't put your measurement in silos', advises Kay. 'It's important to go for a single view of the customer.'

Source: Marketing Direct, 2003, Supplement on Profit through Customer Insight.

This case study emphasizes the importance of finding the right customers.

The three groups of customers which are attractive are:

1. Those who are inherently predictable and loyal, regardless of the organization.
2. Those who are more profitable as they spend more money, pay their bills promptly and require less service.
3. Those who find your offering more valuable than those of the competitors because of a better fit with their needs.

We now move on to examining another way of mapping performance. The balanced scorecard is a well-accepted technique to assess performance. We use it here to assess historic and current performance, other units use it to set objectives, assess future performance and so on.

The balanced scorecard

Exam Hint 2.4

Students are likely to have the opportunity to discuss non-financial business performance measures, the Balance Score Card (BSC) is appropriate to identify the overall causation factors likely to impact financial performance. The balance score card in itself is only one particular tool which identifies specific factors but there many other factors which are missed by the BSC, in this vain it is important for students to appreciate what one is actually trying to achieve with the BSC and to take of the BSC and create specific score cards for specific companies operating in specific contexts. Multifactorial score cards are often developed by consultancies such as Accenture as part of theirs to create High Performance Companies. Students therefore should consider whether the BSC can be applied directly to the company in the question set or does it require adapting in terms of identifying new measurement variables?

It is important that we map our performance against our objectives. One way to do this is to use a framework called the balanced scorecard which was developed in the early 1990s by Kaplan and Norton (1992, 1993). They suggest developing a balanced set of objectives alongside a coherent set of performance measures.

To apply this framework you need to look at the business from four different perspectives:

1. *Financial* – See the organization from a shareholder's perspective and evaluate the success of its strategy and implementation.
2. *Customer* – Put yourself in the customer's shoes. What is important to the customer and how is your organization performing against their requirements?
3. *Internal* – What are the critical internal processes which allow your organization to meet your customers' needs? What are the processes which create satisfaction or dissatisfaction?
4. *Innovation and learning* – To create value, an organization must be able to continuously innovate and learn. How does your organization handle this?

Strategic measures (or performance indicators) are set in each of these areas to provide an objective basis with which to evaluate and formulate strategy.

The balanced scorecard widens the view that managers have by making them look at the business from different perspectives. It forces them to examine inter-relationships between processes and functional areas, and to ensure consistency between objectives.

Table 2.2 gives you an idea of how the balanced scorecard might work within an organization. The objectives and measures are examples and it is for the organization to tailor the scorecard to its own specific objectives and the measures which it sees as relevant and practical. Within the A&E module we will use the balanced scorecard to assess the current position of an organization. In subsequent modules you will use the same framework to move the company forward.

Table 2.2 The balanced scorecard

	Strategic objectives	Strategic measures
Financial	Return on capital	ROCE
	Cash flow	Cash flow
	Profitability	Net margin
	Profitability growth	Volume growth rate vs industry
	Reliability of performance	Profit forecast reliability
		Sales backlog
Customer	Value for money	Customer ranking survey
	Competitive price	Pricing index
	Customer satisfaction	Customer satisfaction survey
Internal	*Marketing*	
	o Product and service development	Pioneer percentage of product portfolio
	o Shape customer requirement	Hours with customer on new work
	Manufacturing	
	o Lower manufacturing cost	Total unit cost (vs competition)
	o Improve project management	Safety incident index
	Logistics	
	o Reduce delivery costs	Delivered cost per unit
	o Inventory management	Inventory level compared to output
	Quality	Levels of rejects
Innovation and learning	Innovate products and services	Percentage revenue from pioneer products
	Time to market	Cycle time vs industry norm
	Empowered workforce	Staff attitude survey
	Access to strategic information	Strategic information availability
	Continuous improvement	Number of employee suggestions

Source: After Kaplan and Norton (1992, 1993)

So, for example, in some sectors such as management consultancy, it may be hard to access a customer ranking survey so another objective or measure may be appropriate, for example percentage of bids won. In SMEs it may be impractical to set up large surveys so other measures may be required.

 Activity 2.2

Apply the balanced scorecard to your organization.

- o What are your key objectives in the four perspectives listed in Table 2.2 above?
- o How would you measure them?
- o Is your organization currently measuring them? And in what way?
- o How are you performing?

A sporting analogy

Bering and Mntambo (2002) apply a sporting analogy to the balanced scorecard. Think football. (This analogy will work equally well with netball, basketball and so on but the terminology may need to change.)

In a football match, the team manager has the responsibility of ensuring that his side wins. The ultimate objective is winning and the ultimate performance measure is the score. But during the match, the manager uses other indicators to decide how well or badly the team is faring, and what action he should take to improve their prospects.

So during the first half, he will see how many scoring chances have been created, how much possession of the ball his team has had and which players are performing well (or badly). The manager can then make adjustments to his tactics on the basis of his analysis. He may substitute players or try a different game plan on the basis of his experience to date.

The aim still remains to win the match but performance indicators such as shots on goal, number of corner kicks and so on will allow the manager to make a more informed decision, which should make his team more likely to succeed.

A balanced scorecard operates in the same way. Where the football team manager wants to win the match/league/cup, the CEO wants to maximize shareholder value. But to do this he/she needs to keep track of other indicators of performance which will help the management team to judge whether changes need to be made to improve the prospects of achieving this.

Continuing with the football analogy, the number of shots on goal can be a useful measure of performance since this is likely to be a predictor of the number of goals scored. But at the end of the day (or match!) the important factor is the number of goals scored, not how many attempts there have been made.

An actual application to technology firm

A major technology organization was investing heavily into sponsoring major scientific congresses and symposia. These congresses were sponsored by many of the big players within the industry but all the companies were unsure exactly how participation into these activities would contribute to the bottom line. Sponsors were allowed to display an exhibition stand but there were also presentations being made by innovators on trials with a company's new technology.

It was accepted wisdom that the congresses had little impact on the current product portfolio but they were considered essential to the success of future products as it was an effective medium to target innovators who would then be utilized to influence other customer groups over the life cycle of the technology. The concern was that an investment today would lead to future cash-flow benefits, but how could one measure the financial return on an investment made today on a product that would not be launched for another 10 years? How could one also develop an appropriate performance tool that would help the company to demonstrate appropriate returns to shareholders for their investment in congresses?

In response to this challenge a marketing strategy consultancy identified, utilizing a hybrid model of the balanced scorecard and Porter's Value Chain (1985), a process for the adoption of a new technology which involved all the steps, including those taking place at the congress, that would influence the purchase of the new technology. Market research with industry experts allowed the consultancy to identify a set of activities considered critical for influencing future purchasing decisions and would help therefore impact on the new technology's financial performance. Various additional activities were identified and included those that needed to be undertaken prior to the congress as well as those following the congress. The results were then developed into an audit which allowed companies to measure their congress activities and spend which in turn allowed them to gain a better understanding of how much return they were likely to be getting from their financial investment. Many organizations found that they completely missed out on the following-up activities after congresses which reduced any long-term relationship benefits between head office, the customers and the local country affiliates.

Summary

In this unit we have seen the main marketing measures used to evaluate performance.

The first point made is that we can only assess the performance of an organization when we know what the organization's objectives are. Performance is the comparison of achievement with objective.

The measures we have considered are:

First, market share. This is a commonly used measure but the issues of market definition need to be considered, as well as the distinction between value and volume and the decision on timescale. The evidence from the PIMS study is reviewed to gauge whether past market share is a useful indicator of future market performance.

Secondly, profitability. This again is problematic since we need to be sure that the measure of profit is consistent. We see the implications of changing the allocation of overheads and see that profitability by line has a degree of subjectivity.

We have then looked at the newer measures of marketing performance which relate to loyalty. Customer acquisition and retention rates are discussed. The benefits of retained customers are explained.

Moving on from these measures the balanced scorecard framework is introduced. This aims to pull together the different elements of the organization, summarizing them into four perspectives – financial, customer, internal, and innovation and learning.

The next unit looks at how we might value brands, increasingly recognized as an important asset.

Forecasting

It is imperative to appreciate that the current performance of an organization and its competitors are measured as part of a SWOT analysis. This is fine when we need to answer the question whether the organization is appropriately positioning its offering currently to its customers relative to the competition. But this is only half the story. Markets are continuously evolving and marketers need to assess whether they have the right resources and capabilities to compete in the future. Therefore a good understanding of how markets are likely to evolve is a very important part of a senior marketer as they will need to minimize risk and uncertainty if they wish to select winning strategies that will maximize shareholder value. There are several ways in which an organization can project the future but the two major ones include forecasting and scenario planning.

Econometric forecasting

There are several techniques available for forecasting with many of them using statistical techniques which use copious amounts of historical data to project what the market is likely to do in the future. These regression econometric forecasts are based on the assumption that history is likely to repeat itself and therefore historical precedence is a reflection of the future and can be used to predict future outcomes. Unfortunately this is only true for very stable markets – an unlikely phenomenon in today's environment. In most economies turbulent markets are the order of the day, caused, by highly competitive pressures with organizations adopting innovating marketing mix strategies to aggressively gain market share.

Scenario planning

Often due to turbulent markets it is very difficult to predict the future state of a market or industry as history is very unlikely to repeat itself. In these circumstances it would be better to assemble a group of experts to brainstorm either together as a group or independently from each other (Delphi technique) a number of possible alternative states.

For example:

The market will quadruple in size over the next 3–5 years. (optimistic)

The market will decline by a considerable amount. (pessimistic)

The market will remain the same. (realistic)

The market will show minimal growth. (realistic)

Having identified the scenarios one could then use a jury of experts to assign probabilities of the likelihood of the scenarios actually happening. Therefore contingencies can then be used to plan for optimal deployment of resources. It is important to continuously scan the external environment to accordingly modify the probabilities of the scenarios.

Activity 2.3

Imagine a tobacco company, an alcoholic beverage company and a company providing healthcare. For each company determine the possible scenarios that are likely to impact each company and assign likely probabilities of their occurrences.

Game Theory and Simulations

You have probably realized that several situations exist where evaluating marketing issues and performance can be extremely complex and difficult due to interacting components which are difficult to separate. In these non-linear situations trying to understand the whole through measuring would be an impossible task. With the advent of computers various scenarios can be simulated and their numerous intricate interactions as well as their outcomes being readily identified. Simulations are being used in marketing and strategy but for the moment they are still primarily within the realm of academia. At some point in the future they should provide some useful insights in determining strategic marketing problems.

 ## Activity 2.4

Think about the performance measures that could be utilized by the New Zealand Tourist Board to measure the success or lack of success of their promotional campaign to raise the profile of the country as a tourist destination following the release of the Lord of the Rings movie trilogy.

 ## Activity 2.5

If you were starting your business and need to get a loan from a bank or attract private investors what would you need to show in terms of performance measures (consider financial as well as non financial) to ensure that they invest in your venture?

Measurement and developing world markets

A major limitation for developing performance measurements is to rely on readility available information in the form of primary or secondary information. Now this information may be readily available for developed economies but in many developing world economies this is not likely to be the case. It is imperative that students appreciate this fact as exam questions can be set on identifying performance measures as well as identifying market research issues relating to gathering data in developing world markets. Creative alternatives are required to analyse and evaluate these particular markets.

Activity 2.6

Think about a major food company setting up a subsidiary in a West African state, what information does it require to effectively launch the subsidiary and what issues is it likely to face in gathering such information?

Further study

Aaker, D.A. (1998) *Strategic Market Management*, 5th edition, Wiley.

Ambler, T., Kokkinaki, F. (1997) 'Measures of marketing success', *Journal of Marketing Management*, **13**, pp. 665–678.

Hints and tips

The examiners will be looking at your breadth of knowledge. So you need to move outside of your own industry and experience. Make sure you do all the activities suggested in this text but that you also read beyond this text. Read the trade press, watch the business news and listen to relevant radio programmes. Be like a magpie, picking up new examples showing how businesses analyse their situation and then apply their findings.

Bibliography

Bering, M., Mutambo, V. (2002) 'Parity Politics', *Financial Management*, February, pp. 36–37.

Kaplan, R.S., Norton, D.P. (1992) 'The balanced scorecard: Measures that drive performance', *Harvard Business Review*, **70**(1), pp. 71–79.

Kaplan, R.S., Norton, D.P. (1993) 'Putting the balanced scorecard to work', *Harvard Business Review*, **70**(5), pp. 134–147.

Reichheld, F.F. (1996) *The Loyalty Effect*, Harvard Business School Press, Boston, Massachusetts.

unit 3 brand valuation

This is a very important unit as it not only considers the issues surrounding brand valuation but also discusses the strategic issues faced by marketers in relation to accountants in justifying the role of marketing in achieving an organization's overall strategic objectives.

Learning objectives

After completing this unit you will be able to:

- Understand the importance of seeing brands as assets

- Appreciate the benefits of brand valuation

- Compare the various methods of valuing brands

- Explain the drivers for valuing brands as assets.

Sections of the syllabus being covered in this unit:

Element 2: Evaluation of business and marketing performance (30 per cent).

2.1 Critically evaluate and use quantitative techniques for evaluating business and marketing performance over current and historic business cycles. Techniques to be covered should include:

- Balanced scorecard, with an emphasis on customer and innovation measures.

- Evaluation of marketing performance including the audit of marketing activities and valuation of marketing assets, such as brands.

- Financial techniques such as SVA (using total shareholder return and economic profit), financial ratio analysis, trend analysis, benchmarking and evaluation of historical financial decisions.

Element 3: Analysis of the internal environment (20 per cent).

3.1 Use and appraise the available techniques and processes for the objective assessment of the internal environment of an organization, including portfolio analysis, value chain, innovation audit and cultural web.

3.2 Critically evaluate the resource-based view of the organization.

3.3 Demonstrate the ability to use appropriate information and tools to evaluate the core competencies, assets, culture and weaknesses of an organization.

3.4 Assess the 'fit' between an organization's culture and its current strategy.

3.5 Summarize the salient factors and insights emerging from the internal analysis.

Branding potentially represents an important way of an organization developing and sustaining competitive advantage and is therefore an important intangible asset of a firm. Brands capture the relationships and reputation of both a firm's corporate, as well as its products' reputation to command a premium price from its customers over the equivalent commodity offering. Building brand equity through marketing activities potentially creates a differential positioning resulting in increasing shareholder value, the main purpose of the new Professional Post Graduate Diploma. Effectively valuing brands would be very important for a company in terms of estimating its true value but it is fraught with controversy due to the fact that they are intangible. For this reason it is worthwhile to have a separate section of valuation of brands and other assets will be reviewed in the following unit.

Exam Hint 3.1

The points mentioned above are very important and students should take note and remember them. Marketing's role is to create superior value to shareholders by being better than the competition at offering customers what they want so that long-term relationships are built and repeat purchasers follow. Marketing achieves this through developing an effective positioning for its offerings utilizing the marketing mix and establishes a perceptual set in the minds of their target audience through promotional activities which develops a brand reputation that eventually creates a brand identity. Branding is therefore the way to build the long lasting relationships amongst customers that will enhance shareholder value, a point that should be mentioned more in exam scripts.

Students need to show that they appreciate the meaning of what stands behind specific brands in specific context; for example why do customers return to a particular supermarket, airline or other business? There are several reasons of why they may do so but whatever the reasons may be, they are captured in the brand and form part of the brand emotional values. Customers can then rest assured that they will consistently achieve their desired emotional values by consistently using the same supplier. Brands therefore provide trust and reliability and take out the potential risk and anxiety from making purchasers. Students in exams should spend a little more time showing an appreciation of what different brand values stand for within different marketing contexts rather than using the term generically.

Brands therefore capture value, create and sustain a differential advantage and represent an asset for organizations. Alas because they are intangibles, branding activities, in the form of promotion, within firms are more often considered as expenses than investments are therefore communicated in the profit and loss accounts rather than the balance sheet. This has a major implication for marketing executives in convincing their colleagues of the merits of an expense rather than an investment. This is particular true in non-marketing-orientated companies.

How will this unit help you and what can you expect to achieve after completing this unit?

As mentioned in previous units, the purpose of the new Professional Postgraduate Diploma is to improve your potential to be a senior strategic thinker within your organization. Your newly acquired skills should support your role which will be to improve your ability to critically analyse and evaluate business situations so as to identify opportunities and threats in addition to recommending on how to best exploit these opportunities and minimize these threats respectively. Organizations require strategic thinkers in order to improve the chances of their future survival through improved decision-making and risk minimization. In order for you to be able to identify, describe and communicate business issues as well as their magnitude, you will have to rely upon your ability to utilize appropriate frameworks as well as defining appropriate metrics. Therefore prior to delving into an evaluation of the external, internal, customer and competitive environment of an organization, Units 2–4 are there to get you to think of analytical tools and measures that you will require as well as thinking about applying them. Remember it is not enough for you just to be able to recite relevant theory but you should also think about its application to the particular situation identifying its potential limitations.

Brands and branding not only play a significant role within marketing, but also have implications for other functions within organizations and can impact upon other stakeholders. It is therefore important to consider branding as a separate unit to see how it impacts upon the other units within the new PPDIPM syllabus as well as its impact upon marketing and business in general.

First, it is important for you to appreciate that brands have economic implications for creating wealth for firms as well as society as a whole. Brands are a means for firms to capture greater value (defined as generating above average returns) for their offerings, through their ability to charge above-average prices than firms offering similar goods and services. Brands are what differentiate an organization's products and services from being perceived simply as commodities which are easily replaceable with substitutes. Customers loyal to specific brands in question perceive them, either rationally or irrationally as being somewhat superior and sometimes inferior (e.g. Skoda's old reputation for poor quality before their acquisition by Volkswagen) than other offerings on the market. Therefore one of the focal points of marketing is applying an organization's capital (shareholders' funds plus any long-term loans) to build brands to capture long-term financial value benefiting all societal stakeholders concerned.

In many instances, customers may not perceive brands as being superior or inferior but simply different and will therefore hold a place in the minds of their loyal target audience. So unless the brand is deemed negative one can see that branding is a means of securing an organization's future cash-flow stream through differentiation. From the customer's perspective this can be seen as a benefit as customers want to minimize risk in terms of getting poor quality from an offering and sometimes more importantly to minimize how an offering is likely to impact upon how others are likely to perceive them, therefore, affecting their personal reputation.

In terms of firms achieving a sustainable differential competitive advantage, brands can be considered as assets and therefore as valuable resources. Unlike other types of resources available to a firm, such as finance and people skills, brands cannot be duplicated or easily acquired, they need to be built over a long period of time. Therefore, building a brand reputation is possibly one of the most secure ways of developing a sustainable competitive advantage.

One of the major functions of an organization's marketing department is to formulate and implement initiatives that will improve the brand reputation of the company itself, its products or services as well as its employees. The organization is likely to benefit financially from its increased brand equity as the desirability for its products, employees and shares (if it is a company quoted on one of the world's busiest stock exchanges) as well as commanding better payment terms from its suppliers. Therefore, considerable direct and indirect financial benefits results from increasing an organization's brand equity that one could say it is one of the most important business activities that occurs in business and should not be understated.

Unfortunately this particular perspective of branding is not shared by everyone within organizations or by many within the financial community. There has been considerable debate as to whether brands should be listed on balance sheets. In the early 1990s, in the wake of some major hostile take-overs in the United Kingdom, several companies felt that the true worth of their company was not being truly represented on their balance sheet and were considered undervalued and making them vulnerable as an acquisition target. In response to this, Rank Hovis McDougall (McSweeney and Steele, 1994) decided to place a value of their brands on the balance sheets. All other company assets are listed on balance sheets so why not brands? It is important that you appreciate that this area is considered as highly controversial and the pros and cons need to be appreciated by the aspiring senior marketing executive as it has considerable implications to their likely actions being successfully implemented. This particular point is examined in greater detail within Managing Marketing Performance which is Unit 3 of the PPDIPM.

Many amongst the financial community have argued that valuing brands due to their intangibility is fraught with difficulty and their value is likely to fluctuate according to how fickle people felt on any particular day which means that they cannot truly represent a company's net worth. This is a fair point but it should be noted that in product-based companies incomplete products called 'work-in-progress' are also valued and placed on the balance sheet. The real value of these items can also be argued as being subjective as if they ever had to be sold in that particular state then the price they would likely fetch would be what the customers were willing to pay on that particular day.

All promotional activities undertaken by marketing departments which lead to establishing brands are treated as expenses rather than an investment and are written off in the profit and loss accounts. A new product development initiative, on the other hand, is perceived as an investment and is included in the balance sheets. Both initiatives are likely to influence long-term shareholder value but promotion is not perceived in the same light.

Marketing executives are likely to have a hard time justifying promotional 'investments' as their impact is likely to be in the longer term, but the perception from being treated as an expense will be to judge promotional impact in the shorter term. Marketing executives should therefore appreciate that their promotional initiatives are likely to have longer-term shareholder value implications which means that short-term profitability is likely to suffer.

Financial statements are powerful communication tools and marketing executives need to understand that their initiatives are not 'pigeon-holed' in the same way within these documents. Therefore justifying marketing initiatives at board level will be dependent on the extent of the marketing versus financial orientation of the organization in question. Marketers should appreciate that considerable internal communications may be needed to justify the benefits of a PR or a Corporate Social Responsibility programme (both can be considered as brand building exercises). Such justifications may involve some deep changes to occur within the values and operating systems of an organization falling within the realm of change management.

61

After reading this unit, you should be familiar with the organizational stakeholder issues surrounding branding as well as acquire the language and appreciation to be able to appropriately place and justify marketing initiatives at a senior level.

Statements of related marketing practice

The main skill or business competency areas which are being developed in this section are likely to be examined:

○ To develop appropriate structures and frameworks to identify appropriate information requirements to define and structure marketing-related business problems.
○ To be able to critically evaluate different analytical perspectives which will lead executives to gain a better understanding of their external and internal environment within the specific context of their industries, thus setting and placing them in a better position to make better informed decisions potentially leading to minimize risks and uncertainties.
○ To promote a strong marketing orientation to influence strategy formulation and investment decisions.
○ Specify and direct the line marketing process.

Key definitions

A brand – is a distinguishing name and/or symbol (such as a logo, trademark or package design) which is intended to identify the goods or services of either one seller or a group of sellers, and to differentiate those goods or services from those of competitors.

Brand equity – is a set of assets and liabilities linked to a brand name and symbol that add to or subtract from the value provided by a product or service to a firm or that firm's customers.

Introduction

Some of the most important assets of a company are intangible.

As King (1989) puts it:

> A product is something that is made in a factory; a brand is something that is bought by a customer. A product can be copied by a competitor; a brand is unique. A product can be quickly outdated; a successful brand is timeless.

Brands represent a long-term stream of future income to an organization. They can survive even when the original company ceases to exist so they are realizable assets albeit intangible.

Brands as assets

If this business were split up, I would give you the land and bricks and mortar, and I would take the brands and trademarks, and I would fare better than you

John Stewart (Former CEO of Quaker)

Since the 1980s, brands have been increasingly regarded as assets to be valued in the same way that we might value plant and machinery. Some companies have gone to the extreme of adding brands to the balance sheet. Early proponents were Rupert Murdoch and News Corporation in 1984, Reckitt and Colman in 1985 (£56 million for Airwick) and Grand Metropolitan in 1988 (£558 million for Smirnoff). The effect of these was to strengthen significantly their balance sheets. Most organizations, however, are reticent, realizing that fluctuations in the valuation of their brands can have major repercussions on their share value. Where accountancy practice in the valuation of concrete assets such as factories is relatively established with widely accepted rules for depreciation and so on, the valuation of intangible assets such as brands is more problematic and tends to be a minefield that companies avoid. Any assessment of a brand's value will include inherently subjective judgements about market position, market prospects, the quality and value of marketing support.

However, a series of high profile takeovers starting with Nestlé's purchase of Rowntree Mackintosh (purchased for £2.5 billion against an asset base of £300 million) has led to companies viewing brands as assets and hence making them work harder. As a result we have seen a proliferation of line and category extensions as companies try to leverage their brands to the maximum.

Case study

A bit of brand equity history

Jacobs Suchard's dawn raid on Rowntree last Wednesday highlighted how little credit the London market gives companies for their strong brand names. The shares, idling at 477p on Wednesday morning, closed at 710p on Friday. With the benefit of hindsight the City admits that Rowntree was underpriced. But it remains true that American institutions, European markets and international conglomerates are all willing to pay a premium for established brands which British institutions will not.

Suchard's actions seem almost a re-run of the General Cinema double raid on Cadbury Schweppes last year which gave the American cinema and drink bottling group around 18 per cent at share prices up to £1 less than the current level. Rowntree is a medium-sized company with very large brands. KitKat is the bestselling sweet in the world, but such is Rowntree's lack of financial muscle it cannot exploit KitKat's full potential and has to allow Hershey to manufacture KitKat under franchise in America. Cadbury is in the same boat, it has to license Schweppes production in America, and so to a lesser extent are United Biscuits and Rank Hovis McDougall. All have risen in the light of Suchard's move, Cadbury put on 21p on Friday to 292p and United Biscuits 12p to 277p, although some re-investment of Suchard's cash could be a factor.

As an investment, branded names are excellent defensive holdings. It can take years to build up a brand name into the position where it can dominate a market and reap the premium profits accordingly. Many people will pay 3p more for a tin of Heinz baked beans than the store's brand, or 30p more for a jar of

Hellman's mayonnaise. In the wrong hands a brand can easily be ruined, Smith's crisps was starved of investment when part of the ailing Huntley and Palmer group, as was Golden Wonder for a time under Imperial Group's ownership.

As far as brand names are concerned the London market knows the price of all things but the value of nothing, to paraphrase Oscar Wilde.

Source: Daily Telegraph, 18 April 1988, p. 22.

 ## Activity 3.1

What do you think are the top ten brands in the world? What do you think they are worth? Go on the Internet or into a library and find out what they actually are. Did your answers correspond? If they did not (or did) what do you think the reasons were for the discrepancy or correlation?

Reasons for brand valuation

Although companies are right to be cautious about valuing brands, there are some considerable advantages to be weighed against the considerable risks. Broadly speaking these benefits fall into five categories relating to the balance sheet, financial markets, separability, management information and internal management.

Balance sheet benefits

The function of the balance sheet is to provide a snapshot of the equity (or investments) in a company. It is intended to be objective and to allow for comparison between companies or within the same company over time. The balance sheet provides a picture of where the company is at one moment in time. We can then compare it to where we were last year, 2 years ago, 5 years ago and so on.

 ## Activity 3.2

The snapshot analogy can be useful. Imagine a photo album.

The current position is a photo of you with your family and friends (i.e. assets and liabilities). Possibly parents, partner, children, whoever – all the people who are important in your life.

Think back 3 years. Who would have been in the picture then?

And in 3 years' time? Who will be there? Who will have changed? In what way? And why?

Apply this thinking to your organization.

Financial markets

Although we have already mentioned the requirements of the Stock Exchange, there is a broader point to be made. We know that much of the interest in brand valuation was triggered by a flurry of acquisitions in the late 1980s. It was obvious from the reaction of the Stock Exchange to these acquisitions that financial markets find it difficult to accurately assess the value of a company. If all brands were valued on a consistent basis it would be far easier for outsiders to make judgements on the relative value of corporate assets. This would mean that transactions in investment, trading and mergers and acquisitions could be handled more efficiently. In essence we would have a common currency which we currently lack.

Separability

By putting a value on a brand we are essentially setting the price that should be paid for it. This means that we can trade in brands. So we could sell or license the brand to third parties and have an objective (ish!) basis on which to start negotiations.

But there are problems here. Not all brands are separable from their parent organization. For a brand valuation to be useful in the marketplace, there must be a boundary between the brand and the company's assets. This is not always the case, for example brands may share joint production facilities where the costings and hence profits are dependent on shared overheads. Or the brand may benefit from corporate endorsement which adds to its value but would be lost if the brand was sold.

SmithKline Beecham (now Glaxo SmithKline) were able to sell their Ambrosia, Bovril, Marmite and Horlicks brands relatively easily since these assets are separable. The consumer base was largely unaware of the corporate parent and the factories were separate with Ambrosia made in Devon and the other brands in Slough, hence not infringing on SB's core business of pharmaceuticals with different brand values and manufacturing facilities.

Exam Hint 3.2

Students should be prepared to use the above arguments for establishing the importance of developing a brand image and reputation for a particular company in its specific marketing context and show how it can lead to increased shareholder value and sustained differential competitive advantage through the development of relationships. This is particularly relevant in companies operating in B2B markets where their products/services form only part of other organization's products or services and they can go completely un-noticed by the end consumer. These supply companies are at risk of losing value by being completely controlled by the demands of their business customers demanding cheaper prices at they have no power in the supply chain or the so-called marketing channel. Many organizations such as Intel brand their micro-chips and processors to end consumers even though they are an intermediary component for other computer manufacturers. This means they can control their prices because they have perceived differential image amongst end users and are not at the mercy of being an unknown commodity component in the marketing channel. Other examples include Nutrasweet, Nylon, Terylene, Teflon who are intermediary products and have used branding to gain power over the marketing channel, Finally McDonalds in the early eighties switched from using Coca-Cola in their stores to McDonald's cola the decision was short-lived as end customers were very unhappy.

There may be questions in the exam where non-marketing-orientated companies have neglected to build an effective brand identity through lack of promotion. Students should use the above theory to analyse and evaluate a situation and show where this action could potentially or has lead to the destruction of shareholder value.

Management information

Although we could see brand valuation as merely a balance sheet exercise, the process can be of clear benefit to managers, whether they are in marketing or in more general management functions. The brand does not have to go on the balance sheet for the process to give benefits to the organization. Most managers spend their time 'fire-fighting', sorting out relatively short-term problems and being reactive rather than proactive. Most companies have never felt the necessity to review their product portfolio simultaneously so brand valuation can provide a useful trigger to encourage this retrospection.

Entering into this process allows managers to undertake a considered review of their brands and allows for a detailed evaluation of their relative competitive positions. In many ways the process of valuing a brand may force managers to adopt a more strategic approach although the operational demands of their job push them towards tactics. At a more senior level (e.g. marketing director), it encourages a more objective allocation of resources by explicitly examining what the brand stands for and its future earning potential. Strategic options can be evaluated against the brand valuation and an assessment can be made of future brand values.

Internal management benefits

Stephen King, the brands guru, was the first to emphasize the internal impact of valuing the brand. He argues that this is the most important reason for valuation. He sees brand valuation as proclaiming the purpose of the company. Whilst this may be important for outside stakeholders such as analysts and shareholders, it can be used to inspire employees and act as a sort of mission statement. So much for the advantages of valuing brands. But how do we actually do it?

Brand valuation

There are a number of factors which can be used to establish the value of a brand. But we always need to bear in mind that any brand valuation will be subjective. We can use the usual accounting techniques but each has its weaknesses in this complex area.

 Activity 3.3

> Read the quality press, cut out examples/articles on brand valuation – they are happening weekly as companies aim to consolidate their position by buying others. Create a file and build your knowledge. On what basis are they valuing the brand? It might prove vital in an examination.

Historic cost

An obvious basis for valuation is that of historic cost, that is the sum of all the investment into the brand starting with research and development costs, and moving onto distribution costs and promotional investments. The use of historic cost is much simpler in the case of recently acquired brands where the value is relatively easily identified since it is essentially the price paid for the asset. But the situation is far more complex in the case of brands already owned by the company. How can we decide which costs are specific to the brand? How do we allocate overheads, management time and so on? And even if we could, would that actually reflect current value? All we would be able to assess would be the *quantity* of investment in the brand not the *quality*. Arguably, weaker brands might require more investment but under this method they would emerge as high value. So perhaps there is a better way.

Current or replacement cost

Again here we are using another widely accepted accounting technique for valuing an asset. Current cost is the price that a third party would pay for a brand, which is theoretically at least the same as it would cost to establish a totally new brand. Difficulties arise here because of the infrequency of brand trading. Since we rarely see brands coming up for sale, it is hard to identify the appropriate price. Brands are not like cars. The second-hand market is relatively limited and every brand is unique by definition. Benchmarking a relevant price is therefore problematic.

If we stick with the current cost accounting approach, a more realistic view might be to look at the current value of the brand in terms of profits generated over the past years (or perhaps a weighted average of the last, say, 5 years). But here we have the problem that we are looking backwards whereas the whole point of investing in a brand as an asset is that we need to have some view as to its future potential. So, from a marketing perspective, this approach is problematic since its retrospective outlook does not help us in assessing the future.

Future earnings potential

This method has proved very popular since it removes some of the disadvantages listed above. It calculates the future earnings or cash flow of a brand, which after all forms the basis of the value to the owner. Normally the current earnings are extrapolated and discounted to present values.

The problem with this is that it assumes that the market will never change. So there will be no new competitors, no changes in the macro-environment and so on. As you can no doubt see, this is unlikely to be the case.

Activity 3.4

Think of a market with which you are familiar.

What has changed in the last year?

What has changed in the last 3 years?

What has changed in the last 5 years?

Incremental value added

Many companies use this as a basis for an internal measure of brand equity. The price of the brand is compared with the price of the generics in the market. The added value is viewed as equivalent to the brand's equity. This added value may lead to superior margin but is not an indicator of long-term performance or of strategic position. Another problem is that this approach undervalues mass-market brands which profit from sales volume and hence economies of scale. And niche brands with small market share will also be overvalued.

The Interbrand model

An approach which has gained popularity is one developed by a consultancy named Interbrand. Its framework is based on a combination of objective and subjective inputs.

Strictly speaking this is more a measure of brand strength, rather than brand valuation but many of the benefits mentioned above still derive from undertaking this process.

The Interbrand model has seven components of brand strength.

Table 3.1 Interbrand model of brand strength

Component of brand strength	Weighting (%)	Comments
Market	10	This is a measure of market stability. Brands in market where consumer preferences are enduring would score higher, e.g. a detergent brand would score higher than a perfume or clothing brand, because these latter categories are more susceptible to fluctuations in consumer preference.
Stability	15	Long established brands in any market would normally score higher because of the depth of loyalty they command, e.g. Rolls-Royce would score higher than Lexus.
Leadership	25	A market leader is more valuable. It is a dominant force and its relative market position gives it power, e.g. Coca-Cola would outperform Pepsi on a global basis.
Profit trend	10	The long-term profit performance can be viewed as a measure of the brand's ability to remain contemporary and relevant consumers.
Support	10	Brands which receive consistent investment and focused support usually enjoy a stronger franchise. However, it is important to note that the quality of the support is as important as the quantity.
Geographic spread	25	Brands that have proven international acceptance and appeal are inherently stronger than regional or national brands as they are less susceptible to competitive attacks and hence are more stable assets.
Protection	5	Securing full copyright protection for the brand under international trademark and copyright law allows for greater stability and encourages investment in the brand.

Source: Interbrand (2004)

As with any model this does have its weaknesses. For example, this does favour older brands and may therefore undervalue new ones such as easyJet, Starbucks and Amazon.

The outcome of this approach is a brand strength score which can be used to determine an earnings multiplier. Interbrand takes earnings to be a three-year weighted average of post-tax profits. The higher the score, the higher the multiplier to be applied to the earnings.

According to Murphy (1991), the relationship between the brand and the multiplier is an S-curve. The perfect brand would score 100 and operate in a risk-free environment. According to Interbrand, this notional perfect brand would be valued at 20 times average annual brand-related earnings. Sadly, of course, it does not exist and the average brand would be valued substantially lower than this.

Birkin (1994) gives the following example of how four brands would be valued using the Interbrand methodology.

1. *Brand A* – This is a leading international toiletries brand operating in a mainstream and stable market sector. The brand has been established for many years and is a brand leader or strong number two in all its major international markets.
2. *Brand B* – This is a leading food brand that operates in a traditional and stable market, but one where tastes are slowly changing, with a move away from traditional products and towards convenience products. The brand has limited export sales, and its trade-mark protection, though quite strong, is based mainly on common law rather than registered rights.
3. *Brand C* – This is a secondary but aspiring national soft drink brand launched just 5 years ago. The market is very dynamic and growing strongly. The brand has been very heavily supported and much has been achieved; it is however, still early days. Even though export sales are still very small, the brand name, 'get up' and positioning have all been developed with international markets in mind. The brand name still has some trademark registration problems in its home market.
4. *Brand D* – This is an established but quite regional brand in a highly fragmented yet stable market.

Based on these profiles, the following scores might be given by Interbrand on the seven strength factors.

Table 3.2 Application of Interbrand brand valuation methodology

Factor	Maximum score	Brand A	Brand B	Brand C	Brand D
Leadership	25	18	19	9	6
Stability	15	11	10	7	11
Market	10	7	6	8	6
Internationality	25	17	5	2	0
Trend	10	6	6	7	5
Support	10	8	7	7	4
Protection	5	5	3	4	3
Total	100	72	56	44	35

Question 3.1

How does your brand compare against this model?

Does the model suggest any ways to strengthen your brand?

As we can see from the examples of brands A to D above, the final composite score is a percentage, known as the brand strength score. This score can be converted into an earnings multiple to be used against the brand's profits to give a valuation.

The following patterns can be seen in the relationship between brand strength and brand value which follows a classic S-shaped curve:

1. As a brand's strength increases from virtually zero (an unknown or new brand) to a position of three or four in the market, its value increases slowly.
2. As a brand moves to a number one or number two weighting in its market or becomes internationally known, or both, there is an exponential effect on its value.
3. Once a brand is established as a powerful world brand, its value no longer increases at the same exponential rate even if the market share improves internationally.

The following case study illustrates the uncertainty that can surround the valuation of a brand. It looks at the case in the United Kingdom of the potential sale of the major broadsheet newspaper group of the Telegraph.

Case study

How much is the Telegraph worth?

Potential bidders for the Telegraph will be looking closely at the accounts of its owners, Hollinger International, to work out what the papers are worth.

Early estimates put the value of the group at anything between around £400 million and upwards of £600 million.

The Telegraph group – which includes the *Daily Telegraph*, *Sunday Telegraph* and *Spectator* magazine – is the plum asset, accounting for nearly half of the group's revenues. Last year the Telegraph's titles had revenues of £320.7 million, with operating profits of £32.3 million, giving it a profit margin of 10 per cent. On that sort of margin, a company is worth an amount equivalent to 10 times its operating profit – giving the Telegraph a value in the region of £320 million. But the group would attract a 'trophy premium', pushing bids to as high as double that, according to analysts.

'It's hard to say what multiples will apply to a national newspaper group that's been through the profit revival of the 80s and early 90s', said one analyst. 'But the brand is strong and people will pay up.'

Analysts also look how companies in the same sector are performing – in this case the *Daily Mail* and General Trust and Trinity Mirror, for example, although neither is a purely newspaper group. DMGT and Trinity Mirror are both valued above their level of turnover. The Telegraph group could be valued similarly – raising its value to around half a billion pounds.

The market capitalization of Hollinger International – which also owns the *Chicago Sun-Times* and the *Jerusalem Post* – currently stands at around £570 million.

'A realistic range might be between £300 million and £500 million', one analyst said. 'But there's the question of debt – that would really affect the price.'

The *Daily Telegraph* is the leading broadsheet newspaper in the United Kingdom, selling more than 900 000 copies per day and would be a prestigious asset. The *Sunday Telegraph* and the *Spectator* are also attractive assets, and if there is widespread interest prices could rise at an auction. But some analysts doubt there are many potential buyers who would want to take on two papers with falling circulation.

'The *Daily Telegraph* is a dying title', one analyst said. 'In terms of the big boys I can't see anyone stepping in. Maybe the Barclay brothers would – they're strong in Scotland, but not much elsewhere.' But another analyst said that the only candidate in the United Kingdom was the *Daily Mail* and General Trust, the owner of the *Daily Mail, Mail on Sunday* and *London Evening Standard*.

'They have got a fair amount of debt, but assets like this come up once in a generation', the analyst said. 'It would be quite a stretch for them, but they could afford it.'

News International is unlikely to be interested since it owns the *Telegraph*'s main competitor, the *Times*, while analysts believe that Trinity Mirror has too much on its plate and too little cash to mount a bid. The last time a major British newspaper group was up for sale, when the Express titles were on the block 3 years ago, Richard Desmond prevailed with a £125 million bid, almost double some of the earlier offers. His price was only half the group's revenues at the time but the Express group was struggling, with the *Daily Express* left behind by its mid-market rival, the *Daily Mail*.

Mr Desmond is a potential buyer of the *Telegraph*, which would give his newspaper portfolio upmarket credibility, although many analysts doubt he has enough cash. Other possible buyers would come from North America – but they would not benefit from cost savings in the same way as British companies.

Source: The Guardian, 17 November 2003, www.mediaguardian.co.uk.

Branding exercise

Case study: Phileas Fogg Travel

Background

The Phileas Fogg snack range is a highly successful brand in the adult snacks sector of the savoury snacks market. Launched in 1982 by a small entrepreneurial independent manufacturer, Derwent Valley Foods, of Medomsley Road, Consett, County Durham, it has since been acquired by the KP Foods Group.

At launch, the range consisted of three varieties: Mexican Tortilla Chips, Californian Corn Chips and Shanghai Nuts. Since then the range has expanded to include Italian Chicettas, Punjab Puri, French Mignons Morceaux, Bagel Chips, Delhi Poppadums and Indonesian Crackers.

In the first 3 years from launch, Phileas Fogg succeeded in reshaping the total snacks market, by identifying a demand for a premium priced, innovative and distinctly packaged selection of savoury snacks. The range aimed to entice the adventurous, cosmopolitan and affluent customer. Ten years later, Phileas Fogg had achieved value sales of over £10 million and a brand share of 21 per cent. By 1996, the brand enjoyed 80 per cent consumer awareness and a consumer penetration of 3 million adults.

In the early years, distribution strategy reflected and fed the premium positioning of the brand. Derwent Foods were deliberately selective in their dealings with the trade. It was conscious of the need to be seen in the 'right environment'. Distribution was sought and gained in the delicatessen trade and the three major multiples which the company considered essential for the long-term development of the brand – Sainsbury's, Safeway and Waitrose. By 1996, the brand had achieved wide-scale distribution in grocery independents, off-licences newsagents and garage forecourts.

Advertising through Bartle Bogle Hegarty was successful in securing brand status and loyalty among a young aspirant target audience. The brand had a clearly defined niche positioning. Its brand personality was readily identifiable to consumers – 'unique, original, exotic, trail blazing, maverick'. The Phileas Fogg world was perceived to be 'far flung, exotic and hot' and to represent 'places known for their food'. The key words used to describe the brand's image were 'pioneering, humorous, foreign and adult'.

In creating a niche positioning, Phileas Fogg also created a new sector opportunity and competing manufacturer and retailer products soon followed, notable among them Pringles, Kettle Chips and World Snacks.

To protect brand credentials and create differentiation from the competition, the brand management team on Phileas Fogg were set the challenge of refreshing and reinventing the brand.

One of the ideas put forward was to launch an independent tour operator – 'Phileas Fogg Travel'. The briefing below provides the overall background.

Briefing notes: Company objectives

Phileas Fogg Travel aims to achieve a 5 per cent share of the total 'holidays abroad' market during the first year of business. This would give an annual turnover of around £800 million.

Marketing strategy

To dominate a single segment of the travel market by utilizing the strong brand identity of Phileas Fogg and creating an offering which reflects the essence of the brand.

Target Market

Age: 25–34 core, extending up to 45

Social Class: ABC1

Location: London and South East

The task

Your task is to develop an analytical framework for 'Phileas Fogg Travel' with reference to the information provided. Specifically you should provide detailed recommendations and rationale for:

1. The current situation analysis for the organization?
2. To what extent is the brand appropriate in both travel and savoury snacks?
3. To what extent is the move from savoury into travel appropriate?

Potential solution

Phileas Fogg is clearly established in the savoury snack market (current situation analysis), clearly it is assumed that Phileas Fogg initially penetrated the market by offering a differential premium priced product in a market that was described as low priced – low variety products such as different flavoured potato crisps and peanuts. The PF offering must have attracted a target audience who had lifestyle aspirations (behavioural segmentation) and were supported by an appropriate marketing mix to support the premium price positioning. Therefore the customers could aspire to the brand image of any product, service or activity that potentially supports the lifestyle. So the brand attributes could possibly be extended to different markets. Therefore the brand could be a transferable asset to introduce new products to existing customers (Ansoffian analysis) but care should still be exercised to identify the similarities and differences between the environments of the savoury snack and package holiday markets.

Summary

Valuation of brands is discussed in this unit. The advent of brand valuation as a new phenomenon is discussed with a brief summary of its history illustrated by examples of major brand sales.

We see that there are benefits for the balance sheet, management information and internal management. The competing methods of valuation are discussed, that is historic cost, future earnings potential, incremental value added and the Interbrand model.

The next unit examines ways in which we might audit marketing activities. Taking the 4Ps as a framework, we look at the ways in which we might evaluate the effectiveness of our activities.

Exam Hint 3.3

Although you are unlikely to be asked to conduct complex calculations to value brands you are expected to be able to qualitatively critically evaluate the different methods in the exam. You should merely describe but demonstrate an understanding of why brands need to be valued and which methods would be more suitable for a manager in the context of the exam question.

Further study

Aaker, D.A. (1998) *Strategic Market Management*, 5th edition, New York: John Wiley & Sons.

Doyle, P. (2000) *Value Based Marketing*, Wiley.

Keller, K.L. (2003) *Strategic Brand Management*, 2nd edition, Pearson Education.

Stobart, P., Perrier, R. (1997) *Brand Valuation*, 3rd edition, Premier Books.

www.buildingbrands.com

Hints and tips

It is important to keep up to date with current trends in brand valuation. Make sure that you have a good working knowledge of the ways brands are valued so that you can apply that knowledge to a specific brand. In particular, you need to think about how the different methods relate to each other, and how using different methods will give different values. Keep up with the top ten brands, understanding the reasons for their strength.

Bibliography

Aaker, D.A. (1991) *Managing Brand Equity: Capitalizing on the Value of a Brand Name*, New York: The Free Press.

Birkin, M. (1994) 'Assessing the Brand Value', in Paul Stobart (ed.), *Brand Power*, New York: University Press.

Buzzell Robert, D., Bradley T. Gale (1987) The PIMS Principles, New York: The Free Press.

King, S. (1989) 'The Brand is the Business', *Brands on the Balance Sheet*, Economist Conference Report, London, March.

McSweeney and Steele: Ranks Hovis McDougall, Brendan McSweeney, Anthony Steele Brand Valuations and intangible assets, in Schweikart, Gray, Roberts (eds), *International Accounting: A Case Approach*, New York, NY, McGraw-Hill, 1994.

Murphy, J. (1991) *Brand Valuation: A True and Fair View*, Hutchinson.

Robinson, W.T. (1988) 'Sources of market pioneer advantages: the case of industrial goods industries', *Journal of Marketing Research*, **25**, pp. 87–94.

unit 4
auditing marketing activities

This unit has a very tight remit, focusing on audit of marketing activities. It:

o Allows you to understand the process in conducting a detailed audit of an organization's marketing activities

o Develops your understanding of the potential measures of marketing performance.

Sections of the syllabus being covered in this unit:

Element 2: Evaluation of business and marketing performance (30 per cent).

2.1 Critically evaluate and use quantitative techniques for evaluating business and marketing performance over current and historic business cycles. Techniques to be covered should include:

o Balanced scorecard, with an emphasis on customer and innovation measures.

o Evaluation of marketing performance including the audit of marketing activities and valuation of marketing assets, such as brands.

o Financial techniques such as SVA (using total shareholder return and economic profit), financial ratio analysis, trend analysis, benchmarking and evaluation of historical financial decisions.

Element 3: Analysis of the internal environment (20 per cent).

3.1 Use and appraise the available techniques and processes for the objective assessment of the internal environment of an organization, including portfolio analysis, value chain, innovation audit and cultural web.

3.2 Critically evaluate the resource-based view of the organization.

3.3 Demonstrate the ability to use appropriate information and tools to evaluate the core competencies, assets, culture and weaknesses of an organization.

3.4 Assess the 'fit' between an organization's culture and its current strategy.

3.5 Summarize the salient factors and insights emerging from the internal analysis.

Study guide

In this unit you will be covering a number of concepts that will be expanded upon in later units. The importance of this unit is to understand the marketing audit in terms of identifying what needs to be measured in order to identify opportunities that will yield increased shareholder value.

Many texts exist which will take you through a checklist approach to undertaking a strategic marketing audit. You should be aware of these and understand the mechanics of this type of audit. This unit builds on these foundations by focusing on an audit of marketing activities. This unit is also closely linked with the concept of marketing orientation introduced in Unit 1 and provides a more formalized approach with measurements to determine the extent of an organization's marketing orientation. It is also linked to analysing the internal environment and competitive environment of an organization as marketing is in essence the start and compilation or output of a strategic marketing analysis. You should, therefore, appreciate the extent of overlap between the A&E course units and to remember that to develop a marketing audit requires analysis and evaluation which can be the same analysis and evaluation considerations used in analysing the internal and competitive environment.

How will this unit help you and what can you expect to achieve after completing this unit?

The expectation of the PPDIPM is for you to be able to analyse any business situation and to identify the issues or business issues likely to impact on marketing. Real-life business is complex and marketing issues are often intertwined with other business issues. As a professional marketer, you will need to understand these other business issues to see how they impact on customer satisfaction as well as being able to effectively communicate with other business professionals to take appropriate action. Therefore, you will require understanding of their language and 'thinking' if you are to influence them in an effective manner. Remember as a marketer you do not have a direct line responsibility over other business functions but they can have a major impact on you, the marketer, achieving your objectives which is primarily customer satisfaction and therefore you will need to influence them. Certain companies are formalizing this process with greater amounts of internal marketing initiatives.

As mentioned earlier, it is important for you as a marketer to appreciate the need to understand business issues to ensure that you are not only able to identify the appropriate issues but are also able to identify appropriate actions (strategic options and implementation issues) needed to be taken to target all relevant stakeholders likely to impact upon future revenue streams of the company which in turn may adversely affect long-term shareholder value. Now in most organizations being able to appropriately analyse business issues and identify areas within the business that are likely to impact on marketing performance is not necessarily automatic. Formalized systems are often needed to be put in place to ensure that these activities are undertaken. These formal systems are audits which are systems that will identify business areas and their associated activities that will impact upon marketing performance. This unit will therefore guide you to developing customized marketing audits for any type of organization and setting.

Note: Although this unit focuses on developing marketing audits, it also contains discussions on other aspects of strategic marketing management particularly pertaining to the marketing mix. In addition, as a student you should already be familiar with the basic principles of marketing management, having studied it prior to the PPDIPM, and should expect questions on strategic implications relating to any aspect of the marketing mix.

Marketing audits and market research

It is imperative that students appreciate the link between marketing audits which are the tools to assist consultants and senior executives assess the extent of an organization's marketing orientation and market research which provides the necessary information for the audits. Marketing audits can also be thought of as the propositions or hypotheses developed from theory or secondary data that will determine the information needs and the data gathering process within the overall market research process. Auditing and market research is intertwined and this needs to be communicated to students in the exam. Market research is not formally covered at this level and the assumption is that it should have been covered in earlier levels. This does not mean that students are not expected to apply the theory of market research if it is relevant.

Exam Hint 4.1

Students will be able to consolidate their elementary marketing knowledge with appropriate theory from this section to analyse and evaluate the extent or lack of marketing orientation exhibited by organizations. For example if a company is performing poorly, marketing mix audits would allow specific identification and evaluation of which part of the mix is contributing to a poor positioning and therefore resulting in poor performance.

Statements of related marketing practice

The main skill or business competency areas being developed in this section and likely to be examined are:

o   To develop appropriate structures and frameworks to identify appropriate information requirements to define and structure marketing-related business problems.
o   To be able to critically evaluate different analytical perspectives which will lead executives to gain a better understanding of their external and internal environment within the specific context of their industries, thus setting and placing them in a position to make better informed decisions potentially leading to minimize risks and uncertainties.
o   To promote a strong marketing orientation to influence strategy formulation and investment decisions.
o   Specify and direct the line marketing process.

Historical perspective of marketing audits

Marketing audits were popularized in the 1960s by Kotler who argued for their usefulness in formulating strategic marketing plans. Audits were considered important for business areas (*defined as any area located within the boundaries of an organization span of control – could be a business function, department or networked alliance of third parties*) within organizations that were thought to drive business performance, predominantly financial performance. These audits were designed to support executives to determine the extent to which the organization's activities within the business area were marketing-orientated, the assumption being that the more marketing-orientated a company was, the more likely satisfied customers would return thereby increasing long-term profitability and hence shareholder value. A number of audits which unintentionally became standardized checklists were used in many organizations to determine the extent of marketing orientation. These audits included a customer audit, an innovation audit and an external environment audit amongst many others.

It is important to appreciate the essence of what an audit is trying to achieve rather than simply transferring generic ones developed from other organizations without evaluating whether the activities being measured in the audit are in fact appropriate to the organization in question. Therefore this unit will get you to think about which business areas within their associated activities and within a specific organization being examined are likely to drive value. In order to evaluate the activities that are likely to drive value within a business area and develop appropriate contextual marketing audits, we need to rely on applying existing theory and formulating hybrid frameworks.

In practice, marketing audits can be thought of as consisting of two types, both of which need to be considered by marketing executives. The first is an audit of activities within other business areas outside the direct control of the marketing department that can impact on marketing activities and the second is an audit of how well the activities of the marketing department are being carried out.

Audit of marketing activities

One approach to assess the overall marketing performance of the organization is to examine each element of the marketing mix in turn. You may choose to use the 4Ps framework (Product, Price, Place, Promotion), 5Ps (add People) or 7Ps (add Process and Physical Evidence). Use whichever you find most useful. Since the 4Ps mix is generally the most accepted, we will focus on that here. In practice, it is often useful to set up a comparator so that we have a measure of how our customers perceive our offering (marketing mix) relative to a comparator. This can be achieved by undertaking independent market research to identify and define the ideal expectations of customer needs in the desired market and to set up the measures of what the customers would define as being well satisfying, moderately satisfying and not satisfying. Therefore, an audit can be set up using each aspect of the marketing mix with a list of factors with clear definitions of what the customers expect from an ideal product. Further studies can then be carried out to test how the organization's offerings (marketing mix) compare to the ideal expectations followed by testing how the competitors compare to the ideal and us.

It is important to bear in mind that the purpose of this A&E module is to give an accurate and objective position of where we are now. The way that a company perceive us is likely to be a function of our communication, that is what we are and have been saying about us as well as what our competitors are and have been saying about us, so we need to review historic performance as well as current. This concept is ideally represented by Ohmae's strategic triangle (Figure 4.1):

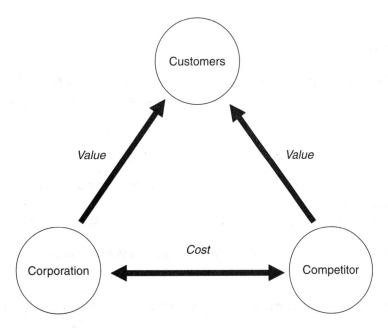

Figure 4.1 The Strategic Triangle
Source: Ohmae, K. (1982) *The Mind of the Strategist*, McGraw-Hill, Inc., p. 99

Ohmae (1982) states that in the construction of any business strategy three main players must be taken into account: the corporation, the customer and the competitor. Seen in the context of the triangle the job of a marketing strategist is to achieve superior performance relative to the competition at the same time ensuring that the strategy matches the key strengths of the organization with the key needs of the marketplace. Positive matching of the needs and objectives of both parties is essential for long-lasting relationships, without which the long-term viability of the firm in terms of shareholder value maybe at stake. Therefore the triangle can be used as the basis of formulating a strategic marketing audit process based on elements of the marketing mix. Ohmae's triangle (1982) can be adapted to form an audit framework (Figure 4.2).

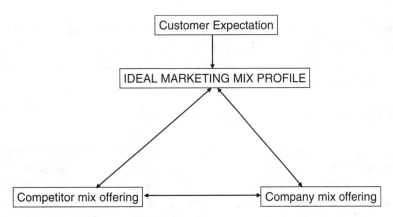

Figure 4.2 Adapted Strategic Triangle
Source: Ohmae, K. (1982) *The Mind of the Strategist*, McGraw-Hill, Inc., p. 91

It is essential for you to appreciate that the adapted framework provides a theoretical framework which can be utilized to formulate a detailed audit using aspects of the marketing mix. The actual audit will then be a checklist with a scoring system developed for a particular company competing in a specific industry setting. Our work is not yet over as we need to decide within each part of the marketing mix the specific attributes along with how will we measure it which will be included in the audit. This is not a simple task and will be discussed throughout the next section.

Product

Primary audit questions:

- To what extent does the product deliver satisfaction of the underlying customer needs?
- What specific attributes are customers looking for to satisfy their underlying customer needs?

Secondary audit questions:

- How close to the ideal does the organizations' product offering meet the needs of the customers?
- How close to the ideal do the competitors' product meet the needs of the customers?

To assess the performance of a product, we can review it on an actual level and a perceived level.

So we need to ascertain whether the product is fit for the purpose it is intended to meet.

Depending on your product, different measures will be relevant. This information can be used as part of an innovation audit to drive an organization New Product Development (NPD) or New Service Development (NSD) where unmet needs by current products can be identified and new products developed to sustain future growth and maintain increased shareholder value.

Question 4.1

What is the purpose of your product?

How can you measure its performance?

Let us assume that you work for a car company. How would you assess the performance of any particular model? Initially you might think sales, market share and profit. But these are dependent on factors other than the product element of the marketing mix. Sales are dependent on distribution, profits on price and so on.

So what factors are solely related to the product?

There are the hard variables – technical factors such as speed, fuel economy, space, number of doors, range of colours and so on. Ironically these hard variables are the easiest to measure objectively. But an additional layer of complexity is added to this. Although we may easily be able to determine these with a fair degree of certainty, we do not know what the consumers think they are. So it may be that a Range Rover has better fuel economy than a Toyota Land Cruiser but if you, as a potential buyer, believe the opposite then Range Rover has the problem, not Toyota.

This brings up the issue of who is the competition. It is useful to see competition as being on a number of levels. These are:

1. Primary (or real)
2. Secondary (or peripheral).

Primary competitors are those brands which are most similar to your own. One of the easiest ways to assess which these brands are is to think about which brands the consumer would buy if your brand was not available. Or ideally ask a sample of your target market that question.

Secondary competitors are brands which are more distant from your own positioning. For example, a Cartier watch might be primary competition to Rolex. However, Rolex might view Swatch as secondary (or even tertiary) competition. Much depends on the need being met; a watch may be used to tell the time or as an expression of affection. In each case the competitive set is different.

Perception could be argued to be more important than reality. What the consumer believes will motivate their buying behaviour.

Activity 4.1

The following information has been collected about the technical attributes of four competing models of car. The target market for all of these is women aged 25–44.

Technical factors	Whitehall Signa	Dazda 3	Wonda Civil	Bandwagen Passe
Maximum speed (mph)	131	114	111	119
Acceleration (sec) (0–62 mph)	8.8	11.0	12.8	12.4
Fuel economy mpg (litres/100 km)	34.9 (8.1)	30.4 (9.3)	57.6 (4.9)	50.4 (5.6)
Maximum load volume cu.ft (litres)	49.8 (1410)	52.6 (1490)	45.5 (1288)	57.5 (1628)
Engine capacity	2.2	2.2	2.0	1.6

Which of these is performing the best on these objective technical attributes? Rank the four cars in order.

Now add in this additional information.

Research shows that women believe that the Whitehall Signa is unreliable and prone to gearbox problems. In addition the target market sees the Dazda 3 as very economical. This is based on their historic perception of the previous model which attracted much publicity at the time of its launch 3 years ago as the most economical car ever.

Now which car is performing best?

Customer satisfaction and service quality

Another measure of product performance is the level of customer satisfaction. Satisfaction can be viewed as the difference between expectation and performance. Generally speaking customer satisfaction is viewed as a short-term, transaction-specific measure whereas service quality is an attitude formed by a long-term overall evaluation of a performance.

These two measures are certainly intertwined but the relationship between the two is unclear with some confusion about the causality.

Services

We have discussed products but what about services; to what extent can we assume that services are similar to products. There is considerable debate amongst practitioners as well and academics relating to the similarity between the two; some believe that there are no differences whilst others feel that they are so different that they need to be treated completely differently. Regardless of where one is positioned in the debate it is generally accepted that services share some differences with products and include:

- Services tend to be a mixture of tangible and intangible offerings and are generally consumed without taking ownership of many aspects of the offering. This means in airline transportation you will occupy a seat but not own it after the journey is complete but you will take ownership of airline meals.
- You cannot store services like you can with products and therefore they are perishable and consumed at the point of purchase.
- It is often difficult to match supply and demand often with companies having too many resources and not enough consumers or too many consumers and not enough resources. Sales promotion using differential pricing strategies are often utilized to smooth demand in these situations.

It is also accepted that for services we need to introduce three more elements to the marketing mix primarily because in most services we cannot separate the service with the operational process designed to deliver the services. With products one does not consider the factory which produces the goods as consumption is usually located at a different geographical location to where it is produced. With so-called front office services customers are involved with operations, with services often being described as 'being factories in the field'. Therefore the operations (called the process) delivering the service need to be considered within the marketing mix as potentially contributing to achieving a differential competitive advantage. People also play a major part in differentiating services therefore they need to be considered as part of the mix. Finally as some services are more intangible than others, physical evidence through imagery and promotion are used to give the physical illusion of a purchase.

Services are therefore more complex than products and need additional strategic tools to evaluate them which are aptly introduced in the next section.

Diagnosing service quality failures

The service quality process can be described in terms of the gaps between customer expectations and perceptions on the part of management, employees and customers. The most important gap is between customers' expectation of service and their perception of the service actually delivered. The goal of the service company is to close that gap or at least narrow it as far as possible.

But before that, four other gaps need to be closed or narrowed. These are:

- *Gap 1* – Difference between what the consumers expect of a service and what management perceives consumers expect.
- *Gap 2* – Difference between what management perceives consumers expect and the quality specifications set for service delivery.

○ *Gap 3* – Difference between the quality specifications set for service delivery and the actual quality of service delivery.
○ *Gap 4* – Difference between the actual quality of service delivery and the quality of service delivery described in the firm's external communications.

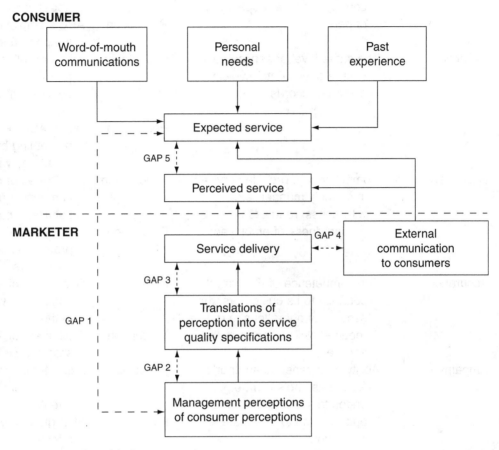

Figure 4.3 Conceptual model of service quality
Source: Berry, Parasuraman and Zeithaml (1994)

Activity 4.2

Apply this model to the gaps in your organization. What are the drivers of these gaps? How might you approach narrowing them?

SERVQUAL

One well accepted research instrument used to assess service quality is a questionnaire called SERVQUAL. It sees service quality as the gap between performance and expectations in the same way as customer satisfaction might be measured. The questionnaire is a 44-item scale which measures customer expectations and perceptions with regard to five quality dimensions. It compares consumer perception of service quality of an organization against the consumer expectation of an excellent company in the same category.

Table 4.1 The five quality dimensions of SERVQUAL

Dimension	Description	E/P	Example item
Tangibles	Tangible evidence, e.g. carpeting, lighting, brochures, correspondence, appearance of personnel	Expectation	Employees of excellent companies will be neat in appearance
		Perception	ABC's employees are neat in appearance
Reliability	The same level of service each time, e.g. accurate invoicing, accurate records	Expectation	When excellent companies promise to do something by a certain time, they will do so
		Perception	When ABC promise to do something by a certain time, they will do so
Responsiveness	Commitment to provide services in a timely manner, e.g. willingness, readiness, preparedness of employees	Expectation	Employees of excellent companies give prompt service to customers
		Perception	Employees of ABC give prompt service to customers
Assurance	The competence of the firm, the courtesy to its customers, the security of operations, e.g. has required skills to perform the service	Expectation	Customers of excellent companies will feel safe in their transactions
		Perception	Customers of ABC will feel safe in their transactions
Empathy	Ability to experience another's feeling as one's own, e.g. understand customer needs and respond to them, are accessible	Expectation	Excellent companies will give customers individual attention
		Perception	ABC gives you individual attention

Source: Adapted from Parasuraman, Berry and Zeithaml (1991)

To deliver a consistent set of satisfying experiences, the whole organization must be focused on the task. The needs of the customer must be understood in detail, as must the operational constraints under which the organization operates. The service providers should be focused on quality and the system must be designed to support that mission. Processes need to be analysed and evaluated to check for problems. The process of blueprinting services can help here. Most service marketing texts carry an explanation of this process. The system must be controlled and delivered to its specification. Finally customer expectations must be managed through communication and pricing.

But what happens if it goes wrong?

Complaining

Despite evidence that many customers are dissatisfied with the service they receive, many seem reluctant to complain. This creates problems for marketers for a number of reasons:

1. Dissatisfied customers may stop buying. Repeat purchase will be reduced.
2. Dissatisfied customers will pass on negative word-of-mouth discouraging other potential buyers.
3. The level of complaints received is likely to dramatically underestimate the actual level of underlying dissatisfaction.
4. Cross-selling is likely to be reduced.
5. Latent dissatisfaction means that the competitive threat may be underestimated.
6. An opportunity is missed for service recovery.

Companies need to set up an efficient complaints handling process. The first stage is to analyse the current complaints. The sources and the factors underpinning them need to be categorized. At a basic level, frequency counts could be made on the following categories:

1. Product quality factors
2. Service quality factors
3. Out-of-stock products
4. Products not delivered on time
5. Products damaged during shipping
6. Errors in invoicing.

You should also look at how efficient and effective the complaints handling procedure is. Research suggests that if a complaint is handled quickly and efficiently, the customer may ironically become more loyal than those who have not complained. Companies need to encourage complaints as a means of free market research on how the product is performing and very importantly an opportunity for service recovery which will encourage loyalty and reduce negative word-of-mouth messages. It is important to prioritize complaints but organizations rarely do so. As a result, treatment of serious complaints tends to get delayed by a backlog of minor complaints. It is good practice to prioritize complaints, from those with serious commercial consequences, through temporary customer distress, to customer inconvenience down to 'trouble making'.

Activity 4.3

Undertake a complaints audit for your organization. What are the implications of your findings for (a) your complaints process and (b) your organization as a whole?

Price

Primary audit questions:

o To what extent does the price of a product or service competing in this marketplace play a role in the customer's purchasing decisions?
o What are the price attribute trade-offs of this marketplace?

Secondary audit questions:

- o To what extent does the organization's price offering meet the expectations of customers?
- o To what extent do the competitor's price offering meet the needs of the customers?

To assess the effectiveness of the price element of the mix we need the following information:

1. The pricing strategy
2. Costs
3. Competitor pricing.

Let us examine each of these in turn.

Mini Case 4.1

Gillette versus Bic – In the late 1980s and early 1990s, Gillette business had started to suffer from severe competition from electric shavers and disposable wet shave razors developed by Bic who were undertaking a similar strategy in this market as they did in the biro pen as well as the disposable cigarette lighter markets by introducing low price, high volume disposable commodities which would be bought on a regular basis by consumers. Without undertaking a thorough review of the marketplace they launched their own version of a disposable razor which had the same heads as high priced premium razors. Instead of taking share away from Bic they found that they were cannibalizing their own business with customers buying disposable Gillete razors as they did not perceive the difference between the disposable and normal razors which meant they were destroying shareholder value from competing against themselves as well as Bic.

This was just too much for Gillette to bear and they reacted by undertaking a complete audit of their customers purchasing behaviour and psychological needs around the shaving experience and they therefore identified all their unmet needs. This allowed Gillette to develop new products and promotion strategies surrounding the key message that Gillette was the 'Best a Man can get' as identifying new target users with different needs such as women. Marketing audits combined with market research completely reversed Gillette's fortunes allowing them to provide value to both their customers and shareholders.

Pricing strategy

We need to understand what the pricing strategy is intending to achieve before we can determine whether it is the right one. Are we aiming for market penetration or market skimming? Is our profit target survival or optimization? What do we want our price to suggest about our quality? Our objectives will set our information requirements to some extent. Any pricing strategy needs to take into account three factors: demand, cost and competition.

Costs

One of price's main contributions to the marketing mix is its effect on profit as profit, is essentially the difference between revenue (i.e. price × volume) and cost. It also affects profit via the mechanism of price elasticity so that normally we would expect that the higher the price the lower the volume and vice versa. Obviously this is not always the case, but broadly speaking this would apply in most markets within certain limits. Price elasticity is specific to product categories and varies over time.

Unit profit = unit revenue – unit variable cost – contribution to overheads (fixed costs)

We need to have this information for each product line so that we can accurately assess the contribution each line makes to the overall profitability. In this way, if appropriate, we can focus our other marketing activities on the more profitable lines, and possibly delete the unprofitable ones.

However, it is not always as simple as to say spend more on the profitable lines and get rid of the unprofitable ones. There are a number of other factors to take into account.

1. *Strategic implications* – Lines may be there for reasons other than simply profit. They may fulfil a strategic purpose such as acting as loss leaders to gain entry to a retailer or to act as complements to other more profitable lines so that a complete range may be offered. They may be there to create an image of being innovative in the market and hence enhance the overall brand image.
2. *Sharing of overheads* – By removing unprofitable lines, we will be sharing the fixed costs between fewer lines hence affecting the profitability of the remaining lines. If we are confident, we can make up the shortfall in volume with the remaining portfolio, which is fine but if the result is of less volume then the effect will be reduced profit overall.
3. *Impact on relative marketing overhead* – If we start to spend more on the profitable lines, then we should allocate a greater proportion of the marketing overheads to these lines, with the result that these lines become less profitable, so we should be spending less on them.

Assessing price competitiveness

We need to be aware that in virtually every market there are competitors. A rare example where most consumers would not see any competition would be the water supply. Normally, however, consumers are evaluating the price of a product against a competitive set. These competitors may not be in the same product class, for example tumble dryers compete with spin dryers to get clothes dry. As we have already stressed, it is important therefore to define your product in terms of needs met.

To determine price competitiveness we need to understand our relative price/quality position in the marketplace. This involves developing a specific positioning map based on value.

To do this we need to measure the quality and price of ourselves and each of our competitors. We can do this in a number of ways. Ideally we would collect lots of customer data on these dimensions focusing on their perceptions. We need to uncover:

1. The dimensions of quality which matter to them, that is what are the attributes on which they are assessing competitive offerings? How important are each of these attributes to them?
2. How do our products and our competitors rate on each of these attributes?
3. What are their perceptions of price?
4. What price/quality combinations are most valued by customers?

We can make an estimate of this data within the organization probably using sales people as they are in closest contact with the customers, but bear in mind that there will be bias in this data as individuals will have vested interests.

Table 4.2 assesses four travel companies on price and quality.

Table 4.2 Assessing the price/quality relationship

Quality dimension	Importance weighting	McGill enterprises	Competitors East meets west	Riley freedom	AWL escape
Reliability	40	6	7	6	3
Efficiency	30	3	5	4	5
Exclusiveness	20	6	6	7	8
Range of locations	10	8	7	6	8
Total weighted score		5.3	6.2	5.6	5.1
Average price per holiday (Euros)		10 000	15 000	20 000	5 000
Market share (value %)		7	35	45	13

The matrix, Figure 4.4, shows the quadrants we would expect to find in a market. The dashed diagonal line represents a notional price/quality relationship since intuitively we would expect there to be a correlation between the two variables.

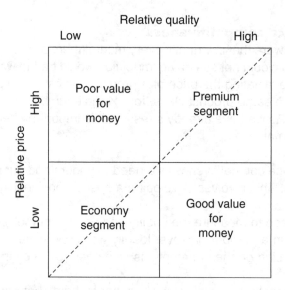

Figure 4.4 Price/quality relationship

 Activity 4.4

Plot the four travel brands above on the price quality matrix.

What are the implications of this analysis?

What might be the shortcomings of this type of analysis?

Activity 4.5

Carry out a competitive price audit.

Find out the prices of all your competitors and evaluate your relative position. Do you command a price premium? Is it reflective of your quality position?

Activity 4.6

Determine the components of final price within your organization.

Breakeven volume and target return on sales

Two useful figures to help you set the price of a product is the return on sales and its breakeven volume. Return on sales is the ratio between sales and profit. Breakeven is the volume at which all costs are met. It is calculated by dividing fixed costs by gross margin per unit.

Activity 4.7

Grossex is a medium-sized manufacturer of scientific instruments which it sells to a variety of private and public sector organizations. One of its products is a measuring device for controlling the emission of gases.

Given that the firm believes that it can sell 2000 measuring devices a year and has a target return on sales of 20 per cent, the product has a variable cost of £25 and associated fixed costs of £50 000, what is (a) the price it should charge and (b) its breakeven volume?

(a)
Target return on sales = profit/revenue

$$0.2 = \text{(Total Revenue} - \text{Total Costs)/Total Revenue}$$

$$0.2 = [(\text{Price} \times \text{Quantity}) - \text{Fixed Costs} - (\text{Variable Costs} \times \text{Quantity})]/ (\text{Price} \times \text{Quantity})$$

$$0.2 = [2000P - 50\,000 - (25 \times 2000)]/2000P$$

$$400P = 2000P - 100\,000 \text{ (after multiplying each side by 2000P)}$$

$$1600P = 100\,000$$

$$P = £62.50 \text{ per device}$$

(b)

$$\text{Breakeven} = \text{Fixed Costs divided by (Price} - \text{Variable Costs)}$$

$$= 50\,000/(62.5 - 25)$$

$$= 1334 \text{ devices}$$

There is a big emphasis in the syllabus that marketers should be more numerate and therefore breakeven analysis is likely to be used extensively across the syllabus at this level and students ought to familiarize themselves with the technique. It is also important that students not only perform calculations but to qualitatively discuss the issues of what one is trying to achieve in using it as well as interpreting the outputs of the calculations. It is also important for students not only to understand the differences between a fixed and variable cost but also to understand that costs can also be semi-fixed as well as semi-variable. This means they either behave as fixed or variable under certain conditions. For example in a restaurant food ingredients ought to be classified as a variable but businesses do not tend to purchase ingredients as they are utilized therefore they are purchased in bulk and are stored. If the ingredients are not perishable they can be treated as variable costs but if they are perishable and are used up by the appropriate sell by date they are therefore fixed or semi-variable costs.

Promotion
Primary audit questions:

- o To what extent does the promotion of the product or service competing in this marketplace play a role in customer purchasing decisions?
- o Which parts of the promotional mix and media are customers accustomed to and which would they prefer?

Secondary audit questions:

- o To what extent is the organization's promotional mix meeting the expectations of customers?
- o To what extent is the organization's promotional strategy deficient?
- o To what extent is the competitor's promotional offering meeting the needs of the customers?
- o To what extent is the competitor's promotional strategy deficient?

The promotional mix can be divided into its separate elements and analysed separately or amalgamated and viewed holistically. Once again the same rules apply. We need to determine first what we are trying to achieve. For a sales promotion it may be an upturn in sales, for advertising it may be an increase in awareness, for public relations it may be an improved brand image or front-of-mind saliency.

The next stage is to determine which measures are appropriate. We may use the same measures for each or alter them according to the characteristics of the element of the mix.

Figure 4.5 Elements of the promotional mix

Sales promotion

So for sales promotion we may rely on invoiced sales over a specified period. These are relatively objective but confounded by the fact that these may merely be sales brought forward. So a period of plenty could then be followed by a period of famine. Once the costs of the promotion are taken into account the initial revenue surge might have actually lost profit rather than generated any. If the promotion was a price promotion then it is possible that, although sales are up in the short run, the brand may have been damaged in the long run. The consumer's reference price (i.e. the price that he has in his mind to pay for a product in this category) may have been shifted downwards. So the consumer may decide to seek a lower priced alternative or only buy your brand when it is on offer, effectively lowering the profit margin.

To decide on whether or not a promotion has been successful it is useful to examine the target markets, likely objectives and the measures we might use.

Table 4.3 Examples of sales promotion evaluation

Target audience	Objectives	Measures
Manufacturer to intermediary	Stimulate intermediaries to try new products	Listings
	Encourage intermediaries to increase shelf space for existing product	Retail audits
Intermediaries to consumers	Generate higher levels of store traffic	Footfall
Manufacturers to consumers	Encourage consumer trial	Consumer market research on trial, frequency, weight
	Increase frequency of purchase	
	Increase weight of purchase	Possible use of panel data
Manufacturers to sales force	Build performance	Performance against targets and historic sales

Public relations

To determine the efficacy of public relations we may be forced to rely on proxy measures such as the number of column inches achieved in the relevant press. This is not ideal since it ignores the quality and type of coverage. Lots of negative coverage in lower quality publications would appear to rate higher than more succinct positive coverage in more prestigious media. Read the following article about a new product from Coca-Cola.

Case study

Dasani

Tap water – it's the real thing.

You are the largest soft drink manufacturer in the world. Sugary drinks are under attack and you need a healthy range.

Then your brainstorming product development sessions come up with a brilliant idea. Tap water. Thames tap water, to be precise. 'The best business opportunities come out of the blue', you tell the grocery trade, as you launch it with a £7 million marketing campaign.

Coca-Cola confirmed yesterday that the source for its new Dasani bottled water was the main supply to its factory in Sidcup, Kent. It said that a 'highly sophisticated purification process' meant that the product was 'as pure as bottled water gets'. Dasani costs around 95p for a 500 ml bottle.

The tap water goes through three filters and then a process called reverse osmosis, which Coca-Cola describes as a technique perfected by NASA to purify fluids on spacecraft. Reverse osmosis filters are more often seen in little boxes under some household sinks that filter tap water. Coca-Cola says it also adds calcium, magnesium and sodium bicarbonate to the water for taste.

The trade adverts for Dasani say that 'pure bottled water makes pure business sense'.

But the UK water industry questions the suggestion that tap water is impure. 'People don't need to buy this stuff to get excellent quality, healthy tap water', said Barrie Clarke, spokesman for UK Water, the umbrella organization for water companies.

Coca-Cola's brand PR manager for Dasani said: 'The source of the water is irrelevant. And we would never say that tap water isn't drinkable. It's just that Dasani is as pure as water can get – there are different levels of purity.'

Source: The Guardian, 2 March 2004.

Question 4.2

How would you assess the effectiveness of this PR from the perspective of (a) Coca-Cola and (b) UK Water?

Direct marketing

In many ways direct marketing can be the easiest to measure. Since by its nature it tends to be micro-marketing, that is, one on one, we can track who responded and who did not. Split mailings whether by snail mail or e-mail can allow us to track the effectiveness of different campaigns simultaneously and judge which campaign to roll out. In some markets, financial services to name but one, minute response rates are an accepted part of blanket mailings. At an average cost of £1 per pack, the economics of these mailings can mean that even at 98 per cent rejection, the mail campaign can be worthwhile. But a recent (2003) survey by the Royal Mail shows that 69 per cent of all B2B mailings contain at least one error. While many items still arrive, having the wrong name, job title or address is just the excuse that the recipient may use to bin the mailing. In 2002, in the United Kingdom, 172 million items of mail were sent to businesses that had either moved or ceased to exist altogether. This cost marketers £163 million in wasted mailings.

If the mailing includes an expensive catalogue, it becomes even more important to spend more time in evaluating the sample and targeting more precisely. The following case study illustrates the point.

Case study

Iceland home shopping

Iceland are a UK grocery retailer who focus predominantly on frozen food and target busy mums. They were early entrants into the home shopping market in 2000, allowing customers a choice of touchpoints to receive their 'Talking Food' catalogue (telephone, Internet or digital interactive TV).

Their initial plan was to send their customers a catalogue based on how recently they had shopped with the company. They analysed their customer base of a million and sent out six mailings a year based on frequency and recency of shopping.

As each mailing cost £4.60, Iceland were concerned to target those people who were most likely to spend and to spend more. Since simple recency and frequency were leading to low response rates, Iceland developed a more sophisticated approach to targeting with the aim of improving order volume and profitability from their catalogue customers.

They used a consultancy to build a catalogue mailing scorecard which uses predictive modelling techniques to select customers based on projected spend. Their scorecard uses historical data to see how much a customer is likely to spend in the next month. Customers are ranked according to their propensity to buy, and any customer falling below breakeven is excluded from the mailing. Every time the model is run the scorecard automatically refreshes itself by analysing transactional data. So the score for each individual customer will go up and down unless their purchasing behaviour is constant.

Since Iceland have introduced this more sophisticated approach to targeting their response rate has quadrupled, with a positive impact on the bottom line.

Source: Direct Response, March 2004.

Case study

BUPA Wellness

As long as companies remain within the law, there is no real limit to the data they can collect on customers online. As long as customers are aware of the use of cookies, marketers can use data from consumers on the website. (Cookies are one of the key tracking tools used by Internet marketers. They are small text files loaded from websites onto the user's hard drive so that the site can recognize visitors when they return.) These files can follow their every move on the site, and gather data through registration forms and online surveys.

BUPA Wellness, BUPA's corporate and personal healthcare division, used this capability to promote its on-site dental service to organizations with more than 500 employees. It appointed an agency who carried out a telemarketing campaign to create a database of human resources managers and gain their permission to send them e-mails. The agency then sent out personalized e-mails that informed prospects how many days their company was losing through dental visits, and how much could be saved by having an on-site dentist.

'One of the key features of the campaign was to a dedicated intranet that tracked the behaviour of e-mail recipients', says Cronan MacMahon, corporate manager at BUPA. 'We were able to measure who opened the e-mail, the time they spent watching it, how many times they opened it, whether it was forwarded and who it was forwarded to.'

According to MacMahon, if it was desirable, his sales team could call people as they were reading the e-mail – something that traditional marketers would need a team of spies with long range lenses to achieve – but he felt that it was too aggressive.

The results from one specific day of the campaign were:

- 70 e-mails sent
- 30 opened
- 12 responded
- 1 lead.

In the campaign as a whole, 52 per cent of recipients opened the e-mail, 21 per cent clicked through and eight per cent clicked the 'call me' button. The campaign resulted in around 50 appointments with potential clients, such as Carphone Warehouse.

Source: Marketing Direct, 2003, Supplement on Profit through Customer Insight, Royal Mail.

Advertising

Advertising has probably the most energy and effort spend on assessing its effectiveness, probably as a result of the amount of money spent on it. Much academic and practitioner time has been spent on writing detailed tomes on the subject which space does not allow us to cover here. Please refer to the further study section which will allow you to delve into this subject in greater depth. Here we will look at basic methods of assessing the effectiveness of advertising based on the Hierarchy of Effects models which predominate in the advertising literature.

The following terms are relevant and would probably benefit from reiterating since many marketing practitioners do not focus on advertising on a daily basis.

Table 4.4 Definition of some common advertising measures

Measure	Definition
Expenditure	Amount spent on advertising
Share of voice	Relative spend compared to competitors within sector – called share of outlays in the US
Exposure	Number of times an ad is delivered to a consumer
Reach	Number of households exposed at least once to an ad in a given time period
Rating	Percentage of the population viewing an ad in a given time period
Frequency	Number of exposures of an ad in a given time period
TVRs or GRPs	Gross rating points are the sum of all ratings. Most common measure for buying media time
Trial	First purchase of brand

Average frequency is the average number of exposures delivered in a period, calculated by dividing GRPs by the average reach of a campaign. It is an abstract value as few households would have been exposed to the ads at exactly the intensity of the average frequency.

One way to evaluate advertising effectiveness is to look at its performance at each stage in the communication process.

Table 4.5 Model and measures of advertising effectiveness

Stage in communication	Type of variable	Typical measures
Firm's advertising input	Intensity	Spend, relative spend, exposures, rating, reach, frequency, gross rating points, share of voice
	Media	TV, radio, newspapers, magazines, telephone, internet, outdoor, mail, classified directories
	Ad content: Creative	Argument and other verbal cues; pictures, sound and other emotional cues; endorsement and other inferential cues
Consumer's mental processes	Cognitive	Thoughts, recognition, recall (prompted and spontaneous)
	Affective	Warmth, liking, attitude
	Conative	Persuasion, purchase intention
Market outcomes	Brand choice	Trial, repurchase, switching
	Purchase intensity	Incidence, frequency, weight
	Financial	Market share, revenue, profits

Source: Adapted from Tellis (2004, p. 44)

Place – **Distribution**

Primary audit questions:

- o To what extent does getting the product or delivering service at the right time and in the right place have on customer purchasing behaviour?
- o What are the expectation of customers in terms of delivery versus the price they are paying?
- o What is the price/product/people/logistics trade-offs in this marketplace?

Secondary audit questions:

- o To what extent does the organization's logistics meet the expectations of customers?
- o To what extent does the competitor's logistics meet the needs of the customers?

Distribution lacks the visibility and glamour of, say, promotion but is still a vital part of an effective marketing mix. Relatively little research attention has been directed towards this important area.

According to Rosenbloom (1999), the most widely used performance criteria for channel members are:

1. Sales performance
2. Inventory maintenance
3. Selling capabilities
4. Competitive products handled
5. Growth prospects.

To this, might be added:

6. Profitability
7. Strategic fit.

Since retailers and wholesalers form part of the supply chain, the value chain may prove useful in exploring where value is added at each point.

Further considerations for developing a distribution audit

A lot of insight can be gained from projects undertaken from the consulting industry. Distribution and logistics is one area that has a significant impact on company profitability. According to one of the authors, it has been reported in many efficiency consultancy projects that re-engineering distribution activities within a company can yield significant cost savings leading to significant increases in profits. Apparently the same profits achieved through reducing distribution costs can only be achieved through significantly increasing the price to customers. As we know from basic economic theory of price/demand, subject to the extent of the price elasticity of the market, customers tend not to like major price increases unless it can be substantially offset with other benefits offered as part of the marketing mix.

For this reason, particularly in times of low growth rates in the economy of most developed nations, corporations are under considerable pressure from the shareholders to deliver at least similar or greater to previous years with the similar revenues. Optimizing distribution costs are seen as one way of achieving this. The significant rise in e-business over the last 10 years can be attributed amongst other things to companies, in an attempt to increase their profits, by trying to reduce the number of levels in the marketing channel with the view of getting closer to the customer and charging them a lower price than they would get from their wholesaler. The companies would make an increased profit by charging the end-customers a higher price than they would to the wholesalers. Additionally a number of organizations, such as banks and super-markets, have also tried to bolster their profits through providing mainly an e-business and marketing medium. The financial attractions of these strategies to senior management can appear obvious as the organization will be reducing a large proportion of their fixed costs by reducing their fixed assets and labour costs but in reality the increased profits have failed to materialize.

The exact cause is uncertain but it appears that likely causes could be that e-business is in fact leading increase costs to the manufacturer as they are having to take on the additional role and activities of the intermediary as well as having to take on increased number of smaller delivery, therefore destroying their cost structure achieved through economies of scale.

In addition, smaller intermediaries such as retailers do not purchase goods from only one manufacturer, and direct marketing e-business purchasers are likely to cause them to lose their wholesaler discount on products purchased from other manufacturers.

Expectation relating to distribution also varies across different nations. The North Americans are very demanding and therefore managing how the product or service gets delivered to the final customer may require different considerations. This situation can be highlighted by the following example from a global communication agency selling international communication solutions. In Europe their clients were happy to have monthly or quarterly face-to-face meeting with all other dealings being effectuated using remote communications such as tele/video conferencing and e-mail. The European clients appreciated the cost implication of changing the design of a communication's project in the later stages, therefore took time in the concept stages to make all the necessary changes and only making amendments in the later stages only if they were essential. The Americans were very different, they expected to incorporate changes at any stage of the project and wanted account executives to be available face to face continuously. So the only way the agency could work was to have a US domestic agency with a higher cost and lower price margins than in Europe.

Another major issue with marketing channels is that often marketing strategies, particularly promotional strategies, are developed primarily with the end-customer and the market channel element is then treated as a separate planning exercise. In reality, distribution issues are interlinked with other parts of the marketing mix and often the strategic objectives of a producing organization may not be the same as the other members of a marketing channel and unless the producer has considerable power within the channel it is unlikely that it will achieve its overall objectives with their final customers. Promotional strategies involving intermediaries and final customers need to be completely integrated with other aspects of an organization's marketing and corporate strategies if is to be effective.

To develop a marketing audit of an organization's distribution capabilities is considerably complex and needs to be carefully thought out if one is to avoid any surprises. Therefore what factors and measurements ought to be considered?

Other important audits

The purpose of this unit has been to provide analytical frameworks to assist with the analysis and evaluation of marketing issues which will enable executives to make sensible strategic marketing decisions. Therefore are there other issues that have not been covered that could severely impact on marketing decisions. The answer is yes and we need to consider:

Any international dimensions – International/globalization audit – There is an assumption with the new syllabus that international issues are pervasive throughout everything that we evaluate. The world is getting progressively more international with the de-regulation of various markets and increased IT connectivity the threat of new entrants from abroad is getting much larger. It is therefore very important that for any analysis that is undertaken we also consider any international dimensions to the issues.

Corporate Social Responsibility (CSR) Issues/Ethics – CSR and Corporate Governance is becoming an important strategic differentiator for many companies, in time it may become a critical success factor for simply being allowed to compete in a marketplace. Various stakeholders are looking very closely at how corporations behave towards a multitude of different stakeholders as well as the manner in which they create shareholder value. Companies need to identify how they maximize not only the wealth of their investors but also maximize value of their other stakeholders. Often like in the pharmaceutical industry different stakeholders may have different and conflicting objectives, patients and the medical community wanting effective and safe drugs, shareholders wanting to increase wealth and government wishing to reduce spending. Ignoring the different stakeholder needs is likely to inhibit future company growth. A CSR audit would therefore be useful to minimize potential risks.

Customer Relationship (CRM)/e-business strategies – The use of IT is revolutionizing the way in which business is being conducted and potentially affecting competitive advantage. From reducing the costs of distribution, to designing new products and improving supplier relationships with Just-In-Time supply strategies one cannot ignore the impact that technology is having on deriving competitive advantage. Improved database technology is enabling companies to develop sophisticated CRM strategies allowing better customer retention as gaining more information regarding their purchasing behaviour. Not considering the potential implication of IT could result in your competitors gaining a significant advantage over you. A CRM/Technology audit would allow you to minimize this risk.

Cultural Web audits – Organizations undertake analysis and evaluate their external and internal environment to generate strategic options which if undertaken should generate an adequate return on investment for investors, measured by positive Net Present Values (NPVs). According to the shareholder value model of organizations senior managers have a duty to select options which generate the highest shareholding value corresponding to the most positive NPV. In reality it may be unwise to select options based on the highest NPVs as the strategy may not fit the organizational capabilities making it very difficult to implement. The strategy may be inappropriate for the company as well as the company not being appropriately structured to implement the strategy.

Therefore strategic choice is a trade-off between what fits the organizational culture and capabilities as well as its potential return on investment. Common sense should dictate that choosing a strategy that would clash with the corporate culture will be riskier and have lesser likelihood of being achieved. Therefore one ought to introduce the concept of Expected NPVs which would be a better measure for determining viable strategic options. This is defined by the value of the option's NPV multiplied by its probability of actually occurring. Very high positive NPVs multiplied by a low probability of occurrence will significantly deflate the overall value of the option.

So what does all this mean in practice. It means when we come to evaluate strategic options not only do we require tools and frameworks to determine financial returns but we also need a way to measure cultural attitudes, values and beliefs of an organization in order to assess the extent to which the various strategy options fit the corporate culture. Culture is a very interesting concept and although we have a good idea of what culture we do find it very difficult to define as well as develop metrics to measure it. Culture in itself is not a tangible variable and is called a construct which means it is not real in itself but its existence is defined through its influence on other measurable variables. Therefore although we cannot see it but we can experience culture through a manifestation of other behavioural actions, cultural constructs are known as reflective variables as culture will determine unique behavioural actions which can be measured in its place. This means that if a company has an audit defining specific behavioural actions defined as dimensions expected from certain cultures one can then gain an idea of the corporate culture.

Specific audit dimensions can be developed such as:

Place a mark X on the scales below that mostly represent the characteristics of the organization!

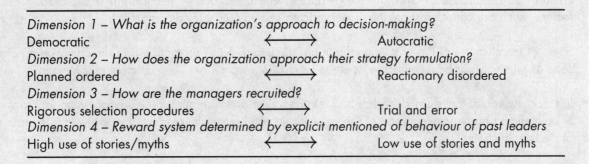

A large number of dimensions can then developed to reflect an organization's culture and then be plotted on multi-dimensional cultural cluster plot (Figure 4.6) which for simplicity is only reflecting four dimensions and two companies. In reality we would expect many more.

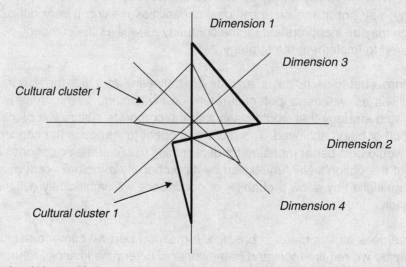

Figure 4.6 Cultural clusters of two companies derived according to dimensions defining culture

Summary

This unit looks at how we might audit marketing activities. Taking the 4Ps as a framework, we look at the ways in which we might evaluate the effectiveness of our activities. A large variety of measures are discussed. It is important when using these measures that you understand what underpins these, that is where do they come from? We use the 4Ps as a structure to analysing marketing activities. This can easily be extended to the 5 or 7Ps.

We examine several measures of assessing product performance. As well as the more obvious measures of actual and perceived performance, we include measures of satisfaction and service quality. A gap analysis model is introduced as a conceptual framework to structure an analysis of service quality. Complaining behaviour is emphasized as a means of understanding levels of consumer satisfaction.

Pricing can be analysed from a variety of angles. The price/quality relationship is explored. Other factors which are considered are the fit with pricing strategy, costs and competitors.

Some of the elements of the promotional mix are discussed. Sales promotion and direct marketing are seen as relatively easily accountable whereas advertising and PR are seen as more problematic.

It is acknowledged that distribution has had relatively little attention but is an extremely important factor in determining business effectiveness. The value chain can be usefully employed to evaluate this section of the supply chain.

A structured and systematic approach to assess marketing activities is important. We need to adopt objective measures to allow us to determine how to allocate limited resources effectively. It also allows us to demonstrate how marketing activities can be made accountable.

The next unit looks at how we might evaluate performance from a predominantly financial viewpoint.

Further study

Broadbent, T. (2000) *Advertising Works 11*, WARC.

McDonald, C. (2003) *Is your advertising working? A guide to evaluating campaign effectiveness*, WARC/Admap.

Reichheld, F.F. (1996) *The Loyalty Effect*, Harvard Business School Press, Boston, Massachussetts, USA.

Rimini, M. (2003) *Advertising Works 12*, WARC.

Hints and tips

Examiners are interested in your ability to see the strategic implications of your analysis. So whenever you conduct a piece of analysis think what it means. Ask yourself the question 'So what?'

Exam questions are likely to ask you to consider a number of marketing activities related to an industry or organizational example and you will need to be able to take a theoretical framework such as the 4Ps, Value Chain or the 7S framework, which are all tools that one can use to create an audit, and analyse as well as evaluate how each part can be used to develop criteria and measures specific to the example or industry setting.

Just because you are not asked for a marketing audit or any other process does not mean that you should not consider it in a question. Remember the exam is trying to test your skills in business analysis and evaluation, so if you feel that an audit could add value to the strategic process as well as demonstrate how it applies to the question then you should go ahead and introduce it.

Bibliography

Berry, L.A., Parasuraman, A., Zeithaml, V.A. (1994) 'Diagnosing service quality in America', *Academy of Management Executive*, **8**(2), pp. 32–52.

Ohmae, K. (1982) *The Mind of the Strategist*, McGraw-Hill, Inc., pp. 91–98.

Parasuraman, A., Berry, L.A., Zeithaml, V.A. (1991) 'Refinement and reassessment of the SERVQUAL scale', *Journal of Retailing*, **67**, Winter, pp. 420–450.

Rosenbloom, B. (1999) 'Channel management' in Michael J. Baker (ed.), *Encyclopedia of Marketing*, International Thomson Business Press, London, pp. 407–419.

Tellis, G.J. (2004) *Effective Advertising:* Understanding When, How, and Why Advertising Works, Sage Publications.

unit 5
evaluating performance: financial measures

"As more firms adopt a customer asset management approach to their business, it has become increasingly important to understand how customer management efforts relate to the financial performance of the firm. Of specific interest to shareholders is the relationship between traditional financial measures and customer-centric measures..."
(Hogan *et al.*, 2002)

Exam Hint 5.1

Students may be expected to interpret simple financial and management accounts and draw key strategic issues relating to the strength and weaknesses of a company or a competitor.

Utilizing quantitative measures, particularly financial data, is very important in business and can significantly affect a number of marketing decisions. Throughout the new Professional Post Graduate syllabus, each unit will build upon your financial awareness. In A&E we will focus on definitions and measures and how to assess financial resources and competences as part of a SWOT analysis. In SMD we will focus on how to use finance to evaluate different marketing options to make a decision and in MMP we will use finance as a means to control and manage marketing performance. This unit is extensive but it provides the basis for other courses and you should spend time trying to get to grips with the concepts. You ought to be able to undertake simple financial calculations or at least to qualitatively describe what you would be looking for; just because one is not asking you for something specific is not an excuse to ignore it.

Learning objectives

'There is also a need to change the way we teach marketing at the undergraduate and graduate levels. Marketing classes can no longer be the refuge for students who "can't do numbers." At the introductory level, students should be exposed to basic models linking marketing assets to shareholder value. This basic understanding can then be leveraged in advanced marketing courses that focus on more complete models of the financial value of customer assets. Such an approach is needed to prepare marketing students to perform effectively in firms where marketing managers come under increasing pressure to justify the potential of their programs to create shareholder value.'
(Hogan *et al.*, 2002)

The previous two units have allowed us to examine performance from a marketing perspective. We now move to look at more purely financial measures which can give us a different insight into how the business is performing. The purpose of this unit is to enable you to understand the importance of financial measures in the strategic decision-making process (without making you into an accountant!). The emphasis is on helping you to understand the range of measures available and their contribution in helping you to reach a decision. A simple explanation is provided of how these measures are calculated but for our purposes it is more important to focus on the implications rather than pure calculation. In an examination you might be expected to calculate a few of the more basic ratios, at most. What is more important, however, is that you understand what they mean and what conclusions they can help you to reach.

In this unit you will:

o   Understand the quantitative techniques which can be used to evaluate business performance (see syllabus 2.1)

o   Examine financial measures (see syllabus 2.1).

Having completed this unit you will be able to:

o   Explain the purpose and contribution of financial evaluation of performance to strategic analysis

o   Use the various financial measures of performance appropriately

o   Use financial ratio analysis, benchmarking, SVA and trend analysis

o   Evaluate performance over current and historic business cycles.

Sections of the syllabus being covered in this unit:

Element 2: Evaluation of business and marketing performance (30 per cent).

2.1   Critically evaluate and use quantitative techniques for evaluating business and marketing performance over current and historic business cycles. Techniques to be covered should include:

   o   Balanced scorecard, with an emphasis on customer and innovation measures.

   o   Evaluation of marketing performance including the audit of marketing activities and valuation of marketing assets, such as brands.

   o   Financial techniques such as SVA (using total shareholder return and economic profit), financial ratio analysis, trend analysis, benchmarking and evaluation of historical financial decisions.

Element 3: Analysis of the internal environment (20 per cent).

3.1   Use and appraise the available techniques and processes for the objective assessment of the internal environment of an organization, including portfolio analysis, value chain, innovation audit and cultural web.

3.2   Critically evaluate the resource-based view of the organization.

3.3 Demonstrate the ability to use appropriate information and tools to evaluate the core competencies, assets, culture and weaknesses of an organization.

3.4 Assess the 'fit' between an organization's culture and its current strategy.

3.5 Summarize the salient factors and insights emerging from the internal analysis.

Statements of related marketing practice

The main skill or business competency areas are being developed in this section and are likely to be examined:

o To develop appropriate structures and frameworks to identify appropriate information requirements to define and structure marketing-related business problems.
o To be able to critically evaluate different analytical perspectives which will lead executives to gain a better understanding of their external and internal environment within the specific context of their industries, thus setting and placing them in a better position to make better informed decisions potentially leading to minimize risks and uncertainties.
o To promote a strong marketing orientation to influence strategy formulation and investment decisions.
o Specify and direct the line marketing process.

How will this unit help you and what can you expect to achieve after completing this unit?

> 'Marketing practitioners and scholars are under increased pressure to be more accountable for and to show how marketing expenditure adds to shareholder value (Doyle 2000). The perceived lack of accountability has undermined marketing's credibility, threatened marketing's standing in the firm and even threatened marketing's existence as a distinct capability within the firm. The Marketing Leadership Council (2001, p. 27) reports that 70 per cent of advertising budgets are in decline, compared with 51 per cent, 47 per cent and 44 per cent for human resources, information technology and general counsel functions: "Having exhausted cost-saving opportunities in virtually every other function," marketing is "next in the line of fire."' (Rust et al., 2004)

This unit will help you understand the importance of financial analysis to business and where does finance sit within the new PPDIPM and within marketing as a whole. Marketing decisions have financial implications and the strategies that marketing executives developed are often judged on financial criteria. Therefore it is imperative that marketers have an understanding of finance if they have any ambitions of getting their plans to succeed in the business world.

First of all, why would it be useful to understand finance and where does it fit within the marketing syllabus? As a senior marketing executive, your task will be to formulate marketing strategies in order to differentiate the offerings of your organization and an understanding of finance is critical in achieving this process, the question you should pose is why? The answer to this question lies within the practice of strategy and therefore you should also ask what help can the discipline of strategic management offer us on formulating competitive strategies for our offerings? According to Mintzberg and Waters (1985), and Mintzberg (1990, 2000), there are several ways in which organizations approach the formulation of strategies but within the different typologies which they use to depict the different strategizing processes two broad categories can be identified to help us as marketers to better understand this process. The first strategy is seen as a process of 'fit' (De-Wit and Meyer, 1994) between the needs of the external environment (customers, other stakeholders and competitors) and the resources that an organization has to compete within the environment. In the second case, the strategy formulation process is perceived as a 'stretch' (Hamel and Prahalad, 1994) of the organization's core competencies around a number of different customer needs. Examples of companies include BIC who define themselves as 'plastic extruders' and apply their competencies in the biro pen, disposable cigarette lighters and razor markets. Honda is a small engine manufacturer and utilizes its competencies to serve specific segments of the car, motorbike, outboard boat engines markets. Although this model of strategy is beginning to be adopted within mainstream marketing it is still the strategy as 'fit' perspective that it is still widely practised in both companies and academia.

The external environment, in the case of strategy as a process 'fit', is perceived in this perspective as being fixed and set by the so-called 'unwritten rules' which dictate the minimum criteria needed to play the resources. (Often these are referred to as critical success factors needed to play this game.) The strategic dictate is that a company has no power to change the external environment but needs to position itself relative to other players according to its resources which it can develop or acquire from third parties. The majority of strategy practice has been centred on this idea of 'fit'. As availability of cash is important in being able to access resources and therefore determining one's position in the game, it is important to understand how to analyse one's financial position in the game. Actually having the cash idle in the bank is not a measure of how much you are truly worth in competitive terms as having access to funds when you need it is also dependent on how much you have already borrowed, relative to how much cash the owners have put in (technically known as gearing) which will in turn determine how much you can borrow from financial institutions and will therefore determine your strategic choices. Having access to spare cash when you need it and how much of it that you have dedicated or have 'tied up' in other projects will influence the strategic behaviour not only of your own organization but that of your competitors as well. Therefore understanding one's competitive financial strength and weaknesses is imperative and should be routinely undertaken as part of a SWOT analysis as it will help you determine possible competitor responses as part of a scenario planning exercise.

So how can a SWOT analysis of our competitive financial standing assist us? One theoretical perspective offered by Porter (1985) with his use of value chain analysis can help us answer this question. The value chain is a means of helping us understand all the activities involved within our organization (value chain) as well as outside organization (the value system), involve getting our products and services to our customers as well as the activities involved in satisfying them. All these activities will incur costs and the objective for a company is to maintain appropriate level of customer satisfaction but with fewer activities than the competitive therefore acquiring an advantage over them. Having access to information regarding a competitor's cost structure and how they can finance these costs can therefore provide significant insight of how the competitors are delivering value and would allow us to appropriately position ourselves relative to them. Unfortunately this is where we meet our first hurdle, this information is only available internally and therefore we would not access it. In some countries like the United Kingdom and the United States, financial information for publicly owned and limited liability companies are available for public scrutiny but again they have been presented in an aggregated format that does not allow you to get the necessary detail. In other countries this information is simply not available. With certain financial analytical techniques insights can be gained on the financial strengths and ability of a firm to deliver value. As Porter (1985) implies in the new preface of *Competitive Advantage*, identifying a competitor's value chain is an ideal, like searching for the 'Holy Grail'. It does not, however, mean that it should be ignored as the process of trying to find it can raise considerable strategic insight which can help in achieving a competitive advantage. Two additional frameworks (Figures 5.1 and 5.2) developed by Hamel and Prahalad (1994) that are similar to Porter's value chain (1985) show a better representation of where financial appraisal sit within the strategy formulation process:

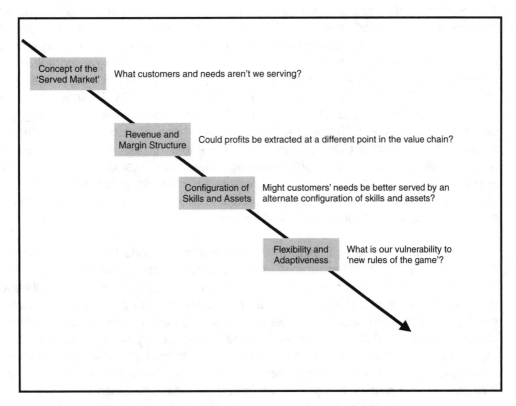

Figure 5.1 Decomposing an organization's economic engine
Source: Hamel and Prahalad (1994)

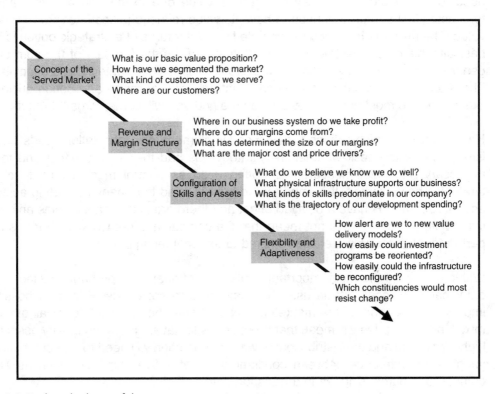

Figure 5.2 Finding the limits of the current economic engine
Source: Hamel and Prahalad, Competing For The Future, Harvard Business School Press, 1994

These models use the analogy of an engine to represent the organization and integrate the marketing, finance and operations functions to provide a framework that can drill into the different parts of the organizations in order to be able to provide an overall strategic competence level of the organization. You ought to get used to different metaphors and similies being utilized to describe organizations. Metaphors from different disciplines such as engineering (mechanistic approaches – systems thinking – 7s Framework) and biological sciences (e.g. the product life cycle) are often used to provide models to study business settings. The trouble is that sometimes we take these analogies too far, that is transition states within the product life cycle are often more in control of management decisions rather than the outcome of their life being seemingly inevitable. Examples of the limitations of such applications include the success of Lucozade following its re-positioning in the late 1980s show the weaknesses of portfolio analyses and product life cycle models emphasizing that they should be used appropriately and cautiously.

Therefore, within the new PPGDIPM financial analysis is undertaken to evaluate the resource capability of an organization as well as its competitors as part of the SWOT analysis of the internal and competitive environment. In the second unit of the course you will need to be able to evaluate the various strategic options open to the company which will then allow management as well as shareholders to determine which strategy is best for all concerned. Strategic choice (Johnson and Scholes, 1997) is a means of selecting which is the best strategy to offer the best financial returns as well as the one which fits best with resources, competencies and capabilities in terms of achieving them. In terms of selecting the strategies with the best financial returns means being able to undertake financial assessments. One of the most common evaluation methods is payback which is the amount of time taken for strategic options to yield profits. Unfortunately the cash flows used in this method have not been devalued to represent the present value of cash due to inflation. As a marketing executive, you will need to understand how to forecast future cash flows and to determine what drives them. You will also need to appreciate that money has a time value due to inflation and that any cash flows forecasted in the future will need to have its value reduced (discounted) to represent it current value. The main method used to evaluate financial returns of a strategic option is NPV which is basically the initial investment outlay subtracted from the forecast of the sum of all the cash generated throughout the lifetime of the strategic option discounted to represent its value today. There are other evaluation tools such as internal rate of return and option pricing but NPV is likely to be the most common evaluation method you will come across throughout the course.

Having decided which options to select and implement, an organization needs control mechanisms in place to check whether the strategy has had the desired effect and to modify it as necessary. Financial measures are often used as control mechanisms to check whether strategies have worked. It is important to bear in mind that many marketing activities such as advertising and PR have a delayed effect and therefore just because sales and profits are not immediately realized does not mean that the campaign is not working. For this reason, other performance measures are also required to test marketing performance.

Within marketing the most important application of finance is probably pricing where financial data, particular cost data is used by companies to set prices. Pricing is possibly the most important component of the marketing mix as it sets the precedence for all other parts of the mix. A premium price will mean that product has to have a premium quality associated with the higher price tag and the distribution as well as promotion will need to reflect the high value. Just imagine the difference between consuming tea at a five star hotel such as The Savoy as compared to purchasing tea in a transport café.

Financial data, wherever available, is also used in segmentation analysis where the financial size of the opportunity potentially offered by the segment should be stated. Whenever financial data is not available, market segments should be represented in terms of volume. This data is then used as part of the strategic planning process to prioritize which segments an organization should target.

You should appreciate that there is a difference between management and financial accounting; the former is an internal process that provides financial information for decision-making and the latter is an external process by which organizations are legally obliged to produce financial statements under a statutory legal framework. Financial accounts are communication documents which are used by various stakeholders, for this reason they potentially do have marketing implications and can have significant influence on marketing activities by determining not only your creditworthiness to suppliers, but also the quality of employees applying and your ability to retain them as well as the future existence of the company in terms of whether shareholders are interested in keeping and buying more shares as opposed to getting rid of them, therefore increasing the chances of being acquired and reorganized by a third party.

Finally, it is important that strategy behaviour is linked to the extent to which an organization is finance-orientated or marketing-orientated. This area was covered in Unit 1 but also fits in nicely with our discussion of financial performance. Finance-orientated companies are likely to have a short-term outlook focus on short-term profitability. There are several ways of affecting financial returns in addition to increasing customer demand and price, and these include improving cost efficiencies as well as reconfiguring the company's financing (borrowing at more favourable terms affecting the cost of capital). This is appropriately represented in Figure 5.3.

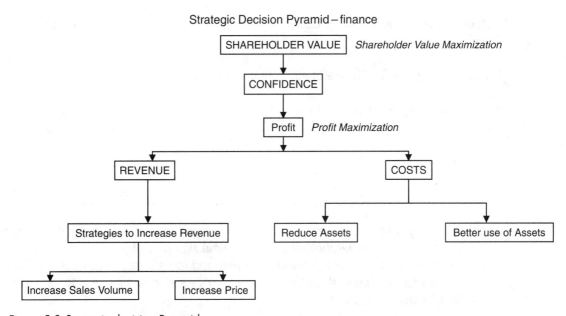

Figure 5.3 Strategic decision Pyramid

Marketing's aim within the corporation will be to convince other senior managers of the necessary trade-offs required between short-term and long-term objectives and that short-term profitability may require sacrificing in order to achieve long-term shareholder value, something which is often 'easier said than done'.

Key definitions

Assets – are the resources that the organization owns and will provide a future benefit to the business.

Fixed assets – are held and used over a long period of time (e.g. land, buildings, plant and equipment).

Current assets – are owned for just a short period (e.g. stocks and cash).

Stock (in the United States, inventory) – is the goods purchased for resale or manufacture (e.g. raw materials, work-in-progress or finished goods).

Debtors (in the United States, accounts receivable) – are both the people to whom the company owes money and the money owed to them.

Liabilities – represent the amount the company owes its creditors.

Creditors (in the United States, accounts payable) – are both the people who owe money to the company and the money it owes to them.

Capital – is the part of the fund of the business provided by its owners.

Capital employed – the sum of shareholders' funds, creditors (over a year), and provision for liabilities and charges. Another way to calculate this is the difference between total assets and current liabilities.

Cost of sales – are operating expenses not treated as distribution costs or administrative expenses.

Net operating profit – is operating profit minus taxes.

PBIT – is profit before interest and tax.

Introduction

> *'For too long, marketers have not been held accountable for showing how marketing expenditures add to shareholder value. As time has gone by, this lack of accountability has undermined marketers' credibility, threatened the standing of the marketing function within the firm, and even threatened marketing's existence as a distinct capability within the firm.'* (Rust *et al.*, 2004)

Marketers are often accused of not viewing the wider picture. Whilst this is often an unfair accusation it is important that marketing managers, particularly those responsible for making strategic decisions, demonstrate a clear understanding of the finances of their organization. This will allow them to evaluate more completely the financial impact of their decisions.

Managers need financial information about their company to manage it effectively. Although information about past profits is useful, in general we need to be more concerned about the present and the future. The two areas we are interested in here are financial statements and management accounts.

Financial statements

Financial statements, such as the balance sheet and the profit and loss account, provide historical information, not current or future information. But history can be useful as an indicator of the future.

A profit and loss account presents information about an organization's financial performance throughout a period. A balance sheet gives information about its financial position at a certain point in time, that is the balance sheet date.

A financially aware manager needs to be able to read through a company's profit and loss account and understand line by line the meaning and significance of each of the items in it.

To give you an idea of what these look like, two simplified versions of financial statements (which might be produced by a UK public company) are shown below.

Diploma plc
Profit and loss account for the year ended 31 December 2004

	2003 £'000s	2004 £'000s
Turnover	199 200	183 900
Cost of sales	(133 800)	(127 200)
Gross profit	65 400	56 700
Distribution costs	(21 600)	(18 500)
Administrative expenses	(32 700)	(26 100)
Operating profit	12 100	10 100
Profit before interest	12 100	10 100
Interest receivable	100	300
Interest payable	(1 500)	(1 400)
Profit before taxation	10 700	9 000
Taxation on profits	(4 000)	(3 200)
Profit after taxation	6 700	5 800
Dividends	3 400	3 300
Retained profits for the year	3 300	2 500
Earnings per ordinary share	0.4p	8.1p
Dividend per ordinary share	4.8p	4.6p

Diploma plc Balance sheet as at 31 December 2004

	2004		2003	
	£'000s	£'000s	£'000s	£'000s
Fixed assets				
Intangible assets		1 200		1 100
Tangible assets		26 100		24 900
Fixed asset investments		500		900
Current assets				
Stocks	6 800		5 500	
Debtors	5 700		4 700	
Investments	100		300	
Cash	600		800	
	13 200		11 300	
Creditors: amount falling due within one year	(7 800)		(5 200)	
Net current assets		5 400		6 100
Total assets less current liabilities		33 200		33 000
Creditors: amount falling due after one year		(300)		(500)
Provisions for liabilities and charges		(50)		(100)
		32 850		32 400
Capital and reserves				
Called up share capital		3 500		3 500
Share premium account		8 000		8 000
Revaluation reserve		7 700		7 700
Profit and loss reserve account		13 650		13 200
		32 850		32 400

Do not panic about these financial statements! You are only expected to be familiar with them and understand the basics. Use the key definitions above and try to understand what the statement is aiming to tell you. Do not worry about the detail. For example, in the balance sheet above you might be expected to understand that capital is important but not to understand the detailed breakdown above. By the way, the distinction between creditors of less than one year and more than one year is purely arbitrary. Accountants! Creditors of more than a year are sometimes referred to as long-term debt.

Financial statements are communication documents targeted at different stakeholders; marketing executives should appreciate this fact. Marketing therefore ought to have an influence in the way that these statements are communicated to the stakeholders as well as appreciate the potential impact that it may have.

Activity 5.1

Get your own organization's financial statements and work out what is going on. What are the key trends? Perhaps talk to someone in the finance department about them. Or alternatively get the company accounts of a major company (some of these can be downloaded from the web). Accounts may have a commentary associated with them to help you pick out the key points. Try just reading the numbers yourself and jotting down your thoughts. Then compare them with the 'experts' view.

Question 5.1

Which groups are likely to be interested in financial statements? What are they likely to use them for?

It is important to remember that in many ways financial statements are incomplete as they are backward looking, focusing on the past when the interested user groups are more often concerned with the future. They also, by their nature, report in purely financial terms without addressing non-financial matters.

We now move to look in a bit more detail at two very important measures contained in the financial statements, namely profit and costs.

Profit

The obvious definition of profit is the excess of revenue (or sales turnover) in a period over costs and other expenditure in the same period.

However, financial statements tend to view profit on a number of levels and it is important to understand at which level profit is being calculated in your organization to make both historic and competitor comparisons. Gross profit, for example, is sales turnover minus cost of sales. Net profit (or operating profit) is gross profit minus distribution and administrative costs.

Already you should be able to see that your choice of measure of profit makes a big difference. If, for example, you work in an industry which has low distribution and administrative costs then the difference between gross profit and operating profit may be relatively little. A small management consultancy may see very little variance between the two measures. But a company exporting fragile goods to a bureaucratic country may see a huge gap between the two. The important thing is that each of these measures is telling a different story.

Costs

It is very important to understand how costs are allocated within your organization. There are many different types of cost and organizations may treat them differently. This can all get very complicated but all we are going to cover here are the basics of fixed and variable costs.

Essentially a 'fixed cost' (sometimes called an overhead) is one which will remain the same for a given period of time (i.e. will be a fixed amount) regardless of the volume of activity in the period. Examples of fixed costs are the cost of renting a building, the cost of equipment depreciation and the salaries of managers and supervisors. These costs increase over time but are fixed for a given period of time. For example, the cost of renting building increases with time and so is more for 1 year than for 1 month, and will probably increase year on year. But the important point is that the cost per period, such as the cost per month, does not vary with the amount of activity. Let us assume that renting a factory costs us £6 million per year. Whatever we do in the building, whether we produce five widgets or five million widgets, the cost is the same. We have to pay £6 million anyway.

'A variable cost' is one which varies in line with the volume of activity. A clear example is the cost of raw materials. If we assume that each of our widgets needs £3 of wood and £7 of metal, then our unit variable cost is £10. So if we make five of them, our total variable costs will be

£50; if we make five million, our costs will be £50 million. A variable cost is a constant amount per unit, but the total increases as the volume of activity rises.

That is the simple version. In many organizations the picture can get much more complicated. You can have more subtle distinctions of cost, for example mixed costs, variable overheads, indirect costs and so on. As you are not doing a module in costing, we will not pursue these here as there are many specialist texts which cover this in more detail. The important thing is that you understand that even costing is subjective. And that you find out how the rules work in your organization.

Management accounts

Management accounting is concerned with providing financial information for the management of the organization. Much of the information comes from within the organization rather than externally.

It is useful to compare the characteristics of financial statements with those of management accounts.

	Financial statements	Management accounts
Regulation	Must meet company law and accounting standards	No regulation or control
Content	Profit and loss statement, balance sheet and cash flow statement	Also may include information on profits, assets, liabilities and cash flow but may also include productivity, stock turnover, orders placed etc.
Time frame	Backward-focused relying purely on historic data	May include historic data but can also be predictive, for example budgets and forecasts
Main users	Shareholders, investors and stock market professionals	Managers
Frame of reference	Focus purely on company performance	Also takes external factors into account, such as the prices of competitive products and services, or the rate of growth in the economy

One of the main ways for us to use financial statements is to analyse the ratios contained within.

Using financial ratio analysis

Ratios can be used very effectively in the analysis stage. They can offer us a snapshot of one point in time. But more importantly, they allow us to make valuable comparisons.

- We can identify trends by comparing a firm's performance over time, or from period to period.
- We can benchmark against the competition since we can compare our performance with others in the industry, or even companies in other industries. We can compare ratios at one point in time or examine comparative trends over time.

When we are making comparisons between firms, we need to decide which type of business we see as comparable; we need to find a business with a similar trading pattern. The following factors might be considered: type of industry, nationality, regional area and size of business.

The golden rule of ratios is, 'Always compare like with like'.

There are many ratios. We are just going to focus on the key ones here but if you refer to other texts, particularly accounting ones, you will find lots more out there! For the purpose of passing this module, it is better to focus on understanding the one we cover here rather than drown in the morass of all the potential financial ratios in the world ever.

Broadly speaking there are five different types of ratio:

1. Profitability ratios (including return on investment)
2. Asset utilization ratios
3. Liquidity ratios
4. Capital structure ratios
5. Investor ratios.

Let us look at each of these in turn.

Profitability ratios

Profit is the return that a company makes on the resources it has invested. Investors expect to see a profit return in line with the amount of money invested. The main measures of profit used therefore are return on capital or return on investment. There are many, many different ways to measure these but you will doubtless be glad to know that we are only going to cover two of the main ones here. These are Return on Capital Employed (ROCE) and Gross Profit Ratio.

o   Return on Capital Employed

The total capital employed in a company can be measured in several ways but these should all give the same figure.

1. Fixed assets plus net current assets
2. Total assets minus current liabilities
3. Share capital plus reserves plus long-term creditors and provisions for liabilities and charges.

Activity 5.2

Use the three methods above to calculate the capital employed in Diploma plc in 2004.

We can move on to calculate the ratio. We are interested here in showing how hard the capital is working, or perhaps more accurately how successfully it is being put to use. So we need to compare what we get out with what we put in, that is profit with capital. Remember our golden rule of always comparing like with like. If we are looking at all the capital, we need to look at all the profit. So PBIT is a good measure to use, as that measures total profit before interest and tax are deducted.

$$\text{ROCE} = \frac{\text{PBIT}}{\text{capital employed}} \times 100$$

So in our example we can see from the profit and loss account that PBIT was £10 100 in 2004. We already know that capital employed is £33 200 because we have just calculated it.

$$\text{So ROCE} = \frac{10100}{33200} \times 100 = 30.4\%$$

Activity 5.3

Work out the ROCE for Diploma plc in 2003.

So why are we doing this? What does ROCE tell us? What should we be looking for?

There are three main comparisons to be made:

1. We can look at changes year on year. In our example we can see that return on capital reduced over the period 2003–2004, from 36.6 to 30.4 per cent.
2. We can compare our ROCE with our competitors and other industries.
3. We can compare ROCE with the market borrowing rate. But we need to be careful here as market yields are not the same as accounting returns. What would be the cost of extra borrowing to the company if it needed more loans? Is it earning a ROCE which suggests that it could make profits to make the borrowings worthwhile? Is the company making a ROCE which suggests it is getting value for money from its current borrowing?

The ROCE ratio is concerned with assessing the rate at which asset values are converted into sales revenue. It shows the ability of the assets to generate profit.

○ Gross Profit Ratio

This is also known as the gross margin ratio. It is used to check the stability of market conditions, by examining the relationship between the two factors relating to the operations of the organization, that is sales and the cost of sales.

$$\text{Gross Profit Ratio} = \frac{\text{gross profit}}{\text{cost of sales}} \times 100$$

Asset utilization ratios

This set of ratios looks at the use of resources by the organization. We will look at three of these: stock turnover, average debtor collection period and asset values to sales.

○ *Stock turnover* – The rate at which a business converts its stock into sales is a critical indicator of business activity. The stock turnover ratio tells us the number of times the stock is completely sold and replaced by purchases during the accounting period.

$$\text{Stock turnover ratio} = \frac{\text{average stock}}{\text{cost of sales}} \times 365$$

This gives an answer in days. But remember the trading cycle may be cyclical, resulting in peak and low stock levels so the timing of this measure may be crucial. Where demand is seasonal, manufacturers may have to hold stock so that they can meet the demand when it arrives. For example, there is no point in an umbrella manufacturer wanting it to rain before he/she starts making umbrellas. He/she will need to stockpile throughout the summer in anticipation of a damp autumn. So the summer may see a low stock turnover ratio which may be remedied in a few months once the rain starts.

    o *Average debtor collection period* – This ratio estimates the number of days of sales which are represented by the firm's debtors.

$$\text{Average debtor collection period} = \frac{\text{value of debtors}}{\text{sales}} \times 365$$

This should be as low as possible, whilst still being consistent with business reality. If it is too high this could indicate inefficient investment by management in unproductive current assets, that is the firm's managers are not ensuring that its debtors settle their debts quickly.

    o *Ratio of asset values to sales* – This ratio looks at the ability of the assets employed by the company to generate sales revenue.

It is calculated by dividing the sales revenue by the total asset base (the sum of fixed assets and current assets).

This ratio gives an indication of the ability of the assets to generate profit.

Liquidity ratios

Liquidity ratios are used to assess whether the organization has enough cash to meet the payments due for its current liabilities. In everyday language, can it pay its bills? This is called short-term solvency and there are two primary ratios used to calculate this.

    o *Current ratio* – This is the standard test of liquidity and is the ratio of current assets to current liabilities.

$$\text{Current ratio} = \frac{\text{current assets}}{\text{current liabilities}}$$

This expression tells us that for every £1 that the company will have to pay in the near future, it can expect to receive £X when its current assets are converted into cash.

A ratio above 1.0 would normally be expected but this varies from industry to industry. Any organization with a ratio of below 1.0 faces a risk of not being able to pay its debts on time. A general rule of thumb is that an acceptable current ratio is 1.5 but this is only a rough guide, depending on the industry. Most analysts would be concerned if a manufacturing firm's current ratio falls below 2:1, but a lower ratio would be acceptable in firms with little or no stock.

The assumption with the current ratio is that the organization is able to convert all its current assets into cash relatively easily. For example, a manufacturing company may hold large quantities of raw materials which it will need to convert into finished goods. If stock turnover is low these assets are not very liquid, that is, it takes some time to convert its assets into cash to pay off its creditors. Construction companies have a particular problem here as their work spends a long time in progress. These types of companies suffer from illiquid assets.

To cope with this problem another liquidity ratio may be used, that is the acid test ratio.

    o *The acid test ratio* – The acid test ratio, or quick ratio as it is sometimes known, takes account of the illiquidity of some assets. It removes stocks from the calculation allowing for a fairer assessment of the liquidity of some companies.

$$\text{Acid test ratio} = \frac{\text{current assets} - \text{stocks}}{\text{current liabilities}}$$

This ratio should be at least 1.0 for companies with low stock turnover. For those with a high stock turnover, this ratio can be lower than 1.0 without suggesting that the company has cash flow problems. An acceptable quick ratio may be 0.8 but again this is dependent on the industry and is just a rough guide.

> Whilst a low liquidity ratio tends to be bad, a high liquidity ratio is not always good. The company may be tying up more money in the business than it needs to be.

The trend in liquidity ratios should also be monitored, whether the organization chooses to use the current ratio or quick ratio or both. Changes in the ratio can show if the company's solvency position is improving or declining.

It is vital in analysing these ratios that you take account of the context and do not read too much into a single figure. That is why it is so important that you understand where the numbers come from so that you can make informed decisions as to what they mean. Although you may not have come into marketing to understand financial ratios and the like, to be a competent marketing director you will need to. Here is an example where deconstructing the ratio can help us to understand it. Different organizations may have exactly the same liquidity ratio, but for one this may be fine and for another disastrous.

Example

Supermarket groups have very low liquidity ratios and yet operate safely. Why?

They have low levels of debtors since they do not give credit. Although you and I may pay by credit card at our local supermarket, as far as the store is concerned that is a cash sale since the burden of credit is carried by the credit card company.

Their stock turnover is high. Although there may be high quantities of stock, these tend to have high rates of sale and sell on quickly.

The grocery multiples benefit from buying their stock on credit from their suppliers, often not having to pay for their stock until they have already got the cash for selling it on.

So what seems like an extremely low liquidity ratio is actually perfectly healthy for them. But for most of their suppliers it would probably be terminal.

Capital structure ratios

The main ratio to interest us in this category is the gearing ratio.

Gearing is a UK term; the US equivalent is leverage. Understanding the meaning of these terms helps to understand what the ratio means. Imagine you are driving a car. If you are in a low gear, say fifth, it will take longer and need more pressure on the accelerator to reach the same speed. If you are in a high gear, say first, a relatively light pressure on the accelerator will dramatically increase your speed.

The same is true of a gearing ratio. In highly geared companies, a small change in the operating profits will result in a much larger percentage change in earnings per share than in a lower geared company.

$$\text{Gearing ratio} = \frac{\text{long-term debt (i.e. creditors of more than a year)}}{\text{total of share capital} + \text{long-term debt}}$$

The way in which a business is financed can have a dramatic effect on its success or failure. An analysis of the financial structure of the company is important to both the owners and the creditors. Gearing is the relationship between debt finance and equity finance. It is important because the amount of debt increases the sensitivity of variation in profit. Investment in a highly geared company carries more risk of low returns but also more possibility of high returns.

A ratio of more than 0.5 would show that lenders are contributing more capital than the owners. For the lenders this would generally be unacceptable. Also the closer the ratio comes to 0.5, the less likely the firm is to raise further long-term loans.

Investor ratios

One of the functions of management is to ensure the best possible return is made to the firm's investors. If the investors are not happy with the return which they are earning, the consequence is that they are unlikely to invest more of their money in the organization. Potential investors are also unlikely to invest their money if they can see a higher return available elsewhere on the market.

Various ratios are used by investors and investment analysts to assess the value and performance of equity investments. Some of these are obtained from or at least partially derived from financial statements. We will look briefly at the most common ones here. You will be glad to know that these are very simple ratios and mostly self-explanatory.

- o *Earnings per share (EPS)* – This is the amount of profit earned by the company during a financial year that can be attributed to each ordinary share.

$$\text{Earnings per share} = \frac{\text{total earnings for the year}}{\text{total number of equity shares}}$$

This is often used by investors as a measure of corporate performance, and can be used to assess corporate trends over time.

- o *Price to earnings (P/E ratio)* – Another commonly used investment ratio, the P/E ratio, expresses the share price as a multiple of the EPS. A high P/E ratio indicates strong investor confidence.

$$\text{P/E ratio} = \frac{\text{current share price}}{\text{earnings per share}}$$

This ratio tries to show the number of years an investor must wait until their investment (cost of a share) is recovered by the earnings. The lower the ratio the better off the investor is, as the cost of the share is recovered more quickly.

119

○ *Dividends per share* – It could be argued that using earnings is misleading since it implies that shareholders actually receive all of the earnings of the company. Very few, if any, companies retain their profits for internal investment – it is only dividends which the owners of shares receive.

$$\text{Dividends per share} = \frac{\text{dividend}}{\text{number of issued shares}}$$

○ *Dividend cover* – The dividend cover is the number of times the annual dividend is covered by earnings.

$$\text{Dividend cover} = \frac{\text{earnings per share}}{\text{dividends per share}}$$

A dividend cover of 2 times would indicate that the company paid 50 per cent of its distributable profits for the year as dividends to its shareholders, and retained 50 per cent in the business to finance future operations.

A significant change in the dividend cover from one year to the next needs close examination. If the cover falls sharply, you need to investigate why this has happened. It may be that the organization's profits have fallen but the directors want to maintain the dividends to match shareholder expectations.

Activity 5.4

Calculate the dividend cover for Diploma plc in 2004. What does this tell you?

○ *Dividend yield* – We can also measure the yield compared to the share price. This is the dividend return a shareholder currently expects on the share of a company.

$$\text{Dividend yield} = \frac{\text{dividend per ordinary share}}{\text{market price per ordinary share}} \times 100$$

Equity investors look for both dividend yield and capital growth. Obviously dividend yield is an important aspect of a share's performance.

Activity 5.5

Look in the share information service in a newspaper and find the range and the typical size of the dividend yield for companies.

Limitations of ratio analysis

Ratios are very valuable but need to be used with caution. The calculation of ratios is objective and accurate, but that does not mean that financial analysis is similarly objective. Once calculated, the ratios have to be interpreted and this interpretation must involve an individual's subjective assessment and judgement.

It can be easy to make misleading comparisons. This can come from:

1. *The two-year problem* – Comparing only 2 years where one may be atypical, that is especially good or especially bad and unlikely to be repeated.
2. *The snapshot problem* – Using figures from a balance sheet will only tell you what the situation was on one particular day, the day of the financial year end. These figures can be atypical as they can have been massaged to give the best possible view of the company.
3. *The apples and pears problem* – No two companies are the same even if they operate in the same industry. If you are using ratios to compare companies, you need to be sure that you know how the figures are calculated. The same may occur in your own company if accounting procedures have changed between accounting periods.
4. *The history problem* – Information needs to be up to date. If historic cost (the price paid for the asset) has been used in asset valuation, the value of assets may be out-dated particularly for land and buildings. Ratios are invariably calculated from past data so they will only analyse how well a firm has performed. They may be used to indicate what might happen in the future but they are not crystal balls.

In summary, bear in mind that ratios are largely subjective and their analysis still remains more of an art than a science. As long as you understand the potential biases in the data, you can use them to make an informed judgement.

Ratio analysis is only an analysis of the financial affairs of a company; it is not an analysis of the company itself. It cannot analyse subjective elements or non-financial matters such as improving customer relations, potential labour difficulties and so on.

These problems do not make ratio analysis unusable, but you do need to bear in mind its limitations. You will not be able to get a clear picture from any one set of accounts. For a clearer picture, you need to go back a number of years and analyse those annual reports. In this way you can gain a better understanding of the firm.

Another approach to analysing the financial impact of marketing decisions is to examine the amount added to shareholder value and economic value. We now examine each of these in turn.

Shareholder value analysis

Shareholder value analysis has evolved as a result of the shortcomings of the other valuation techniques.

Asset-based valuations, for example, have limitations. They:

o   Do not take into account the future potential use of those assets
o   Use subjective assumptions about marketability, replacement cost and so on
o   Are often only useful if the business is going to be cannibalized and the individual assets sold off on a piecemeal basis. If the business is being taken over as a going concern, the intangible assets are likely to be underestimated.

Profit-based valuations are also limited. They:

o   Are less useful in assessing future potential cash flows
o   The multiplier used for profit is subjective.

The advent of SVA has probably been one of the major influences on corporate strategy in the last two decades. Major companies have adopted this approach to place value on firms to be divested and acquired, and also to evaluate business units and their strategic options within the company. SVA can be used directly to evaluate a business or strategy.

So what is different about shareholder value?

First it is a long-term measure. Do not confuse it with share price which may see dramatic rises and falls even within a short period. Speculation about a possible takeover of Manchester United Football Club by an American entrepreneur it led to impressive increases in their share price which were wiped out when the potential bidder backed out. Shareholder value on the other hand remained relatively unchanged giving a more realistic picture.

Secondly it gives a better view of the future as it is less susceptible to short-term blips. This should make for better strategic and operational decision-making.

Put simply the business or business unit is evaluated with respect to the value it creates for the shareholders. This is the true bottom line for the business. Since we in marketing tend to focus on the top line, that is revenue and sales contribution, this requires a change in orientation.

How do we work it out?

Calculating SVA is somewhat less simple! The following description is entirely for your information. You will never be asked to do this in an examination! But you should have an idea of the complexity of the method.

How to calculate SVA

1. Calculate the annual after-tax cash flows for a specified planning horizon
2. Determine the discounted value of the profit stream
3. Estimate the residual value of the business unit at the end of the planning horizon
4. Determine the SVA which is the sum of the present values of future cash flows and residual value less the market value of any debt associated with the business. A positive value means that the business is creating shareholder value. A negative value means that shareholder value is being eroded.

To assess the potential impact of a new strategy, the value is calculated with and without the new strategy. Its value is determined by the difference between the two measures, once again positive is good and negative is bad.

Economic value added

Economic value added (EVA) goes beyond SVA by adding in the idea that every business employs capital in some way. That capital may be plant, stock, working capital and so on. It does not matter what sort of capital it is but the important issue is that it comes with a cost. The EVA builds on SVA by adding the additional variable of cost of capital into the mix. Essentially EVA uses an SVA perspective to evaluate business performance taking into account profits, cost of capital and capital employed.

We calculate EVA using the following formula:

$$EVA = \text{net operating profit} - (\text{costs of capital} \times \text{capital employed})$$

So we are deducting the cost of the capital employed from the organization's net operating profit to give a truer measure of the firm's business performance. Again if the result is positive the business has contributed positively to shareholder value. A negative value means that the shareholder has lost value.

EVA's important contribution to analysis is to include capital in the equation. Until the advent of EVA capital was viewed as free and so there was no incentive to reduce it. This analysis can be extended to include intangible assets such as human assets. So if we take an organization such as a management consultancy where the asset base is predominantly people, we can add in replacement cost. Brands can also be included.

To increase EVA we need to:

o   Earn more profit by reducing costs or increasing revenue without using more capital
o   Invest in high-return profits
o   Reduce the cost of capital by increasing debt ratio or reducing the risk of the portfolio of businesses
o   Use less capital.

As an effective strategic marketer you need to make the connections between the economic measures that drive the bottom line and the practical marketing activities that deliver them.

This is not easy ... One of the true tests of a strategic marketer is to make that connection. You need to develop a real understanding of what drives shareholder value in your organization. These value drivers will differ from market to market and also over time. If you look to economic value analysis, it will also be dependent on the capital employed in the business.

One technique is to imagine shareholder value as a tube of future cash flows. We need to make the cylinder as long, as wide and as fast flowing as possible. The greater the volume contained in the tube, the more shareholder value.

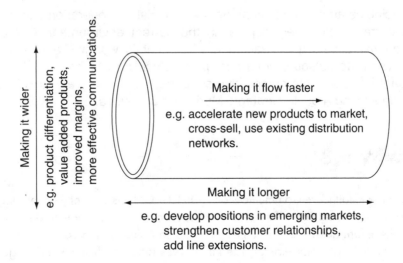

Figure 5.4 The shareholder value tube

Activity 5.6

Figure 5.4 gives examples of how the shareholder value tube may be made wider, longer and faster. Develop your own examples.

Although it is a simple visual model, it does emphasize the role of marketing in generating greater shareholder value. Process efficiency alone, for example, will never create a fatter, longer, faster tube.

A value-based marketing strategy identifies the marketing actions that generate the best returns in the future. It identifies which operational levers to pull, for example advertising, pricing, new product development.

The next activity is the most important in this unit and will help you to hone your skills as a strategic marketer. You may wish to use the idea of the shareholder value tube to do this. It is important that you remain objective about the contribution of each marketing activity.

Activity 5.7

Critically analyse and evaluate your organization.

What are the key drivers of shareholder value?

Which marketing activities underpin them?

How should you change your allocation of resources to deliver shareholder value more effectively?

Outsourcing

Outsourcing as an activity to improve the financial and operational efficiency of an organization is currently extremely popular in the current environment. Companies are therefore auditing their assets and evaluating whether it is worthwhile to undertake the activities themselves or to outsource to a third party. Deciding whether to outsource or not can have significant impact on the competitive advantage of the firm and this issue will be examined within the second module Strategic Marketing Decisions.

Activity 5.8

Outsource Healthcare Communications (OHC) – OHC is currently developing a resource kit for a major pharmaceutical client providing healthcare professionals in developing world markets with the information and resources required to calculate the social and economic impact of diseases in a particular market. The kit involves tools and frameworks to gather relevant data, analytical tools and appropriate theory from the health economic literature to support the data. All this information is collected, written up and printed on A4 size paper, which is copied, collated, hole punched and inserted in A4 ring branded ring binders. The agency usually undertakes all the activities leading to the creation, production and delivery of finished binders to a destination named by their clients. The agency outsourcers the printing and binding to other firms.

The client wishes for OHC to complete the development costs but they would like to commission the printing and binding themselves.

Question 5.2

To what extent do you think that the client should manage this activity themselves or should they outsource it and how would you analyse and evaluate its feasibility?

Discussion

This is not a complete answer but any plan should include a discussion regarding the fact companies activities are not both in printing and binding and therefore this activity is not core to their business. Both companies should outsource to a third party as they do not have the economies of scales as well as the experience to gain financially from undertaking the activity. The question is really about whether the agency could be in better place to manage this activity? The answer ought to be yes, as they should be commissioning more print jobs which means that they would benefit from the economies of scale and be in a better position to negotiate better deals than the pharmaceutical.

Summary

In this unit we have explored the use of financial measures. We looked at the differences between financial statements and management accounting.

We have examined the main ratios which we can use, categorized as:

1. *Profitability ratios* – which attempt to measure the efficiency of the enterprise in the generation of profit
2. *Asset utilization ratios* – which attempt to indicate the relative efficiency with which the firm's resources have been employed
3. *Liquidity ratios* – which attempt to predict the firm's ability to meet its financial obligations and so prevent the possibility of insolvency
4. *Capital structure ratios* – which attempt to determine the financial implications of the firm's capital structure
5. *Investor ratios* – which attempt to relate the firm's earnings to the performance of the capital markets as a whole.

Their value is explained alongside their limitations.

We end with SVA and EVA, as newer approaches to measuring the financial impact of marketing. An emphasis is placed on understanding how marketing activity contributes to shareholder value. Strategic marketers need to understand the value drivers of their business to allocate marketing resources effectively. You need to understand the strategic implications of any analysis you undertake whether it be financial or otherwise.

Setting prices

Mini case – Bombay Tricycle

Bombay Tricycle is a famous restaurant, located in South London, specializing in premium quality Indian cuisine.

The establishment originally started as a traditional restaurant targeting high-income individuals, but after a short time the company diversified by opening several take away establishments in prime locations within southwest London, reaching a wider customer group as well as those affluent customers who could not quite afford their high restaurant prices.

The take away operations would take orders over the phone as well as serve those who would turn up in person at the store. Motorbike couriers would then be used to deliver phone orders to customers in a pre-defined area. Unfortunately the take away service still could not reach many potential customers who are disgruntled that they cannot use the service.

In response to this challenge one of the managers has decided to create Bombay e-cycle, where customers can pre-order food at any time of the day or night, over the Internet, stating exactly when and where they wanted it delivered. In order for the system to work, food would need to be ordered at least 6 hours before it was needed. Orders would be processed at a number of single room locations across the city and they would be supplied from a larger centrally located warehouse. Food would then be transferred to mobile vehicles that had the facilities of heating up the food prior to delivery.

Management appreciated they would need to adjust their product offering as well as position themselves differently to their traditional restaurant and takeaway offerings as they were likely to appeal to a different customer segment.

The management are putting together their marketing plan and need to determine the prices at which to set for their range of dishes.

Questions

1. How could market research support Bombay e-cycle in determining the optimal prices for their service?
2. What factors should the management of Bombay e-cycle consider in setting prices for their dishes?
3. What role would other parts of the marketing mix play in establishing Bombay e-cycle's pricing strategy?

Outline case solution:

Although in this case there is no financial data provided, one can always adopt a qualitative approach explaining the financial issues potentially impacting on marketing within the case. This is as important as undertaking any financial calculations, whenever data is provided, and students should bear this in mind when it comes to the exam; any financial question should involve a qualitative critical evaluation of the situation as well as the implications of the quantitative calculations.

The case demonstrates a situation where a company would like to make a strategic decision to exploit an opportunity offered by the new e-economy (Internet-based companies) to expand its potential customer satisfaction capabilities well outside its current area of operation cost effectively without incurring major costs. Setting up new takeaways and restaurants in different towns are likely to be capital intensive requiring major investment making entry into new areas which are cost prohibitive.

An e-marketing solution, utilizing a heavily branded virtual restaurant representing a customer ordering system offset by non-branded back room operations consisting of smaller unbranded kitchens dotted around the capital delivering food to customers using mobile kitchens in the form of vans, could provide an attractive alternative lower cost proposition. It is anticipated that customers will need confidence to initiate orders and the business is likely to rely on its brand reputation from its offline business, namely the restaurant and takeaway operations.

1. Market research provides critical information for managers to minimize risk as well as uncertainty in making decisions. The company requires information to set the price which will determine the rest of its marketing strategy in relation to product, place and promotion and as we are dealing with a service we need to consider the extended marketing mix which includes people, process and physical evidence. The marketing mix in this case will not only determine the differential positioning of Bombay e-cycle but is likely to impact upon the overall positioning of the group. Therefore, it is important for management to get it right.

2. Management need to know the process to set the optimal price for its dishes that will not compete with its other outlets. This criterion is the strategic intent of management and is a constraint which we need to work within. One could suggest re-structuring of the business and getting rid of the takeaway part of the business but that will involve you putting together a change management implementation plan (which is part of the Managing Marketing Performance syllabus) potentially involving changing the operating values and beliefs of management which is likely to be a difficult task.

The first step (see Figure 5.5) in setting a price involves knowing the minimum price that we can set for a product. This is often referred to the 'floor price' which is the minimum price that an organization should charge as it represents the cost of producing, delivering and marketing the product. Unless one's business is for charitable purposes, organizations will usually want to recoup their costs so will never charge less for a product or service than its cost of production, delivery and marketing. There are exceptional cases when organizations do charge less for their product or services than its costs which include 'dumping', a practice which is usually frowned upon where companies try and gain rapid access of a market and getting rid of existing competitors by out-pricing them followed by putting up their prices once they have gained controlled. Other cases include 'loss leaders' where organizations for promotional reasons such as minimizing negative PR will offer products at a loss. In certain situations if a product or service is making a loss within a mixed portfolio it is sometimes advisable to maintain the product line going as it is contributing to the organization's overheads. Unless alternative profit-making uses can be made of the assets and resources, it is usually best to keep the line functioning as a 'going-concern' as it is putting less pressure on the other products or services in recovering overheads.

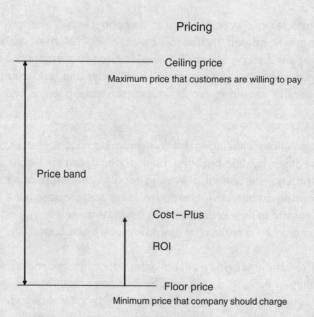

Pricing

Ceiling price
Maximum price that customers are willing to pay

Price band

Cost – Plus

ROI

Floor price
Minimum price that company should charge

Figure 5.5 Generic pricing process

Therefore in the case of Bombay e-cycle the company needs to work out its total costs for producing, marketing and delivering its dishes before it can get an idea of the minimum price it can set. The first thing that management need to do is to identify all the costs that are likely to be incurred and then to classify them according to whether they are fixed costs (costs associated whether you are preparing or not preparing any dishes) and variable costs (costs only associated with preparation and delivery of dishes). Different prices can then be determined and fed into a cost–volume–pricing evaluation model otherwise known as break even analysis to determine the minimum price for different cost–volume forecasts. For Bombay e-cycle the fixed costs such as the website and vehicles are likely to be easy to identify but the variable costs are more likely to be difficult to identify. One of the advantages of an e-business model is having less fixed costs (balance sheet items) and more variable costs items (profit and loss items) therefore improving the financial management of an organization. Unfortunately due to the way that restaurants purchase ingredients (in bulk so as to gain cost savings in terms of economies of scale) and the fact that Bombay e-cycle is likely to need committed and motivated staff to reflect its premium positioning, it is unlikely to benefit from seasonal casual labour and therefore will still have high fixed costs.

As mentioned the 'floor price' is the minimum price one should consider and usually most companies will place a 'mark up' on their costs for profit and this tends to be the most common type of pricing method in use today across the world. Unfortunately this method does have shortcomings as it does not take into account competitor activity as well as customer's willingness to pay. Companies should therefore undertake an analysis of competitor prices and positioning as well as undertake a 'willingness to pay' study amongst their potential target audience in order to evaluate what is commonly termed 'the ceiling price'. This is the maximum price that customers are willing to pay for a mixture of offerings. Conjoint analysis tends to be the major analytical market research technique often used to determine ceiling prices. In these studies customers' attitudes and reactions to a number of attributes are determined, the aggregate of these attributes are assumed to determine behaviour which in turn is then utilized to determine optimal pricing.

The organization therefore has a price band between the two points to which it can select its optimum price. Several things are to be considered before a price is set, one of them is the desired strategic intent of a firm. For example, does it wish to rapidly recoup its investment costs by charging the highest possible price, therefore adopting what is known as a skimming price strategy, or does it want to establish market share by attaining maximum penetration of the market, otherwise known as penetration strategy? Additionally the organization needs to consider its desired position relative to its available resources to effectively serve the market. All these factors will play a role in pricing.

3.   As previously mentioned Bombay e-cycle cannot ignore other aspects of the marketing mix when it sets its price as price will impact upon the other elements. Therefore, one will expect all other elements of the service mix to be representative of the premium image. A problem that the company may have is cannibalizing their other businesses. The main restaurant is not likely to be affected as it is believed that customers using the restaurant have different needs and wants to the same individuals using a takeaway service. The problem is that the e-takeaway business is likely to be seen as similar to the traditional takeaway and additional market research is likely to be necessary to evaluate how perceptual differences can be created to differentiate the two businesses to meet the needs of the management.

Further study

Arzac, E.R. (1986) 'Do your business units create shareholder value?', *Harvard Business Review*, January–February, pp. 121–126.

Day, G.S, Fahey, L. (1990) 'Putting strategy into shareholder value analysis', *Harvard Business Review*, March–April, pp. 156–162.

Simms, J. (2002) 'Business: FDs and marketing directors seeing eye-to-eye', *Accountancy*, London, February.

Tully, S. (1993) 'The real key to creating wealth', *Fortune*, 20 September, pp. 38–50.

Wenner, D.L., Lesser, R.W. (1989) 'Managing for shareholder value – from top to bottom', *Harvard Business Review*, November–December, pp. 52–68.

Hints and tips

Learn to calculate the basic ratios: gearing ratio, acid test ratio and current ratio. Understand the others and their implications. Do not get in a flap about the more complex ratios. The examination is designed to test your overall understanding of the basic concepts and for you to demonstrate that you can see the importance of financial measures of business performance.

You also need to understand how these relate to marketing activities.

Bibliography

De-Wit, B., Meyer, R. (1994) *Strategy – Process, Content, Context – An International Perspective,* West Publishing Company.

Hamel, G., Prahalad, C.K. (1993) 'Strategy as stretch and leverage', *Harvard Business Review,* March–April, pp. 75–84.

Hamel, G., Prahalad, C.K. (1994) *Competing For The Future,* Harvard Business School Press.

Hogan, J.E. Lehmann D.R., Merino M., Srivastava R.K., Thomas J.S. and Verhoef P.C. (2002) 'Linking customer assets to financial performance', *Journal of Service Research,* JSR. Thousand Oaks: **5**(1), p. 26 (13 pages).

Johnson, G., Scholes, K. (1997) *Exploring Corporate Strategy,* 4th edition, Prentice-Hall Europe.

Mintzberg, H. (1990) 'The design school: Reconsidering the basic premises of strategic management', *Strategic Management Journal,* **11**(3), pp. 171–195.

Mintzberg, H. (2000) 'Strategy, blind men and the elephant', *Mastering Strategy,* Prentice-Hall pp. 11–16.

Mintzberg, H., Waters, J. (1985) 'Of strategies, deliberate and emergent', *Strategic Management Journal,* **6**(3), 257–272.

Porter, M.E. (1985) *Competitive Advantage: Creating and Sustaining Superior Performance,* with a new introduction written in 1998, New York: The Free Press.

Rust, Roland T. (2004) 'Measuring marketing productivity: Current knowledge and future directions', *Journal of Marketing,* **68**(4), p. 76, ISSN 00222429.

unit 6
analysing the external environment

Learning objectives

In this unit we highlight the importance of understanding the external environment in which the organization operates (syllabus references 4.1, 4.2). There are external factors beyond every organization's control to which they must respond. The first stage to determining how to respond to these is to understand what these forces are and how significant they are to your organization. In this unit you will:

- Appreciate the difference between the macro- and micro-environment

- Evaluate the techniques available to allow the objective assessment of the external environment including frameworks such as PEST and Porter's Five Forces

- Understand the tools used to evaluate an organization's competitive position

- Study the means of analysing potential and current customer bases to gain understanding.

Having completed this unit you will be able to:

- Define the organization's intelligence/research/resource needs to support a rigorous environmental audit

- Undertake customer and competitor analyses at the micro-level

- Assess the political, economic and social and technological trends at the macro-level

- Assess the organization's competitive position in relation to them

- Draw together the results of the internal and external analyses to give a summary of the organization's competitive position.

Sections of the syllabus being covered in this unit:

Element 1: Strategic management and the role of marketing (10 per cent).

1.1 Demonstrate an understanding of the role of marketing in creating exceptional value for customers and shareholders.

1.2 Demonstrate an understanding of the role of marketing in organizations that are driven by performance measures other than shareholder value, for example not-for-profit organizations.

1.3 Critically evaluate the characteristics of the marketing models and criteria for success used in organizations with a strong market orientation.

1.4 Critically evaluate the characteristics of marketing models used by, and the challenges facing marketing in, organizations with a weak market orientation.

1.5 Give examples of the strategic planning process used in organizations and evaluate marketing's role within it.

Element 2: Evaluation of business and marketing performance (30 per cent).

2.1 Critically evaluate and use quantitative techniques for evaluating business and marketing performance over current and historic business cycles. Techniques to be covered should include:

  ○ Balanced scorecard, with an emphasis on customer and innovation measures.

  ○ Evaluation of marketing performance including the audit of marketing activities and valuation of marketing assets, such as brands.

  ○ Financial techniques such as shareholder value analysis (using total shareholder return and economic profit), financial ratio analysis, trend analysis, benchmarking and evaluation of historical financial decisions.

Element 4: Analysis of the external environment (20 per cent).

4.1 Use and appraise the available techniques and processes for the objective assessment of the external environment covering the macro-environment, competitive environment, customers, channels and evaluation of the organization's offers against customer needs.

4.2 Define the organization's intelligence needs, research needs and resources required to support an analysis of the external environment.

4.3 Acquire and use appropriate information and tools to evaluate the organization's current competitive position, position within the value chain and sources of competitive advantages.

4.4 Develop customer insights by analysing potential and current customer bases and developing an understanding of their needs, preferences and buying behaviours (as prelude to segmentation).

Exam Hint 6.1

The techniques that you will learn are applicable throughout the whole syllabus and you will be applying them again in Strategic Marketing Decisions, Managing Marketing Performance as well as Strategic Marketing in Practice. Even within the Analysis and Evaluation examination you should anticipate to apply certain aspects, maybe not in its entirety, of the techniques to the majority of problems set in the Part A and Part B sections of the exam.

Statements of related marketing practice

The main skill or business competency areas are being developed in this section and are likely to be examined:

o   To develop appropriate structures and frameworks to identify appropriate information requirements to define and structure marketing-related business problems.
o   To be able to critically evaluate different analytical perspectives which will lead executives to gain a better understanding of their external and internal environment within the specific context of their industries, thus setting and placing them in a better position to make better informed decisions potentially leading to minimize risks and uncertainty.
o   To promote a strong marketing orientation to influence strategy formulation and investment decisions.
o   Specify and direct the line marketing process.

We have already covered a large component of this section in previous units but it is important that we have a unit dedicated to analysing and evaluating the external environment of the firm. As we have already identified, marketing audits are a means of identifying what external forces that need measuring as well as the financial and non-financial measures that can be used to measure them.

In strategic marketing one is attempting to identify opportunities that will differential competitive advantage options and at this level one is trying to find measures and tools to identify and frame such opportunities. One major driver of competitive advantage is the external environment and in many industries the external and dynamics of the industry is what drives strategic positioning. Therefore the critical success factors of competing in such industries are driven primarily by the external characteristics and not the internal capabilities of the firm. Commodities and utilities are prime examples of these industries. For this reason, understanding the external environment is critical. In the next unit we will see the other extreme of strategy where differentiation is likely to be achieved through a unique deployment of bundles of both tangible and intangible resources, that is the internal and not the external perspective of the firm. In the majority of cases it is the belief of many authors that competitive strategies are formulation as a function of both the external and internal environments, the extent of which is determined by the specifics and uniqueness of each industry.

How will this unit help you and what can you expect to achieve after completing this unit?

The first five units were intended to provide an understanding of different business orientations and the language and techniques for identifying and measuring business issues. You are now in a position to bring the whole lot together and to analyse the different business situations to identify opportunities and threats facing the organization from an analysis and evaluation of its macro-environment and in the following unit the strength and weaknesses facing the organization from analysis and evaluation of its micro-environment.

You should appreciate that at the end of the day the unwritten rule for organizations and individuals within them is survival (Ansoff, 1988). Marketing is often seen as necessary as many customers have choice and corporate survival often depends on an organization to meet their customer needs and wants better than their competitors. The theory used to explain the behaviour of managers pursuing their self-interest rather than those of shareholders is known as Agency Theory (Shleifer and Vishny, 1994). Although this viewpoint can seem cynical, an understanding of actual organization strategizing processes being far from being rational can be very important and help develop effective implementation plans (this is the purpose of the third unit – Managing Marketing Performance). The behavioural theory of firms acknowledging deviation from the rational economic view of the firm was first put forward by Cyert and March (1963). Since then, several authors such as Pettigrew (1977) and Mintzberg and Waters (1985) have put forward their perspective of strategy formulation as being a socio-political process where final strategy outcomes are being considered as negotiated settlements between customers and suppliers as well as other stakeholders. Optimized behavioural outcomes of a strategy between parties can be analysed and evaluated using Transaction Cost Analysis (Williamson quoted in Kay, 1993) and it is the strategic options with the lowest Transaction Costs which includes financial and psychological pay-offs that are most likely to prevail.

Therefore, as customer behaviour is a primary determinant of cash inflow into the organization anything that is likely to interfere with the so-called 'lifeblood' should be of great interest to everyone within the organization as it is likely to impact on future survival. There is considerable debate within the strategy literature (Whittington, 1993) as to whether it is possible for an organization to effectively manipulate its external environment but what is accepted is that knowledge of the likely impact factors, even though we may not be able to identify and evaluate all of them, will increase the chances of an organization being selected by the environment. It is therefore imperative for marketing to be able to set up market research process and methods for scanning their external environment in order to anticipate changes and adapt accordingly therefore increasing their chances of survival.

Key definitions

Marketing environment – is the set of uncontrollable external forces to which a company must adapt.

The macro-environment – consists of macro-factors and their trends such as politics, economics, societal and technological.

The micro-environment – consists of trends at the industry level such as suppliers, competitors and customers.

Environmental scanning – is the process of monitoring the environment, and gathering relevant market intelligence to ensure that the organization remains up to date with trends.

Study guide

This unit builds on the internal environmental analysis but turns to the organization's competitive position in relation to the external environment. Again the available techniques and processes are examined. The macro- and micro-environments are covered, with an emphasis on the quantification of trends. We will use the well-known PEST framework to structure our macro-analysis, and Porter's Five Forces model to enable an analysis of the micro-environment.

Introduction

We explore the environment in which marketing decisions are made. Since the macro-environment is largely unchangeable, its analysis offers an assessment of the risk associated with marketing decisions. The scale of the task of monitoring both the macro- and the micro-environments means that the effective management of information becomes essential.

The marketing environment constitutes the arena in which organizations go about their business – the multitude of largely uncontrollable factors that affect their daily activities. It provides opportunities for organizations to market products and services as new or changed demands emerge. But it also exercises constraints, such as the activities of competitors, limitations imposed by legislation, the physical environment or the availability of raw materials. And it harbours threats in technological advances, population movements, changes in customer preferences and many other forms.

Exam Hint 6.2

It is important for you to appreciate that examiners will be expecting you not to simply draw out the models as depicted in textbooks but to apply them to the specific problem. So a Five Forces diagram drawn in the exam should not look exactly as it does in the textbook but resemble one that represents an analytical output (i.e. representing your analysis).

Environmental monitoring

Of all the functions an organization performs, marketing is the one which is closest to the external environment, because it has the job of looking outside to the needs and wants of customers. Consequently, environmental monitoring in an organization is often a marketing responsibility.

Because it is never static, the environment requires continual monitoring and evaluation by marketers. This constant change also demands corresponding changes to the marketing mix – the more controllable factors – so that the organization remains in tune with the environment, providing the most appropriate product or service in the most appropriate way.

The process of environmental monitoring is carried out alongside those of general business planning and marketing planning. Environmental monitoring consists of the following steps:

o Selection of the driving forces, or drivers, among the many environmental variables – those that are most likely to have an impact on the organization's activities. This first step is the most crucial, as it determines the influences that will be watched most closely, and those that may be ignored. Key drivers are usually selected for particular attention as it is not possible to monitor all factors closely.
o Collection of information on these factors.
o Evaluation of information and forecasting of likely environmental changes.
o Assessment of how the changes will affect the organization.
o Adjustment of marketing strategy and mix to minimize the negative impact and maximize the positive impact.

Scanning can take three forms. Organizations should consider a mix of these, given the varying nature of change.

o *Continuous* – Companies should always monitor their main stakeholders of customers and competitors to identify changes and trends.
o *Periodic* – It makes sense for organizations to undertake periodic research when appropriate, for example at the beginning of a planning cycle.
o *Irregular or ad hoc* – Tailored research may be undertaken for a specific project, for example determining the direction of new product development.

Changes in the environment may be either continuous or discontinuous. Continuous changes are called trends and may be either fast or slow. These are relatively easy to predict since we can extrapolate existing data to make an assumption about a future trend from an historic one. Discontinuous changes are one-off events or environmental shocks and are by their nature hard to predict.

European airlines

The macro-environment in which European airlines operate illustrates both types of change.

Since deregulation in the 1990s, we have seen low cost carriers enter the market. Companies such as easyJet, Buzz, Go and Ryanair have transformed the marketplace with their no-frills offerings. Customers can now fly from London to Faro for under £30 provided they are willing to forego a meal and travel to a London regional airport such as Stansted or Luton rather than the main hubs of Heathrow and Gatwick. They have gradually eroded the market share of the main airlines and reduced industry profitability. Profits have further been reduced by continuing legislation prohibiting mergers which would have generated economies of scale but were not deemed to be in the consumer interest. These changes are continuous and largely predictable.

However, the events of September 11 were not. A single discontinuous event dramatically reduced passenger numbers as people, Americans in particular, avoided air travel fearing another terrorist attack.

Environmental scanning has a number of advantages:

1. Early identification of opportunities
2. Better decision-making arising from objective up-to-date information
3. Improved corporate image as the organization is seen as responsive.

The macro- and micro-environments

Exam Hint 6.3

All models and frameworks in strategic marketing represent a description or understanding of issues as well possible explanations of the interrelationships between variables identified by the researcher in their particular setting. This means whenever you use the 'five forces' model or a PEST framework as well as any of the other techniques, you ought to appreciate that they were developed by the author in one particular setting and that you are applying it in your setting. Students who will score higher marks are those who will explicitly demonstrate the purpose or intention of what the analytical frameworks will attempt to evaluate followed by applying them to the setting and carefully interpreting the outputs. All models have operational components which allow managers to evaluate their particular settings followed by telling their story about their setting. A model is simply a torch that shines light and allows different managers to see in the dark, what each manager potentially sees in the dark having switched it on will be different from each other. Students should therefore emphasize these differences when answering their questions. They should also ensure that they spend explaining the situation or problem they are trying to resolve and justify why a particular framework would fit the evaluation of the problem rather than simply introducing a model as written in the textbook without any explanation to the examiner of why it is appropriate. The exam is not a test of how many theories you know listed in bullet points but a way for you to demonstrate that you can analyse and evaluate business problems which means using models appropriately and justifying their usage.

The marketing environment is divided into two areas:

1. The 'macro-environment' consisting of those factors furthest from the organization which it can neither control nor influence.
2. The 'micro-environment' consisting of those factors close to an organization which, although it cannot control them directly, it may be able to influence indirectly through marketing campaigns.

Figure 6.1 provides an overview of the marketing environment.

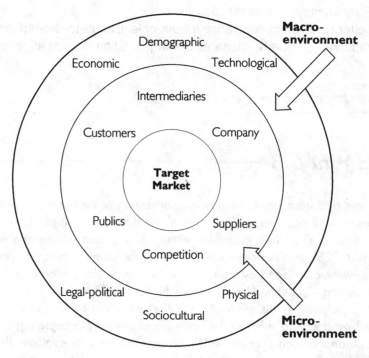

Figure 6.1 The marketing environment

This unit will examine each of these categories, starting with those in the macro-environment using the PEST framework, sometimes called STEP and sometimes augmented to PESTI. Then we look at the micro-environment. The section on the micro-environment ends with a summary of a model which can help in our judgement on the attractiveness of markets. This is Porter's Five Forces model.

The macro-environment

The macro-environment includes the following:

- o Demographic factors
- o Economic factors
- o Social and cultural factors
- o Legal and political factors
- o Physical factors
- o Technological factors.

This is sometimes called a PEST analysis, which is an acronym for Political, Economic, Social and Technological factors.

Demographic factors

Demography is the science of population and demographics concerns itself with populations, sizes, structures and trends. For organizations marketing directly or indirectly to consumers, demographics quantifies their marketing opportunities by showing how large the various sections of the population are, which are growing and which are declining in numbers. A key demographic trend in many mature economies is the decline in the size of the youth market, that is the population aged 10–19, and the growth of the mature market, people aged 55 and over. This has important implications for a number of markets, such as CDs and cassettes, sports shoes and soft drinks, which have traditionally found most of their buyers from the youth market and which will now have to reposition themselves to appeal to older people.

Economic factors

The state of the economy has a profound impact on marketing both in consumer and industrial markets. Disposable income, the money which the consumer has available to spend after taxation and housing costs are deducted, is affected by a number of factors, such as money supply, interest rates and exchange rates. Interest rates affect a person's propensity to borrow and hence to spend.

Unemployment has a major impact on consumer spending. Changing patterns within labour markets affect the amount of disposable income and also the way in which people choose to spend it; the decline of manufacturing and the rise of the service sector as an employer have brought with them an increase in the proportions of both women and part-time workers, leading to demands for longer and more flexible retail opening hours.

Social and cultural factors

The sociocultural environment is arguably the most important part of the macro-environment, because it determines the lifestyles and values of consumers and, hence, plays a major part in determining their needs and wants. Here are some key cultural trends of the past 20 years, and some of the products which have evolved in response to them:

- o *The growth of dual income households* – resulting in the growth of convenience foods such as ready meals
- o *Interest in health and fitness* – growth in the number of sports facilities, boom in sports clothing and equipment, plethora of 'lite'/diet food and drink products
- o *Unacceptableness of drinking and driving* – development of alcohol-free/low-alcohol drinks
- o *Need for speed and flexibility in communications* – advances include e-mail, the mobile phone and courier services.

There are other general trends.

Consumers are becoming more 'knowledgeable'. The role of the Internet is very important here as it allows for fast assimilation of information, making price comparisons which would have taken hours now literally available in seconds.

Consumers are also becoming more 'demanding'. Greater disposable income in many industrialized countries, coupled with their increased knowledge, has led to increased customization of product ranges and fragmentation of markets. Take the shampoo market as an example. In the 1970s, it was commonplace to have a single bottle of shampoo for a family. Now it is commonplace in many households to have multiple brands and products. Shampoo for thinning hair for dad, shampoo for coloured hair for mum, shampoo for straight hair for daughter, shampoo for blonde hair for other daughter, sports shampoo for son and so on. And that is without looking at the myriad of conditioners and other hair care products available.

As consumers have become more exacting, organizations have responded with an 'increased level of service'. Next day delivery has become commonplace in many product categories, for example. And with the American enthusiasm for litigation spreading across the world, organizations need to be even more careful to meet their promise.

The cliché that we live in a 'global village' is increasingly true. The Internet, improvements in communications technology and logistics infrastructure mean that most organizations are competing in an international marketplace, whether they have chosen to or not.

Legal and political factors

Changes in the legal and political environment can give rise to both opportunities for an organization and threats to its activities. New legislation may affect product design, such as the requirement that all cars be fitted with rear seatbelts. Harmonization across the EU (European Union) affects organizations in a number of ways, from packaging and labelling to the composition of food and drink products.

New laws can affect the way products are produced, for example the restrictions on chloro-fluorocarbons (CFCs) as propellants in aerosols in the EU. And similar legislation applies to refrigerators leading to a fridge mountain in Europe as governments struggle to find ways to dispose of old refrigerators in an environmentally friendly way.

Case study: Data protection legislation in Europe

Privacy and Electronic Communications Regulations (EC directive)

This directive came into force in December 2003. There are several regulations which have implication for direct marketers.

o No e-mail or SMS marketing can be undertaken unless the recipient has consented, or under the soft opt-in rule, if the sender has obtained contact details in the course of a sale, or negotiations for the sale of a product or service and if the sender uses them to market similar goods and services.

o The opportunity to opt-out must be given when the data is collected and in every subsequent communication.

o Senders must identify themselves and provide a valid return path.

o Owners of websites employing cookies should provide a clearly accessible privacy policy explaining their use, the consumer data they store and make accessible, to whom that data is accessible to, how to refuse or disable cookies, and how doing so will affect their use of the site. Compliance with this means that there is no need to obtain opt-in to the use of cookies unless they are being used for intrusive purposes, such as tracking another's web use.

Case study: Regulations governing UK alcohol advertising

Non-broadcast media is covered by voluntary guidelines in the Code of Advertising Practice, overseen by the Advertising Standards Authority. Under the code, ads should not encourage excessive drinking, exploit the young or those who are mentally or socially vulnerable. They should not be directed at anyone under 18, nor should they depict anyone under 25 consuming alcohol. Most importantly, ads should not suggest that any alcoholic drink can enhance mental, physical or sexual capabilities, enhance popularity, masculinity, femininity or be linked to sporting achievements.

Content of advertising on radio and TV is regulated by statute overseen and implemented by Ofcom, the successor to the Independent Television Commission and the Radio Authority. The rules are almost identical. Drinking should not target the under 18s and anyone associated with drink should appear to be over 25. Drinking must not be linked with social success, daring, toughness, bravado or sexual attractiveness nor must it appear to overcome boredom, loneliness or other problems. Scenes showing drinks consumed in one swallow or a few large swallows are unlikely to be acceptable.

The drinks industry's own code of practice, introduced in 1996, is administered by The Portman Group. Under the code, the naming, packaging or promotion of a drink must not suggest any association with sexual success; nor should it encourage illegal, irresponsible or immoderate consumption such as binge drinking, drunkenness or drink-driving. It must not appeal to anyone under 18 or feature images of anyone under 25.

All guidelines must conform to European Commission regulations and although scare stories about EC bans continue to abound, the Commission issued reassurances last year that it had no intentions of bringing forward recommendations to restrict or ban alcohol ads in the foreseeable future.

Source: Campaign, 27 February 2004, p. 25.

Activity 6.1

Compare the UK regulatory framework on alcohol with that of another European country and a country from South East Asia.

Assume that you work for a drinks manufacturer operating in the United Kingdom. How would you prepare for a ban on alcohol advertising in the United Kingdom?

Physical factors

The physical environment of the world in which we live affects organizations and their marketing activities. Crops of agricultural produce can be drastically affected by weather; in the past several Mediterranean olive crops have been destroyed by severe winter frosts, thus restricting the supply of olive oil. Oranges, coffee and wine have been similarly affected. Global warming and the changing weather patterns which it brings with it can only increase the number of harvests affected by weather – not to mention the sales of carbonated drinks and suntan lotions!

The impact of climate may not always be obvious. For example, the sales of toilet paper go up in cold weather. This is because customers use toilet roll for blowing their noses rather than the just the more obvious primary use! Car theft goes up in the rain as potential thieves prefer not to walk home. And domestic violence increases with the temperature as people drink more alcohol.

In many countries, there is tremendous pressure on space and a corresponding shortage of prime land available for retail and office developments. This has been a major contributor to the spiralling costs of such developments and restrictions on the building of new superstores.

Millions could die from global warming by 2020

Climate change in the next 20 years could result in a global catastrophe costing millions of lives, a leaked Pentagon report claims. The study predicts a combination of nuclear wars, droughts, famine and riots across the world. Cities will be engulfed by rising seas and Britain's weather will resemble that of Siberia by 2020.

Climate change should be elevated beyond scientific debate to a national security concern say the report's authors Peter Schwartz, a CIA consultant, and Doug Randall of the Global Business Network in California. Their key findings were:

○ 2007: violent storms will smash coastal barriers, rendering some parts of the Netherlands uninhabitable. Cities such as The Hague could be abandoned.
○ Death from war and famine could run into millions.
○ 2010–2020: Europe will be hit by climate change as the average temperature drops by 6 degrees Fahrenheit. Britain will become colder and drier.
○ Access to water becomes a major battleground. The Nile, the Danube and the Amazon are all at high risk.
○ Rich areas such as Europe and the United States will become virtual fortresses to prevent millions of migrants from entering after they are forced from their homes by rising sea levels.
○ There will be a significant fall in the planet's ability to sustain life within the next 20 years.
○ Riots and internal conflict could tear apart India and Indonesia.
○ Droughts could affect the world's major sources of food.
○ More than 400 million people living in subtropical regions will be at risk.
○ Future wars will be fought over the issue of survival rather than religion, ideology or national honour.

Source: The London Metro, 23 February 2004, p. 5.

Question 6.1

How will the predicted changes above affect your organization?

How might you react to them? How could you prepare to minimize the impact?

Technological factors
Technological developments present some of the most exciting new opportunities for marketers. The development of the silicon chip, for example, opened up a whole new market for low-cost, small-scale electronic gadgets. The appearance of the microwave oven fuelled the development of the ready meals market. The arrival of videocassette and DVD players has given birth to a new type of retail outlet where tapes and discs are available for rental. The Internet and mobile phones have created opportunities for low-cost services, for example online and telephone banking.

New technology also poses threats. The decline of the cotton and wool industries in Europe was due to replacement of these materials by man-made and synthetic fibres such as polyesters. Technological developments such as computer-aided design and robotics helped to give European and Japanese car manufacturers an edge over their British and US competitors. Direct sales of airline tickets and holidays are threatening travel agents.

Question 6.2

In what ways is the Internet changing your life?

Broadband destination: Thomas Cook

The travel industry has been altered dramatically by the advent of digital, following an outbreak of dot-com entrants, for example Travelocity, Expedia, ebookers, lastminute.com and Opodo. It is very competitive with venerable old brands such as Thomas Cook battling it out with the entrepreneurial newcomers. Times have been tough for the industry with airlines lowering commission on flights as low occupancy has resulted from terrorist activity and war. The reaction of the industry has been to develop dynamic packaging online allowing users to build their own trips. This fits with increasing consumer sophistication as world travel experience has grown, and offers travel agents the opportunity to gain high margins for a tailored product.

The travel industry has relatively low entry costs, even on the high street, and this is echoed online. This emphasizes the need to maintain competitive advantage. Thomas Cook claim to have invented the package holiday 160 years ago and adopts a similar pioneer strategy with new technology. It was the first UK travel agent to launch its own website in 1996, albeit with limited offers and prices. 1999 saw the relaunch of the holiday website and the addition of a flight website. Online booking was added in 2000, offering real-time availability, pricing and booking for inclusive tours. In the same year a WAP site was introduced but discontinued within the year as a result of low takeup and high costs.

In 2002, Thomas Cook launched a dedicated broadband site (www.Thomascook.com/broadband), resulting from research showing that broadband consumers use the web differently and want a more exciting experience. A major advantage of broadband is that it allows consumers to do things quicker and alleviates some of the problems of page weight. The new Thomas Cook site uses content from Thomas Cook TV and allows visitors to get blended search results for scheduled and chartered flights. Some 13 million products are now offered on line.

But Thomas Cook is not alone in seeing the advantages of broadband.

Competitor Kuoni has spent a six figure sum on building a network of holiday destination sites, full of audio-visual content. Its aim is to give access to some 5000 virtual tours and 3000 minutes of streaming video. The site uses images from video, audio and 360 degree all round views of the chosen destination and even their chosen hotel room. Most Kuoni sales (85 per cent) go through travel agents, and the new broadband experience is seen both as a way to increase Internet sales and to support the travel agent network by offering a 'try before you buy' experience.

Source: Revolution, January 2004, pp. 30–34.

The micro-environment

The micro-environment includes the following factors:

- Customers
- Competition
- Suppliers
- Intermediaries
- Publics
- The organization itself.

We will look at each of these in turn.

Customers

An organization's customers form a key component of its micro-environment. These include direct customers and more indirect consumers further down the distribution chain.

Monitoring questions include:

- Who are our customers?
- How many of them are there?
- Is that number growing or declining?
- Is the customer base static or changing?
- What do they want?
- Who, apart from us, do they deal with?

As customers are the focus of marketing thinking and action, we ought to concentrate most of our analysis on them. The more we understand them, the greater empathy we have with their lives and the part our products play in them, the better we will be able to serve them. This section discusses the quantitative and systematic aspects of customer analysis, but it is important to remember that there is no substitute for personal contact with real, live customers.

What we need to understand above all is the product in use – not just ratings of lists of brand attributes, or recall of the latest advertising campaign, but how our customers actually use the products day to day. What are their objectives, what problems are they trying to solve, how can our product help them, what are the realities of practical application on the factory floor or in the kitchen?

Why e-shop?

One of the most important changes in buying behaviour in our lifetimes has been the advent of e-shopping. So what do we know about how consumers choose one website over another? Surveys conducted at the end of 2003 by two different market research agencies show different results. Directline.com commissioned TNS to survey 1002 adults and eDigital research questioned 670 adults. The studies provide contrasting results.

TNS probed brand awareness by finding out whether consumers bought from websites of household names, brands they knew or just any website. Over half (55 per cent) preferred to buy from a trusted brand, although over a quarter (28 per cent) said they would be comfortable buying from an unknown brand.

Age appears to have an effect. Older consumers (55–64) are more likely to trust high-street brands (53 per cent) than unknown brands (23 per cent). However, younger users favoured online-only brands: 37 per cent of 16–24 year olds preferred to buy online if they trusted the brand, even if it was online only, and over a third (34 per cent) said they buy online even if they had never heard of the retailer.

The eDigital research found that brand awareness was less important than other factors such as usability, price and security. Consumers were asked for the top three reasons for buying from a website (Table 6.1).

Table 6.1 Top three reasons for buying from a website for the first time

Response	% of respondents
It's quick to find what I want, order and pay for it	27
It's cheaper online	24
I'm confident that I am dealing with a secure site	13
I trust the brand name	5

Source: eDigital Research (2003)

A similar picture emerged when respondents were asked why they returned to a website. Trust of the brand name came last with 3 per cent. Fulfilment came highest with 24 per cent, usability scored 20 per cent and price 19 per cent. When consumers were asked if a site's good service would encourage them to buy from its high-street store or catalogue, 29 per cent agreed that it would, and 44 per cent agreed that bad service would discourage them. The implication is that even if price and usability are more important than brand, the online experience will reflect on the brand image overall.

Question 6.3

Summarize the findings of these two studies. What do you think of the inconsistencies? Why do you think they have occurred?

What do we want to know about customers?
All information collection and storage has a cost, so practicality will limit what we can actually do. This list is indicative; what you want to know will vary according to your industry and budget.

Identity
For each individual buying unit (person, household or organization):

- Name, address and postcode.

For organizations:

- Description of location (branch, factory, office)
- Ownership (parent company name etc.)
- Decision-making unit (DMU).

The decision-making unit is basically the group of people responsible for making a buying decision.

For each individual within the DMU:

- o Name
- o Position (title, and in hierarchy)
- o Role in DMU
- o Level of authority (products, monetary value)
- o Media habits
- o Suggested channel of communication (salesperson contact, technical, board level, media etc.).

For the DMU:

- o Any information on rules, procedures, culture
- o Demographics
- o Age, marital status, social class, family stage, any other relevant data (leisure, interests, membership of clubs etc.)
- o Media exposure
- o Geodemographics.

For companies:

- o Industry, size (volume and value, number of employees), products, technology
- o Financial data (summary of last few years, main ratios)
- o Soft data.

For consumers:

- o Attitudes, feelings, culture, values (as relevant).

For companies:

- o Information on strategy
- o Likely new product development
- o Competitive stance
- o Buying patterns.

General buying in this market:

- o Quantity and value bought this year (or relevant period)
- o Frequency, timing
- o Brands/suppliers
- o Where bought (channel, distributor).

History with us:

- o Transactions
- o Detailed record of purchases in last year (or relevant period)
- o Quantity and value by product (transactions and total)
- o Timing
- o Returns
- o Delivery record
- o Discounts agreed, claimed, given
- o Payment record (time, method).

(There may be much more detail for companies.)

Response:

(a) Exposure and (b) response to:

- Product ranges
- Price levels
- Price offers
- Promotional offers
- Direct mail appeals
- Advertising.

Profiling mail-order companies

As an example of customer profiling in action, here are some extracts from profiles of customers of four well-known mail-order catalogues – Next Directory, Racing Green, Innovations and Kaleidoscope. The data is from a national survey, and the companies themselves would add to such information the detailed purchasing data discussed above.

All four groups are similar in some ways. They already buy books and wines by mail order, share a common interest in theatre and the arts, have taken or are interested in taking sport or weekend breaks and have a current bank account... Spookily, they also share a love for cats, a lack of enthusiasm for dogs and are members of the AA, or, failing that, the RAC.

There are differences between the customer groups.

Next Directory buyers have strong profiles featuring many significant likes and dislikes. They are almost certainly young and single and are very unlikely to be aged over 65 or retired. Indeed, they are quite unlikely to be aged over 55 or childless. These young go-getters, who earn more than £15000 a year, stay trim with aerobics and keep fit, and take self-catering or villa holidays in Europe. Racing Green customers are similar in many ways, but they have even stronger profiles and are more mature and richer – very likely to have a household income of more than £40000. They too take European holidays, but are likely to stay in a cottage, or gite, or take their children skiing or for a break in the United Kingdom... They have strong views on newspapers – they definitely do not read the *Sun*, *Star*, *News of the World*, *Daily/Sunday Mirror* or *The People*.

Innovations and Kaleidoscope customers also share many lifestyle activities. Both dislike clubs, dancing, listening to music, walking and hiking and dining out... Both sets of customers are steady, responsible citizens, likely to own their home which they adorn with roses, shrubs, plants and bulbs bought by mail order... They have already made a will, invested in government privatizations and other stocks and shares and use a Visa card.

Online research: How to use it?

We have already seen how new technology can change how consumers buy in the Thomas Cook case study above. But it can also help us in understanding consumers better. With traditional methods of market research it is hard to be quick and cheap. Data collection costs in particular are high with traditional surveys. Since online surveys have no data collection costs, resources can be concentrated on making the questionnaire better and more efficient. In the last few years the number of users in major markets has increased dramatically making it more representative of the population as a whole. In markets such as the United States, United Kingdom and northern Europe over 50 per cent of the population is now online.

Online research can be attitudinal or behavioural. Basic behavioural data can come from weblog analysis which reports on the user's journey from point of arrival to actual sale. Click-maps can be used to show where users are most likely to click through on web pages, mouse trails can chart users' scrolling and reading habits, hotspots indicate the most viewed areas. The result is that we can build a full picture of consumer behaviour on the web and potentially redesign our site to be more visitor friendly and profitable.

The Department of Trade and Industry (DTI) in the United Kingdom used a multi-pronged approach to redesign its website (*Revolution*, December 2003, p. 67). It used browser-based measurement of site traffic (www.dti.org.uk), discussions with current and potential users including SMEs, large businesses, consumers and other opinion-leading stakeholders, a pop-up survey on the site to identify user segments and understand their use of and satisfaction with the site. It also used a spider (called Red Sheriff Insight) that crawled across the site to allow the DTI to audit pages available to users plus broken links, consistency of branding and depths of clicks.

Case study

Profiling websites

High profile sites such as handbag.com and iVillage may fight it out to claim the title of best women's portal, while brands like Saga and 50connect might want to corner the older demographic but the battle to target the young male market seems far less adversarial.

If the United Kingdom follows the United States, young men will be online like never before. In the United States, young men spend more time online than watching the TV. A recent survey shows that 18–34-year-old men spend an average of 21 hours online per week compared with 16 hours watching TV. They access news, information and entertainment sites.

A viral game using young males' usage of sports and gaming sites has been used to drive sales of Nivea for Men. The game, Ball Skillz (www.ballskillz.co.uk), has over 200 000 plays in a week and a half. Young men have been traditionally hard to target as they evade mass marketing communications and need precise targeting.

Watch for trends in the market and adapt your communications strategy and budget accordingly.

Competition

Identifying who your competitors are is a crucial task within marketing, but it is not always as easy as it may seem. We need to know what competes for our customers' interest, time and money – directly and indirectly. For example, the obvious competitors of Burger King are other burger chains such as McDonald's and other forms of fast food, from Kentucky Fried Chicken to fish and chips. But it also competes with indirect substitutes for the consumers' leisure time and money, such as cinemas and sports centres. The first group are called primary or real competition, the second group are secondary or peripheral.

Porter identified four components of competitor analysis:

1. Future goals
2. Assumptions
3. Current strategy
4. Capabilities.

As strategic analysis is concerned essentially with the future, we must look at where the competitors are going. What are their aims, geographically, in products and markets? Frequently these are openly stated, in annual reports or press statements. In other cases we must deduce goals from our intelligence gathering.

Assumptions underlay strategies and action. Often they are implicit, but again we can usually interpret signals – from their action and reactions, from statements, articles and conference speeches, from industry sources – about how the competitor thinks about the industry. What do they think are the major drivers? What do they see as their own strengths and weaknesses? Are they complacent about the industry and their place in it?

Their current strategy should at least be clear – at least in so far as they have an explicit strategy. Although it is decreasingly common, many firms do not seem to have thought through what they are doing and why, they merely carry on as before and react to events. Where a strategy is evident, we probably already know from day-to-day experience what it is, and how competitors are likely to compete in the immediate future. This makes it easier for us to plan, even if the competitive strategy is an aggressive one.

Capabilities we also probably have a good idea about, but it is helpful to take a more formal approach. A SWOT analysis applied to the major competitors is a simple initial approach. A more quantitative method is to take the critical success factors (CSFs, or key success factors, KSFs) and rate ourselves and the competitors on each. An example is shown in Figure 6.2.

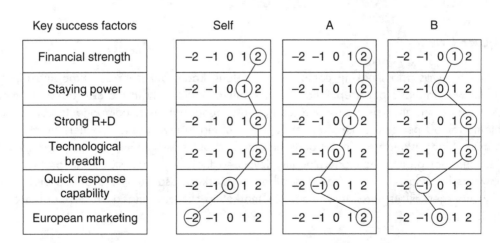

Figure 6.2 Competitors' capabilities
Source: Hooley and Saunders (1993, p. 125)

In this example, the company identified six key factors, and rated the competitors on a scale of −2 to +2. Using a graphic presentation makes it easy to see the relative profiles. From a marketing point of view, we might want to concentrate more on the specifically marketing-related aspects of their capabilities, leaving the more general factors to the corporate planning stage. We might rate them on the 4Ps, or on a longer list such as:

- ○ Quality of current products
- ○ Skill at product improvement
- ○ New product development (NPD) record
- ○ Balance, depth and breadth of product portfolio
- ○ Pricing strategy and tactics
- ○ Advertising skills: spending, media planning, creativity
- ○ Use of promotional tools
- ○ Salesforce effectiveness
- ○ Channel management: relationships, power, service levels.

The list can be adapted to the industry. As with the CSFs, it is probably sensible to limit the number of factors, perhaps by compressing subunits into a more general heading. Six to eight seems to be the number of variables a human mind can comfortably cope with at once, so that would make a good limit.

The more difficult task is to forecast future capabilities, particularly of new competitors. This can only be done through a careful analysis of their current competencies and resources, together with your view of their future goals. Past history may be a guide, if for instance they have successfully developed new capabilities before.

Suppliers

Without the suppliers of raw materials, components, business services and so on, most consumer and industrial products and services would not exist. Suppliers are crucially important, therefore, in ensuring a steady flow of products from the producer to the end user. They can also be a source of new developments and information about the marketplace. Traditional views that we 'do battle' with suppliers in order to negotiate the lowest price are being replaced with notions of partnerships which can help both buyer and supplier.

Case study

Jaguar Cars

Jaguar Cars was a loss-making company when John Egan took over as managing director. A key problem was Jaguar's poor reputation for reliability, particularly in the crucial export market of the United States. An analysis of customer complaints found that faulty components from suppliers were to blame for 60 per cent of key failures. Egan decided to involve the suppliers in improving quality to a much higher standard. He not only renegotiated purchasing contracts, but also invited suppliers to join internal groups monitoring quality levels so that they understood the problems more fully. Four years later sales had increased in all major markets, especially the United States, and Jaguar finally shrugged off its unreliable image. Its marketing success hinged on developing a partnership with its suppliers.

Intermediaries

Intermediaries are key links in the chain that moves a product from the producer to the end user or consumer. The main types of intermediaries are:

o Wholesalers
o Agents
o Brokers
o Retailers.

Most consumer and industrial products and services reach the end user via at least one intermediary, if not several.

These intermediaries play an important marketing role in penetrating the market for a particular product and any changes to the way in which they operate can be crucial.

Case study

Smith's Crisps

Smith's Crisps was the household name for crisps in the United Kingdom in the 1950s and 1960s. Famous for their little blue salt packets, Smith's products sold extensively through many small outlets such as grocers and public houses. By the 1970s, distribution of food products was changing rapidly with the growth of multiple retailers and supermarkets. The popularity of out-of-town superstores in the 1980s reinforced the concentration of retailing into fewer, much larger outlets. At first Smith's did not change fast enough to cope with this rapidly changing environment. The short shelf life of its crisps was designed for distribution through localized outlets such as the corner shop and pubs and instant or rapid consumption once purchased. The new supermarket chains needed longer-life food products in larger sizes suitable for more leisurely, family consumption. Competitors such as Golden Wonder crisps, ready salted in family-sized, longer-life plastic packs, took an increasing share of a rapidly growing market. By the 1980s, Smith's failure to respond to changes in the distribution environment had reduced its share to 14 per cent of a market it had once dominated.

It has since responded with new marketing strategies more suited to the changed needs of the intermediaries in the marketplace, restoring Smith's to a leading position in the snacks market (interestingly, these strategies also included a nostalgic appeal to previous consumption habits by relaunching the blue salt packet in the 1990s).

Publics

A public is any group which has an interest in an organization and its activities, and which has a potential impact on the organization's ability to achieve its objectives. There are many types of public.

The financial community

An organization's reputation and image affects its ability to raise funds. The organization will attempt to build a favourable image with financial institutions through managing its own finances shrewdly, and through devices such as the annual report.

The media
It is obviously beneficial to an organization if it receives frequent positive media coverage. Some organizations do everything possible to provide the media with information that will show their activities in a good light.

The government – central and local
Organizations need to take likely future government policy into account when formulating their plans. It is common practice to lobby against legislation which might be harmful to an organization's interests. Local government is also influential, for example, in determining planning applications, setting local business rates and local economic policies.

Consumer action groups
Many types of consumer groups are likely to have an interest in an organization's activities. For example:

- Environmentalists will campaign for 'green' products and manufacturing practices
- Ethnic minority groups will seek to be fairly represented in advertising and so on
- Animal rights groups will demand cruelty-free products
- Local community groups may protest against the development of a new manufacturing plant or a new retail outlet.

Question 6.4

What publics have had an impact on the tobacco industry in recent years, and in what ways?

The organization itself
Every aspect of an organization has a potential effect in the marketplace. Its corporate objectives, resources, structure and culture all affect marketing activities. For this reason, internal marketing, which seeks to ensure common objectives, understanding and motivation throughout an organization, is often needed before external marketing campaigns can be considered. This becomes particularly significant in people-intensive organizations and also in services where the performance of an organization is linked most closely to that of its staff.

Porter's Five Forces

Porter's model of the forces that interact to produce the competitive situation in an industry is one of the most famous in business literature. It is reproduced as Figure 6.3. Porter identifies the five forces as:

- Threat of new entrants
- Bargaining power of suppliers
- Bargaining power of buyers
- Threat of substitutes
- Intensity of rivalry.

Porter (1980) gives detailed suggestions for analysing each of these.

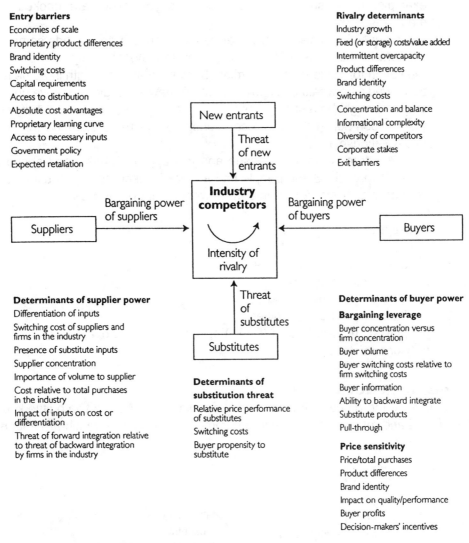

Entry barriers
Economies of scale
Proprietary product differences
Brand identity
Switching costs
Capital requirements
Access to distribution
Absolute cost advantages
Proprietary learning curve
Access to necessary inputs
Government policy
Expected retaliation

Rivalry determinants
Industry growth
Fixed (or storage) costs/value added
Intermittent overcapacity
Product differences
Brand identity
Switching costs
Concentration and balance
Informational complexity
Diversity of competitors
Corporate stakes
Exit barriers

Determinants of supplier power
Differentiation of inputs
Switching cost of suppliers and firms in the industry
Presence of substitute inputs
Supplier concentration
Importance of volume to supplier
Cost relative to total purchases in the industry
Impact of inputs on cost or differentiation
Threat of forward integration relative to threat of backward integration by firms in the industry

Determinants of substitution threat
Relative price performance of substitutes
Switching costs
Buyer propensity to substitute

Determinants of buyer power

Bargaining leverage
Buyer concentration versus firm concentration
Buyer volume
Buyer switching costs relative to firm switching costs
Buyer information
Ability to backward integrate
Substitute products
Pull-through

Price sensitivity
Price/total purchases
Product differences
Brand identity
Impact on quality/performance
Buyer profits
Decision-makers' incentives

Figure 6.3 Porter's Five Forces
Source: Porter (1985)

Consolidating your analysis

The previous units have focused on external and internal analyses, with an emphasis on using appropriate models and developing rigorous measures of performance. But now we need to pull this altogether in a situation analysis which allows us to assess the implications for our strategic options. There are several frameworks we can use. These are not mutually exclusive and may be usefully combined to pull out key themes.

1. *SWOT analysis* – This well-known framework can be used to distil the analysis, summarizing the outcomes of the internal analysis into strengths and weaknesses, and the external analysis into opportunities and threats. It has the potential to be a powerful tool in communicating the organization's current position. But...it is often misused and can result in a list of all factors covered in the analysis without any sense of priority. When writing a SWOT analysis make sure that you focus only on the items that are important. This means that you may have to disregard an area on which you have spent a lot of time but the results are unhelpful. And also make sure that you are objective in your summary and do not delude yourself about your strengths, for

example. Make sure that any assertions you make are backed up by objective measures.

2. *Issue analysis* – This is a broader-based approach and avoids some of the problems inherent in the classification required by the SWOT analysis. For example, whilst a reputation for value for money might be viewed as a strength in some markets, it might be viewed as a weakness if the company's new strategy is to move upmarket. Low-cost structure might be a strength but not if it results in low quality. Identifying issues, rather than pigeon-holing them into categories, allows us to examine the complexity of the inter-relationships.

3. *The 6Cs framework* – The issue analysis approach described above is a very open ended approach. Some people find a more focused approach useful to structure their summary analysis. A possible framework is that of the 6Cs.

These are:

o Customers and the market
o Competitive position
o Core competencies and assets
o Chances and opportunities
o Critical success factors (CSFs) or problems to be overcome
o Constraints.

Process of strategic audit

To summarize the process, it is shaped like a diamond. We start with little knowledge, gather lots of data and refine it, ending with a summary of the issues which are important.

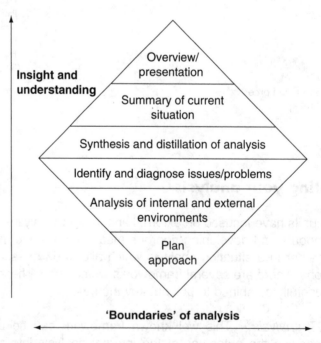

Figure 6.4 Process of strategic audit

Summary

Since the environment is largely beyond our control, we need to understand it so that we can plan for it.

In the unit we have:

- Explained why a regular and detailed audit of the micro- and macro-environments is important
- Looked at how environments are changing
- Explained the key elements in the environments
- Identified appropriate frameworks for analysis, for example PEST and Porter's Five Forces.

The unit concludes with a discussion of how to synthesize the results of internal and external analyses. This is a very important skill to develop. There is a danger that the analysis results in a mass of data, the trick is to distil all this data down into a meaningful summary which allows for a proper evaluation of strategic options. Analysis is not an end in itself, its value lies in its use in allowing us to objectively evaluate our future options.

Further study

www.broadband-travel.co.uk

Hints and tips

When talking about trends in the environment, it is important to be able to quantify the trends. So, for example, when talking about demography do not just talk about an ageing population but be prepared to quote actual figures. Examiners will appreciate your depth of knowledge.

The examiners will be interested in your ability to synthesize information and prioritize. You need to be able to demonstrate your ability to 'see the wood for the trees'.

Bibliography

Ansoff, I. (1988) *Corporate Strategy*, Penguin.

Cyert, R.M., March, J.G. (1963) *A Behavioural Theory of the Firm*, Prentice-Hall, Englewood Cliffs, NJ.

Kay, J. (1993) *Foundations of Corporate Success*, Oxford University Press.

Mintzberg, H., Waters, J. (1985) 'Of strategies, deliberate and emergent', *Strategic Management Journal*, **6**(3), pp. 257–72.

Pettigrew, A.M. (1977) 'Strategy formulation as a political process', *International Studies of Management and Organization, Summer,* pp. 78–87.

Porter, M.E. (1980) *Competitive Strategy: Techniques for Analyzing Industries and Competitors* with a new introduction written in 1998, New York: The Free Press.

Shleifer, A., Vishny, R.W. (1994) *Takeovers in the 1960s and 1980s: Evidence and Implications* in Rumelt, R.P., Schendel, D.E. and Teece, D.J. (eds), *Fundamentals Issues in Strategy,* Imprint Boston Mass, Harvard Business School Press.

Whittington, R. (1993) *What is Strategy and Does it Matter?* International Thompson Press.

unit 7
analysing the internal environment

Exam Hint 7.1

As mentioned in Unit 6 the techniques that you learn in this section will be applicable to all the other course units at the Professional Post Graduate level. You will be expected to remember and use them to build on your knowledge as you progress through the units of the course.

Learning objectives

In this unit you will explore the first stage in objectively analysing an organization's position, that is, how to review the organization's internal capabilities. The available techniques and processes will be examined, with an emphasis on the need for objectivity. You will:

o Appraise techniques and processes such as portfolio analysis, value chain analysis and innovation audit

o Evaluate the resource-based view of the organization

o Learn how to evaluate the core competencies of an organization

o Appreciate the importance of organizational culture in determining success.

At the end of this unit you will be able to:

o Assess the internal environment of an organization using appropriate techniques

o Use relevant information and tools to evaluate the core competencies of an organization

o Summarize the salient factors and insights arising from the internal analysis.

Sections of the syllabus being covered in this unit:

Element 1: Strategic management and the role of marketing (10 per cent).

1.1   Demonstrate an understanding of the role of marketing in creating exceptional value for customers and shareholders.

1.2 Demonstrate an understanding of the role of marketing in organizations that are driven by performance measures other than shareholder value, for example not-for-profit organizations.

1.3 Critically evaluate the characteristics of the marketing models and criteria for success used in organizations with a strong market orientation.

1.4 Critically evaluate the characteristics of marketing models used by, and the challenges facing marketing in, organizations with a weak market orientation.

1.5 Give examples of the strategic planning process used in organizations and evaluate marketing's role within it.

Element 2: Evaluation of business and marketing performance (30 per cent).

2.1 Critically evaluate and use quantitative techniques for evaluating business and marketing performance over current and historic business cycles. Techniques to be covered should include:

- Balanced scorecard, with an emphasis on customer and innovation measures.

- Evaluation of marketing performance including the audit of marketing activities and valuation of marketing assets, such as brands.

- Financial techniques such as shareholder value analysis (using total shareholder return and economic profit), financial ratio analysis, trend analysis, benchmarking and evaluation of historical financial decisions.

Element 3: Analysis of the internal environment (20 per cent).

3.1 Use and appraise the available techniques and processes for the objective assessment of the internal environment of an organization, including portfolio analysis, value chain, innovation audit and cultural web.

3.2 Critically evaluate the resource-based view of the organization.

3.3 Demonstrate the ability to use appropriate information and tools to evaluate the core competencies, assets, culture and weaknesses of an organization.

3.4 Assess the 'fit' between an organization's culture and its current strategy.

3.5 Summarize the salient factors and insights emerging from the internal analysis.

Exam Hint 7.2

It is essential that you understand that the context that the models and techniques were developed in one setting and that you are applying in another. All models and frameworks have operational significance as it allows managers to operationalize their problem-solving activities by giving them the means to analyse and evaluate their strategic marketing environments. It is important for students to describe these settings and justify the use of the models that they have chosen in the exams rather than simply describing them.

Statements of related marketing practice

The main skill or business competency areas developed in this section and that are likely to be examined are:

- To develop appropriate structures and frameworks to identify appropriate information requirements to define and structure marketing-related business problems.
- To be able to critically evaluate different analytical perspectives which will lead executives to gain a better understanding of their external and internal environment within the specific context of their industries, thus setting and placing them in a better position to make informed decisions potentially leading to minimize risks and uncertainties.
- To promote a strong marketing orientation to influence strategy formulation and investment decisions.
- Specify and direct the line marketing process.

We have already covered a large component of this section in previous units but it is important that we have a unit dedicated to analysing and evaluating the internal environment of the firm. As we have already identified, marketing audits are a means of identifying what internal resources and competences need measuring, and financial and non-financial measures can both be used to measure them. Understanding the internal environment can be important in formulating differential strategies and it is the viewpoint of many proponents of strategy that the unique way that resources and competences are leveraged within organizations is what gives rise to competitive advantage. These unique ways tend to be intangible and include managerial culture, style and the means by which value creating activities are bundled together that often they are difficult to measure or even identify. They form the resource-based view or core competency perspective of strategy and they are beginning to be predominantly more accepted than the traditional perspectives.

How will this unit help you and what can you expect to achieve after completing this unit?

Exam Hint 7.3

All models depicted pictorially in exams should be simply the ones simply copied from the textbooks but should include information regarding the context in which it is being applied. They should represent analytical outputs.

Having analysed the external environment and its implication for the organization you need to be able to undertake an internal audit of the firm's current resources, competencies and capabilities to identify whether it has the appropriate ones to serve its current customers as well as identifying whether it has the right set of competencies to serve its customers in the future. As mentioned in Unit 4, there are different approaches to strategy formulation and one school of thought is that the external environment is rigid and inflexible, and competitiveness is about having the right resources and competencies to position oneself in the market. In this perspective of strategy, organizations define themselves around a set of customer needs or customers requiring a product (i.e. automobiles, chemicals and pharmaceuticals). The alternative view of strategy is to define oneself around a set of competencies and resources and to serve any customer groups requiring those competencies (i.e. consultancies, advertising agencies and other service organizations).

Whatever strategic perspective, an organization that selects it needs to determine the capabilities required to achieve a competitive advantage in the future. Now several techniques are available to an organization in order to assess its capabilities of how it delivers value and you should be able to apply these techniques to any organizational setting to determine this.

The McKinsey 7S – Framework (Figure 7.1) is a very useful tool to identify whether the organization has the right mix of skills in terms of its people (staff), the right business and IT processes in terms of its systems, the right leadership style to support the structure and strategy intended to be implemented.

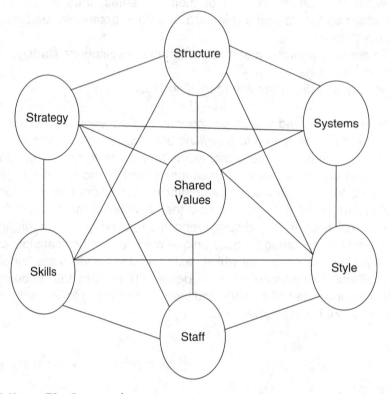

Figure 7.1 The McKinsey 7S – Framework
Sources: Peters, T. and Waterman, R.H. (1985) *In Search of Excellence*, Harper Collins Business; Pascal, R.T. and Athos, A.G. (1981) *The Art of Japanese Management*, Simon & Schuster, New York

The final part of checklist is whether the organization has the appropriate culture, in terms of its shared values, otherwise what does it need to do in change management terms and, therefore, what are the implications of this?

Key definitions

The internal environment – is the set of factors within the organization which affects its success within the marketplace.

Portfolio analysis – involves assessing the relative attractiveness of products within the range (or businesses within the company) to allow for informed decisions on resource allocation.

Value chain analysis – divides organizational activities into five core activities and four supporting activities, which allows for a detailed evaluation of how value is added.

Resource-based view (RBV) – suggests that high performance depends on historic resources.

Resource-based view of the firm

We have seen in Unit 1 what a market orientation means. It emphasizes the superior contribution of companies with high quality and responsiveness to market needs. An alternative perspective is the resource-based view (RBV). Whilst market orientation is outward looking, RBV is inward looking. It focuses on the organization's resources.

Models to assess attractiveness of products and markets

The next section discusses models which integrate some of the factors covered above. These are the portfolio analysis models and Porter's value chain framework.

Portfolio analysis models

Two of the more commonly found models are described here – the Boston box and the directional policy matrix.

Portfolio models really came to the fore in the early 1970s, when they became almost synonymous with strategic market planning. The dramatic increase seen in the complexity of businesses fuelled that need. Their appeal was apparent to managers wrestling with the problems of diversified firms with large numbers of products in an equally large variety of markets. Portfolio models provide these managers with a clear framework within which to make their decisions. They are an objective measure for assessing products and markets in terms of their attractiveness to the firm. And from that analysis, rational decisions about objectives, strategy and resource allocation could be made.

All portfolio models involve a classification and display of the current and potential positions of businesses and products according to the attractiveness of that market and the ability of the business to compete within that market. The first of these to gain widespread acceptance is the growth–share matrix, also known as the BCG (Boston Consultancy Group) grid after its developers, and the cash quadrants model.

BCG growth–share matrix

As you would guess from its name, the two principal factors with which the BCG grid is concerned are

1. market share
2. market growth.

Before we examine the model in depth, we will consider the reasoning behind choosing these two factors out of so many potential candidates. Why not chose profit, for example? Or potential market size?

Let us look first at market share – why is that judged to be so critical?

Market share
To understand the importance of market share, you need to understand the impact of the learning curve, which suggests that the more often we perform a certain activity, the more efficient we get at doing it. This is for several reasons.

161

o *Labour efficiency* – Those actually performing the function understand what they are supposed to be doing and perform it more effectively as they become more experienced.

o *Work specialization* – As the volumes increase, companies can afford to specialize units of work into smaller units. Again, this would normally lead to more efficiency.

o *Methods improvement* – The more often a company has to produce a particular product, the more likely it is to find a better (quicker, cheaper) way of doing it.

o *Economies of scale* – As the company produces more, the costs of raw materials and so on should go down.

The Boston Consultancy Group wanted to quantify this learning curve effect, to give some idea of the cost advantage a company producing more would have over one producing less. Its work suggested that a decline of up to 30 per cent in costs would occur for each cumulative doubling of output (Figure 7.2).

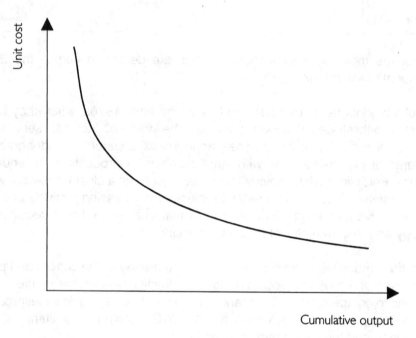

Figure 7.2 Learning curve effect

So unit costs would initially start very high, as there would be a high wastage rate, initial products would spend a long time in manufacture, raw materials would be relatively expensive due to small order sizes and so on. Then, as output increases and the company 'settles' into the new manufacturing process, the learning curve will take effect. Costs will progressively decline until a minimum cost is reached. Obviously costs are not going to decline to zero, however much you produce.

What this suggests is that the greater the volume produced over time, the lower the costs. In any one market, the greater the market share, the lower the costs. So in that market the company with the largest market share should have the lowest cost structure, and hence an advantage over its competitors. But the size of that advantage will be dependent on the difference in market share between the largest company and the one closest to it. For example, let us assume that our company has 40 per cent market share and is the market leader. If that market is very fragmented, that is, has lots of companies with very low market shares in it, then that is a major advantage. If our nearest competitor has a 7 per cent share, then we should have a very significant cost advantage over them. If, on the other hand, our nearest competitor has 39 per cent, the differences in our cost structures are likely to be minimal – and we do not really have an advantage.

We can therefore see that market share is not sufficiently specific as a variable. What we need to know is relative market share, that is, the ratio of our share to that of our largest competitor. This is more likely to give us a more realistic measure of our cost structure advantage, and hence hopefully our profit advantage.

So in the first case (we have 40 per cent, they have 7 per cent), our relative market share would be $40/7 = 5.7$; and in the second case (we have 40 per cent, they have 39 per cent), it would be $40/39 = 0.9$. Obviously, 5.7 suggests a far superior position to 0.9.

This choice of measurement was given added credibility by a PIMS study showing the importance of market share in determining return on investment. Let us look now at why market growth is deemed so important.

Market growth

Whereas relative market share is essentially a measure of our ability to compete within a market, market growth is a measure of the attractiveness of the market. You will already be familiar with the product life cycle as a concept – the idea that products move through a series of stages throughout their lives, each with its own characteristics. They will begin life in the introductory phase, a period of relatively slow sales growth and very low sales. The growth rate then increases dramatically as more and more people come on to the market and the product begins to recoup its development costs and move into profit. After a period of time (and this can almost literally be of any length) sales will start to flatten out as the market becomes saturated and the product is deemed to have entered the mature phase. Eventually, the product's sales will start to decline as new products take its place.

Markets could be said to act in a similar way, as the sales in a market are merely the aggregation of the sales of all the products within it. Market life cycles tend to be longer than product life cycles, but are still thought to go through all the same stages.

In the mature phase of the market, when it is saturated, the growth rate is by definition low. A few firms tend to dominate after price competition has shaken out the weaker competitors. It is hard to increase market share because of the static nature of the market and the dominance of a few large firms. This type of market should therefore be viewed as unattractive unless you already hold a commanding position within it.

By contrast, the growth phase of the market life cycle is a period of rapid growth. It should be easier to increase share, although it may be expensive, as this is the period when companies tend to have a relatively high advertising-to-sales ratio. Money is spent on advertising and promotion to build awareness and encourage trial of the product.

Price competition often occurs in the mature phase of a market. This will remove the weaker competitors, so that it is only the companies with the lowest cost structures who can afford to survive in this market.

This underlines the need to be very wary of complacency in the growth phase. It is easy in a period of rapid growth to become complacent as long as your business continues to grow. Let us assume your business is growing by 50 per cent year on year. You would be pleased, would you not? But you really need to view that growth rate in relation to the market growth rate. And if the market is growing by 75 per cent year on year, you have a problem. You are losing market share. You can survive that during the growth phase, but what happens when the market growth rate slows down? Price competition will increase and you will not be in a position to survive it, because your cost structure will be relatively weak. This is the classic mistake that the UK motorbike industry made when Japanese competition came in during the growth phase. Where are these UK manufacturers now?

In the same way that market share is used as a relative variable, so market growth should be. It should be corrected for the level of inflation to give a more realistic idea of the rate of growth.

How the growth–share matrix works

The previous sections have explained to you the importance of relative market share and market growth in determining the attractiveness of the market and your competitive position within. Let us now look at how the BCG grid works.

The BCG grid (or growth–share matrix) uses the two factors of relative market share and market growth to position products within the portfolio. Four quadrants are used to designate product types within the grid, each with its own strategic implications. Each product within the portfolio is evaluated on the basis of its market share, relative to its largest competitor, plus the rate of growth within the market.

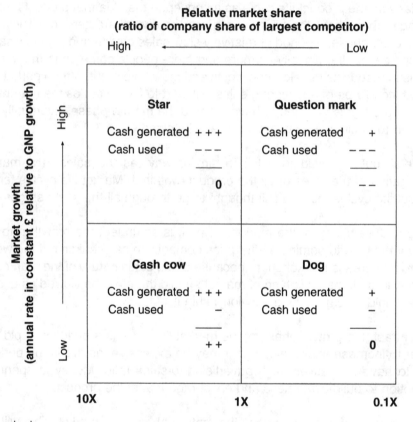

Figure 7.3 Growth–share matrix
Source: Boston Consultancy Group

We shall now examine the characteristics of products lying within the different quadrants. A major difference between the product designations is their implications for cash flow, provided that market share and growth behave as expected. Market share represents the ability to generate cash, and market growth the need for cash.

Cash cows

Cash cows have dominant positions in slow or no-growth markets, that is, markets in their mature phase. They are profitable and cash positive. They need some investment as their position of dominance must be maintained, but the excess cash can be siphoned off to fund other categories. They provide the money to pay interest on the corporate debt, pay dividends, cover corporate overheads, finance research and development and help other products to grow.

Stars

Stars also tend to be profitable because of their strong share position. They may be self-financing or may provide or require cash at the margins. This depends on the need to fund additional capacity and/or new products to maintain rapid growth. However, the present cash needs will tend to be modest in scale and will be more than compensated for when the growth rate of the market slows. Then the product, provided that it has maintained its dominant position, will move down into the cash cow category.

Problem children

This category is also known as 'question marks' or 'wildcats'. They have a low relative market share but operate in markets of rapid growth. The low market share means that there is a relatively weak cash flow from operations, but unfortunately this is compounded by the expensive process of operating in a market of rapid growth. It is costly just to maintain share but an obvious objective for 'question marks' is to build share to a dominant position.

Dogs

Dogs are products with a low share in a low or no-growth market. They are best regarded as 'cash traps' as they are unlikely to ever generate cash themselves. As there can only be one leader in a market and most markets are mature, the greatest number of products and businesses fall into this sector.

Strategic implications

Over time, products will move because of market dynamics and strategy decisions. The objective is to analyse the current portfolio matrix and understand the natural dynamics of the portfolio so that a strong portfolio will result in the future.

Movements in the vertical direction, up and down the matrix, are largely outside the firm's control and must be anticipated when planning strategic decisions. Over time, all products would fall down the grid so that 'stars' become 'cash cows' and 'question marks' become 'dogs' – provided that the relative share position has been maintained.

If the growth rate of the market is outside your control, as is normally the case, then portfolio analysis is limited to determining market share strategy.

Money from the 'cash cows' will be used to fund share increases for at least some of the 'question marks'. If this is successful, these 'question marks' will become 'stars' and then the 'cash cows' of tomorrow.

Unfortunately, many companies view investing in 'dogs' and 'cash cows' as 'safer', investing less than is needed in both 'question marks' and 'stars'.

Sales volumes and forecasting

The BCG grid has been adapted to include the impact of sales volumes. Obviously, it is of fundamental significance to understand whether the mass of company revenue comes from 'cash cows' or 'dogs' or whatever.

Sales volumes can simply be included on the grid by the technique of using proportional circles. The size of the circle illustrates the size of the sales volume. This can be done by using the area of the circle (πr^2) or the radius. Both approaches are employed, although the area technique could be viewed as having an advantage, in the sense that the visual impact of the circle relates more to area than to radius.

Strategic alternatives

The outline strategic alternatives for each of the quadrants in relation to marketing strategy are as follows:

- ○ *Cash cows* – use profits to maintain position; fund stars/question marks.
- ○ *Stars* – maintain/increase share.
- ○ *Question marks* – either intensify efforts, or maintain current strategy, or leave the market.
- ○ *Dogs* – reduce efforts, maintain, divest.

Weaknesses in the BCG grid

The BCG grid is a very useful tool, but it needs to be used with caution. One of the main problems is how the measures are determined.

Product-market definition

For the purposes of portfolio analysis, a business segment or product market is correctly defined if it is possible to establish and defend a competitive advantage in that segment alone, without the need to participate in other segments. This is easier said than done.

Market share estimates

Whenever market share is used to evaluate performance, managers become adept at moving the market boundaries to show a static or increasing share. The resulting narrow view of the market may result in threats and opportunities being overlooked.

Market growth rate

This can also be manipulated where wishful thinking may lead to a higher growth rate being predicted than is realistic.

Relationship between share and profitability

The BCG grid assumes a direct causal relationship between market share and profitability. This is, to say the least, an oversimplification of the issue.

It is important to remember that the learning curve effect relates only to relative profitability within the industry. It takes no account of the fact that some industries are inherently more profitable than others.

Market share can be important, but other factors need to be considered in evaluating its role in profitability:

- ○ *Size of business* – In some industries both niche and multinational companies prosper.
- ○ *Type of industry* – Market share appears to be more important in high-tech industries. In the service sector, diseconomies of scale can occur leading to reduced profitability.
- ○ *Stage in the product life cycle* – PIMS research has shown that profitability differentials narrow as the market matures. On average, a company with twice the share of its leading competitor (relative market share of 2.0) would have a direct cost advantage of 3.5 per cent in less mature markets and only 1.2 per cent in mature markets.
- ○ *Unionization* – This appears to mitigate the effect of large market share by ensuring that a larger percentage of costs end up as wages.

Perhaps the causality of the relationship does not come from market share – perhaps it lies in the relation of profits to market share. Perhaps a third variable such as quality of management or perceived quality of product jointly influences both market share and profits. Maybe there are many influences on profit, of which market share is only one. More recent reviews of the PIMS data suggest that the direct causal impact of market share is much less than is commonly assumed and may account for only 10–20 per cent of the relationship.

Empirical evidence from Porter and others suggests that companies with a strong share of a tightly defined/niche market have high return on investment (ROI). In the PIMS study, which looked at total rather than served markets, such companies would have been defined as having low market share. To counteract many of these criticisms, and to support that planning process more effectively, new portfolio models have been developed. The BCG grid can be viewed as an oversimplification of the market and, as a result, multifactor models have been developed that can be adapted to a variety of industries.

Directional policy matrix (DPM)

The most commonly used multifactor model is one often referred to as the directional policy matrix. This is very similar to the GE matrix. The sectors are determined by assessing the strength of the strategic business unit (SBU), product group, individual product or segment on the two composite factors of market attractiveness and competitive (business) position. Why have these two variables been chosen?

Market attractiveness reflects the difference in average long-run profit potential for all participants in the market. Competitive position evaluates the profitability of the business relative to the competition.

We need to classify businesses on both these dimensions to gain a realistic picture of the portfolio, and we need to look at each business now and in the future.

One of the main strengths of the multifactor matrix lies in its flexibility in adapting to a variety of industries. The managers responsible select the factors that they believe are important in determining market attractiveness and competitive position. Hence managers become very committed to this technique as they are closely involved in its evolution – to a large extent it is their theory.

There are two possible complementary approaches to developing the lists of factors. One is to select from a standard checklist that has been developed from those factors that have historically determined either industry or relative profitability. The other is to select a series of pairs of units (businesses) – one in each pair to be deemed attractive, and one unattractive to the company. Factors are then derived from noting the important differences.

Factors contributing to market attractiveness

The following factors contribute to market attractiveness.

Market factors
- Size, volume and value
- Size of segments
- Growth rate

- o Stage in market life cycle
- o Diversity of market
- o Price elasticity
- o Bargaining power of buyers
- o Seasonality of demand.

Economic and technological factors
- o Investment required
- o Nature of investment
- o Industry capacity
- o Level and maturing of technology
- o Utilization
- o Barriers to entry/exit
- o Availability of raw materials.

Competitive factors

- o Types of competitor
- o Structure of competition
- o Substitutes
- o Degree of differentiation.

Environmental factors

- o Legal/regulatory framework
- o Social acceptance
- o Unionization and so on.

Once we have decided which factors we are going to use we need some method of consolidating them into a single composite score. The section below outlines an approach we could take.

Assessing market attractiveness

1. Determine the relevant factors which affect market attractiveness. These factors will apply to the market as a whole, not just our particular SBU or brand. Generally it is best not to exceed five or six factors.
2. Decide how important each of these factors is and allocate an appropriate weighting. The total weighting should add up to 100. For example, we might decide that market growth rate is important and allocate it 25 but that market size is even more important and allocate it 40.
3. Next give a score which reflects how well the market performs on that particular factor. It is important here to make sure that the scales always work in the same direction, for example that 0 is always low/poor and that 1 is always high/good. This can sometimes be a bit confusing. Take a factor like the degree of competition. If levels of competitor activity are high then this is bad in terms of market attractiveness so we might score this variable as a 0 or 0.25. The level of investment required is similarly schizophrenic! Scores between the two extremes of 1 and 0 indicate an intermediate performance. One decimal place is likely to be the most that people can visualize to any degree of accuracy. Or it may be worth limiting scores to a restricted range, for example 0, 0.25, 0.5, 0.75, 1. For some respondents attaching a semantic scale may be useful, for example 0 = not at all, 0.25 = to some extent and so on.
4. Multiply the weighting by the score to give a ranking of how each market performs on each factor.
5. Sum all the rankings to give a total score for the market.

Table 7.1 offers a simple example of how we might assess the attractiveness of a market.

Table 7.1 Assessing market attractiveness

Factor	Score	Weighting	Ranking
Market size	0.5	30	15
Market growth	0.5	20	10
Level of competition	0.0	20	0
Barriers to entry	1.0	15	15
Investment required	1.0	15	15
Total		100	55

Factors influencing the strength of competitive position

The following factors could influence the strength of competitive position.

Market position

- o Relative market share
- o Rate of change of share
- o Variability of share across segments
- o Perceived differentiation of quality/price/service
- o Breadth of product range
- o Company image.

Economic and technological position

- o Relative cost position
- o Capacity utilization
- o Technological position
- o Patented technology, product or process.

Capabilities

- o Management strength and depth
- o Marketing strength
- o Distribution system
- o Labour relations
- o Manufacturing efficiency.

Once all the significant factors are agreed, the next stage is to weigh each according to its relative importance – it would be very unusual if all were equally important. Problems can occur when factors are interrelated – relative market share and cost position, for example. A factor also may be very significant in one market and not in another, so weights may be ignored if it is felt that they do not add anything other than a spurious scientific objectivity.

Assessing competitive position
Here we repeat the process undertaken in assessing the attractiveness of the market with one important difference. When we were assessing market attractiveness we assessed the factor relative to the market, now we need to look at how we are performing compared to the strongest competitor.

So the profile of a unit with regard to its competitive position could look something like Table 7.2.

Table 7.2 Competitive position profile

Factor	Score	Weighting	Ranking
Relative market share	0.75	40	30
Manufacturing efficiency	0.50	20	10
Relative cost position	0.50	20	10
Distribution strength	1.00	20	20
Total		100	70

Once composite scores have been calculated on both dimensions, the present position of the unit can be plotted on the grid in Figure 7.4. In the same way that proportional circles are used on the BCG grid to incorporate sales volumes, they can be used on the multifactor grid. But this time the area of the circle should be related to the size of the total business segment, with perhaps a shaded area included, as shown in Figure 7.4. This will correspond to the market share currently achieved in this segment.

Evaluation of the future position will involve making judgements about the changes likely to occur in the factors underlying the composite scores for market attractiveness and competitive position.

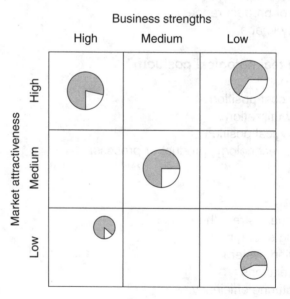

Figure 7.4 Directional policy matrix

Figure 7.4 illustrates an example of a completed DPM.

We can make parallels here with the BCG grid which we discussed earlier.

The SBUs/segments/brands which appear in the top left hand of the matrix are the stars. Those in the bottom left are the cash cows which generate income for the organization. Those in the centre and top right are the equivalent of problem children, that is they have a question mark over their future. For these, a decision needs to be made to jump one way or another; either we decide to invest in them or we cut our losses.

Products in the bottom right fall into the category of dogs and are unlikely to succeed. In most cases the best decision is to withdraw them or sell them to another company. Since this matrix is very specifically tailored to the organization, it may well be that what we view as a dog may be a cash cow to another company.

The multifactor grid can offer some generic strategic options according to the position of the unit on the grid. But in fact it is better to analyse the feasible strategic options for each business, based on the realities of its current situation.

Be careful when using these generic strategies. They tend to assume that SBUs/brands and so on are autonomous, whereas a degree of interdependency is more likely to be the case.

Strategic implications

Organizations need to review the performance of each of its SBUs, products or segments in the context of its overall mix. The relative position of each will help determine the appropriate strategy. The organization has broadly a choice of four strategies. It may decide to:

o *Build* – increase the market share/develop further.
o *Maintain* – stabilize current market share/use resource to maintain the status quo.
o *Harvest* – sell off or pull off after milking the brand (or SBU etc.) for its last potential profit.
o *Divest* – drop or sell as soon as possible.

<table>
<tr>
<td rowspan="3" style="writing-mode: vertical-lr">Market attractiveness</td>
<td>High</td>
<td>Protect position
o Invest to grow at maximum rate
o Concentrate effort on maintaining strength</td>
<td>Invest to build
o Challenge for leadership
o Build selectively on strengths
o Reinforce vulnerable areas</td>
<td>Build selectively
o Specialize around limited strengths
o Seek ways to overcome weaknesses
o Withdraw if no indications of sustainable growth</td>
</tr>
<tr>
<td>Medium</td>
<td>Build selectively
o Invest heavily in most attractive segments
o Build up ability to counter competition
o Increase profit by raising productivity</td>
<td>Manage for earnings
o Protect existing investment
o Focus investment on segments where profit is good and risk low</td>
<td>Limited expansion or harvest
o Explore means of expansion without high risk
o Minimize investment and rationalize operations</td>
</tr>
<tr>
<td>Low</td>
<td>Protect and refocus
o Manage for current earnings
o Concentrate on attractive segments
o Defend strengths</td>
<td>Manage for earnings
o Protect position in most profitable segments
o Upgrade product line
o Minimize investment</td>
<td>Divest
o Sell when cash value is maximized
o Cut fixed costs and avoid investments in the interim</td>
</tr>
<tr>
<td></td>
<td></td>
<td>Strong</td>
<td>Medium</td>
<td>Weak</td>
</tr>
<tr>
<td></td>
<td></td>
<td colspan="3" style="text-align:center">Business position</td>
</tr>
</table>

Limitations of the multifactor model

The multifactor model overcomes many of the criticisms of the BCG grid by adding greater complexity rather than relying on the simplicity of share and growth, but increased complexity leads to problems of its own. These are on two levels.

Conceptual

There is a danger that the outcome of all this analysis is merely to recommend that invest-ment takes place in those areas of greatest market attractiveness and strongest competitive position.

Measurement

The problem of having to reach a consensus on the factors and/or their weighting tends to bias results towards the 'medium' categories. Managers who disagree will compromise to reach a solution. The matrix will then lose its discriminatory power.

The use of composite scores can also mean that differences are lost in the process of generating a single score.

Furthermore, care needs to be taken in the choice of individual factors so that the composite score is not unintentionally biased towards a certain area of market attractiveness or compe-titive position. For instance, it might be possible to have four factors relating to the market position and one to technological and economic, when both are judged to be equally significant.

Both portfolio analysis techniques have their strengths and weaknesses. What is important is to be aware of their shortcomings and take them into account when making use of these manage-ment tools. The end objective is to have a balanced portfolio in terms of the cash flow generated and the degree of risk involved. Both of these techniques should be used as an aid to your decision-making in this area rather than as a substitute. If you are intending to use portfolio analysis to evaluate your business over time, it is important to ensure that the variables and weightings are constant so that you are comparing like with like. You cannot decide that market size is weighted 50 per cent and then six months later decide that actually it is only 40 per cent. If you are going to make the comparison you need to compare apples with apples so one set of data will need to be reworked to take account of your change in thinking.

Also bear in mind many other models of portfolio analysis exist. Research these as well.

Value chain analysis

Porter (1985) developed a useful tool to analyse current activities of competitors and your own organization, namely the value chain. The value chain divides activities into five primary clusters, namely:

1. *Inbound logistics* – how the company manages the flow of products into the company.
2. *Operations* – how the company changes the inputs into a saleable product and adds value.
3. *Outbound logistics* – how the company distributes its product to its buyers.
4. *Marketing and sales* – activities which communicate to and motivate the buyers. This also includes market research which can be used to inform decisions on the other activities.
5. *Service* – the activities to keep the product working effectively for the buyer after purchase.

These five primary activities are underpinned by four support activities.

1. Procurement
2. Human resource development
3. Technological development
4. Infrastructure.

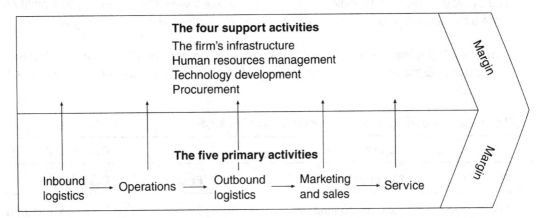

Figure 7.5 The value chain
Source: Porter (1985)

These support activities feed into the primary activities.

Value chain analysis can provide an insight into:

1. Competitors' relative cost structure
2. Ways to add value cost effectively
3. How to look beyond operations as a means of adding value.

This area has been extensively discussed. Read around this subject.

The innovation audit

Successful companies innovate. They may innovate to create new products and services or be innovative in the way they operate, creating efficiencies within the value chain. Innovation may be natural to an entrepreneur running his own small business but within larger companies managers may need to make more of an effort to encourage individuals to be creative. The innovation audit provides us with a framework to uncover whether the necessary assets and competencies are available. It is divided into four main areas.

1. The current organizational climate and its impact on creativity.
2. Measures of current performance in innovation.
3. Policies and practices used to support innovation.
4. Balance of the cognitive styles of the senior management team.

Let us look at each of these in turn to understand how we might implement an innovation audit.

Organizational climate

We can approach this in two ways. First, we need to conduct an attitude survey amongst staff to see how they feel about the organizational climate. Secondly, we can use the technique of the metaphor to gain a more qualitative view of employee perception.

Attitude survey

The survey is decided to look at how the employees view the organization's ability to support innovation and also to see what barriers exist to prevent staff from being creative.

Burnside (1990) lists 12 factors which are important in determining the level of innovation within a company. Eight of these are supportive of innovation and the remaining four are potential constraints.

Table 7.3 Supporting and constraining factors on innovation

Support		Constraint	
Factor	**Description**	**Factor**	**Description**
Teamwork	Level of commitment, level of trust, willingness to help each other	Time	Lack of time to consider alternative approaches to work
Resources	Access to resources such as facilities, staff, finance etc.	Status quo	Traditional approach, unwillingness to change
Challenge	Challenge in work. Is it enough?	Politics	Territorial battles within the organization
Freedom	Amount of individual autonomy	Evaluation	Focus on criticism and external evaluation
Supervision	Management support in goal setting, clear communication and morale		
Infrastructure	Level of senior management support and structures necessary for creativity		
Recognition	Level of recognition of and rewards for creativity		
Unity and co-operation	Collaborative and co-operative atmosphere, shared vision		

The staff survey should also include two other overarching factors of productivity and creativity. Staff should be asked how productive they think the organization is and how creative they feel it to be.

Metaphors

There are a number of well-established tools to encourage creativity; the use of the metaphor is one of these (Morgan, 1993). Using metaphors works because it moves us away from literal language and allows us to describe a much richer picture in a succinct way.

Employees should be asked to describe their organization in terms of a metaphor. For example: 'This company is like a cougar. Fast and lean.' Or 'This organization is like a dinosaur. Slow and lumbering and destined for extinction.'

Activity 7.1

Describe your own organization in a metaphor. What does this tell you about your company's culture? How does it affect innovation within the organization?

Measures of innovation orientation

As with any activity, we need objective measures to monitor our performance. Innovation is no different.

We can tailor these measures to our business.

We might look at the number of innovations in a specified timescale, the percentage success rate, the percentage of sales attributed to new products, the payback period for new products. We need to assess these measures over time to determine our success in encouraging innovation. In many ways these are like the multifactor matrix. We can decide which factors are important to us as an organization and possibly even weight these to give a total innovation score.

Table 7.4 An example of innovation trend analysis

Innovation criterion	2004	2001
Number of new products launched in the last 3 years	25	15
Number judged a success	3	10
Percentage success rate	12	67
Percentage of total sales accounted for by new products	15	30
Average annual sales per new product ($m)	1	12
Average payback period (years)	3	1
Average cost saving for innovation in process ($'000s)	30	150

Question 7.1

Summarize your conclusions from the above data. What do you think the company should do?

Policies and practices to support innovation

Within the innovation audit we need to review the policies and practices already in place to support innovation. There may already be schemes which encourage creativity. Some organizations offer employees a percentage of the cost savings gained if they can identify potential cost savings in process. Others run schemes which encourage the generation of new product ideas. Rewarding individuals for creativity is very important in promoting an innovation culture and encouraging individuals to put in additional effort. If schemes are not already in place to encourage employees to 'think outside the box', the company should think about putting them in place.

Cognitive styles of the senior management team

Much work has been done on how our personality affects the way we work and manage. This is an area of great complexity and is hard to summarize in the space and time we have here. But here is a simple attempt.

Although we are all individuals and have complex personality profiles we tend to have a dominant side or preference in the way we work.

Much of the research in this area uses the Myers Briggs Type Indicator (MBTI) which summarizes personality into 16 different types. For the purposes of the innovation audit we can look at four different cognitive styles and think about the impact these may have on the organization.

Table 7.5 Cognitive styles

Cognitive style	Focuses on	Tends to be
Intuitive	Patterns, possibilities and ideas	Ingenious and integrative
Sensing	Here and now	Adaptable and practical
Thinking	Logic and objectivity	Pragmatic
Feeling	People and values	Empathetic

The ideal senior management team would have a mix of these styles, although in reality many are headed by thinking types.

Question 7.2

What do you think are the cognitive styles of your senior management team? How do they interact? What is your style?

How might you improve to encourage innovation?

We are now at the end of this unit. The next section summarizes the main learning outcomes of this unit in preparation for moving on to the next one.

Summary

The marketing environment constitutes a set of largely uncontrollable factors that can affect, positively or negatively, an organization's ability to achieve its objectives. As it is dynamic, it presents a continually changing set of opportunities and threats to an organization and so monitoring the environment is a key marketing activity. The marketing environment can be divided into:

o   The macro-environment of factors further from an organization's control or influence – such as demographic, social, cultural, legal, political, physical and technological factors.

o The micro-environment – those factors closer to an organization that it may be able to influence, such as suppliers, intermediaries, customers, publics, competitors and the organization itself.

Portfolio analysis and the Five Forces model are explained as useful frameworks to help in the analysis of the micro-environment. The BCG and DP matrices are explained in some detail, together with their strategic implications. We also look at an innovation audit which helps us to assess the extent to which an organization nurtures creativity amongst the individuals it employs.

Further study

Buzzell, R.D.A., Gale, B.T. (1987) *The PIMS Principle: Linking Strategy to Performance*, New York: The Free Press.

Davidson, M. (1997) *Even More Offensive Marketing*, Penguin.

Porter, M.E. (1980) *Competitive Strategy: Techniques for Analyzing Industries and Competitors*, New York: The Free Press.

Stokes, D. (2002) *Marketing*, London and New York.

Hints and tips

Throughout this module we stress the importance of using examples. But do not just quote ours – think of your own ones. Originality will be rewarded in the examination.

An important part of the module is in the application of theory in a particular context. Marks will be gained for applying the theory rather than just describing it.

Bibliography

Burnside, R. (1990) in M.A. West and J.L Farr (eds), *Innovation and Creativity at Work*, Wiley.

Day, G. (1986) *Analysis for Strategic Marketing Decisions*, St Paul MN: West.

Morgan, G. (1993) *Imaginization, the Art of Creative Management*, Sage.

Porter, M.E. (1985) *Competitive Advantage: Creating and Sustaining Superior Performance*, New York: The Free Press.

unit 8
characteristics of the global marketplace

Exam Hint 8.1

It is important to appreciate that international issues are assumed to be throughout the course. Students should keep this in mind whenever they are answering an exam question in any parts of the course units.

Learning objectives

Sections of the syllabus being covered in this unit:

Element 5: Characteristics of the global and international marketplace (20 per cent).

5.1 Assess the variances in key factors influencing customer buying behaviours and competition in global and international markets.

5.2 Identify the specific challenges in collecting and interpreting information to develop a detailed understanding of customers and markets in a foreign market and explain how they may be overcome.

5.3 Identify and assess the processes, techniques and factors to be used in assessing the attractiveness of international markets (e.g. assessing rate of development of economic development, cultures, consumer profiles etc.).

5.4 Assess the position of an organization working in an international or global marketplace.

5.5 Critically assess the capability of an organization to expand in international markets taking into account factors such as its cultural expertise, organizational structure issues, current strategic objectives (defending home market from attack, operating in foreign market etc.) and so on.

5.6 Critically evaluate the effectiveness and value of ICT in cross-border marketing.

Exam Hint 8.2

All the techniques that you use in the course will have international applications, please be aware of that fact. It is also important for you to revise the basic principles behind buyer behaviour theory as well as adoption theory and diffusion theory market research as they will be applied throughout the course.

Statements of related marketing practice

The main skill or business competency areas which are being developed in this section and are likely to be examined are as follows:

- o To develop appropriate structures and frameworks to identify appropriate information requirements to define and structure marketing-related business problems.
- o To be able to critically evaluate different analytical perspectives which will lead executives to gain a better understanding of their external and internal environment within the specific context of their industries and setting thus placing them in a better position to make better-informed decisions potentially leading to minimize risks and uncertainty.
- o To promote a strong marketing orientation to influence strategy formulation and investment decisions.
- o Specify and direct the line marketing process.

Key definitions

Culture – is patterned ways of thinking, feeling and reacting, acquired and transmitted mainly by symbols constituting the distinctive achievements of human groups including their embodiment in artifacts; the essential case of culture consists of traditional ideas and especially their attached values.

Marketing Intelligence System – is the systematic approach used to gather market intelligence.

Introduction

There are now over 250 countries in the world, almost all of which trade internationally.

We all live in an increasingly global market. Look around you. Most of us are surrounded by products from all around the world. Furniture from Sweden, computers from America, clothes from Italy, food from everywhere!

And although the same principles of marketing apply wherever we are practising the discipline, there can be additional challenges in dealing in international markets.

Porter (1986) divides the forces which drive international marketing into two: currents and cross-currents. Figure 8.1 gives examples of these two types of force. Essentially the currents are governed by macro-forces, and the cross-currents by emergent trends. The cross-currents interact with the currents to alter their direction to some extent. The cross-currents drive organizations to behave in new and sometimes innovative ways to change the basis of international competitive advantage.

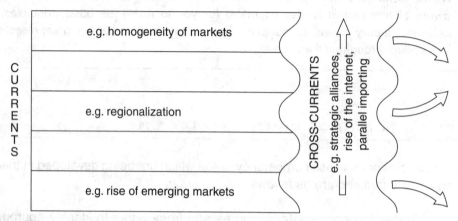

Figure 8.1 Forces driving international marketing
Source: After Porter (1986)

Although international marketing is not conceptually different from domestic marketing, there are factors which may require additional attention.

1. *Culture* – markets can often be culturally diverse which can provide challenges particularly in the communications arena. Rules of business may differ.
2. *Markets* – these can be geographically disparate leading to distribution and control problems.
3. *Data* – market intelligence can be difficult and expensive to obtain, with problems of comparability.
4. *Politics* – the relative stability of countries varies dramatically. Also the relative power of governments in regulating foreign trade.
5. *Economic* – economies differ in levels of development, their finance systems, their regulatory bodies and the stability of their currency.

Exam Hint 8.3

You are very likely be examined on issues relating to international marketing so please ensure that you are aware of them. Particularly be aware of the differences in culture and approach as well as availability of data across different countries. You ought to appreciate what you would do in circumstances where limited data is available.

Highlights of world trade

The World Trade Organization (WTO) makes the following points about the WTO International Trade Statistics 2003 (www.wto.org):

○ A weak trade recovery in 2002 was followed by a near stagnation of trade flows in the first half of 2003. The sluggishness of international trade reflects the weak economic growth in the OECD countries and in particular Western Europe. Uncertainty about the global economic prospects increased in the early months of 2003 due to the emergence of SARS and the tensions in the Middle East. Whilst the economic impact of SARS was largely confined to one region (East Asia) and a few sectors (the tourism and air transportation), the situation in the Middle East contributed to an increase in energy prices worldwide and therefore had an impact on the global recovery.

o In 2002, world trade recovered from its steep decline in 2001. The average annual rate of merchandize trade expansion in 2002 was limited to 3 per cent in real terms, only half the rate of the 1990s.

o The trade recovery in 2002 benefited from strong import demand in developing Asia, the transition economies and the United States. Sluggish import demand in Western Europe and a sharp contraction of Latin America's imports constituted a drag on global trade expansion.

o A combination of declining exports and rising imports by the United States has led to a record trade and current account deficit, the latter equivalent to 5 per cent of its GDP.

o China's trade expansion (both exports and imports) remains outstanding. In the 1990s, China's trade growth was three times faster than global trade and between 2000 and 2002 its exports and imports rose by 30 per cent while world trade stagnated.

o Chemicals emerged as the product group with the strongest trade growth over the last two years. Driven by the pharmaceutical trade among the developed countries, its share in world merchandise rose above 10 per cent exceeding both automotive and agricultural products.

o In the first half of 2003, world merchandise exports rose by 15 per cent in dollar terms over the corresponding figure in 2002, a strong acceleration compared to the average 4 per cent annual growth in 2002. The depreciation of the US dollar and higher oil and non-fuel commodity prices contributed to the dollar price and value increase in international trade.

o Adjusted for price and exchange rate changes, a different and less bright trade picture emerges. The OECD countries' real exports in goods and services have stagnated from the fourth quarter of 2002 through the second quarter of 2003 (on a seasonally adjusted basis).

o Developments in the first half of 2003 and the improvements of the leading indicators in the third quarter led to a projection of world trade merchandise growth of 3 per cent, basically unchanged from the preceding year's rate.

Activity 8.1

Visit the World Trade Organization website and acquaint yourself with the patterns of world trade and the trends.

International market Intelligence gathering

The first stage in any market research programme is always to decide on the research objectives which need to be defined in terms of information requirements. International market research is no different. A basic list would be:

1. Where to go?

   o Assessment of global demand
   o Ranking of potential by country/region
   o Local competition
   o Political risk

2. How to get there?

    o   Size of markets/segments
    o   Barriers to entry
    o   Transport and distribution costs
    o   Local competition
    o   Government requirements
    o   Political risk

3. What shall we market?

    o   Government regulations
    o   Customer sophistication
    o   Competitive stance

4. How do we persuade them to buy it?

    o   Buyer behaviour
    o   Competitive practice
    o   Distribution channels
    o   Promotional channel
    o   Company expertise

Table 8.1 adds to this basic list and shows how domestic firms need to adopt a structured approach to gathering international marketing intelligence.

Table 8.1 The task of global marketing research: what should it determine?

Differences across countries and regions of interest

The marketing environment	The competition	The product	Marketing mix	Firm-specific historical data
Political context: leaders, national goals, ideology, key institution	Relative market shares, new product moves	Analysis of users. Who are the end-user industries?	Channels of distribution: evolution and performance	Sales trends by product and product-line, salesforce and customer
Economic growth prospects, business cycle stage	Pricing and cost structure, image and brand reputation	Industrial and consumer buyers; characteristics: size, age, sex, segment growth rates	Relative pricing elasticities and tactics	Trends by country and region
Per capita income levels, purchasing power	Quality: its attributes and positioning relative to competitors	Purchasing power and intentions	Advertising and promotion: choices and impacts on customers	Contribution margins

The marketing environment	The competition	The product	Marketing mix	Firm-specific historical data
End-user industry growth trends	Competitors' strengths: favourite tactics and strategies	Customer response to new products, price, promotion	Service quality: perceptions and relative positioning	Marketing mix used, marketing response functions across countries and regions
Government: legislation, regulation, standards, barriers to trade		Switching behaviour, role of credit and purchasing Future needs, impact of cultural differences	Logistics networks, configuration and change	

Source: Terpstra and Sarathy (1997)

Case study

Car security systems in Pakistan

Lasman Electronics in Lahore, Pakistan, felt that there was a latent demand in Pakistan for electronic car security systems.

The objective of their market research study was to test this perception and to carry out an assessment of the market for the electronic car security systems in Pakistan and to examine the feasibility of launching the product into that market. At the time of the study, such systems were not available in the Pakistani market.

The project was being administered from the United Kingdom and so had all the problems attendant with long and cumbersome communication channels. Furthermore, the project was being carried out in a country which was seen as a researcher's nightmare. There was no recognizable research infrastructure and there were few reliable sources of secondary information, a multiplicity of languages, a mistrust of interviewers and a fierce instinct to protect privacy. The conditions were not seen as being conducive to a successful market research exercise.

Whilst wanting to satisfy the client's need for marketing information, the researchers were interested in whether it was possible for a small company to conduct primary research on a limited budget in a country such as Pakistan.

It was found that it was impractical to carry out a full country-wide study of Pakistan. It was assumed there would be difficulties with the sampling plan and it was argued that in such cases the more targeted the consumer sample, the easier it would be to formulate an effective sampling plan.

Preliminary research showed that it was only the affluent consumers who owned reasonable new cars and, therefore, would have an interest in security systems, and that the vast majority of these individuals could be found in the vicinity of the capital city of Lahore.

The particular social and cultural problems with carrying out the survey were identified as the following:

o A marked reluctance to talk to strangers and admit strangers even with proper references – this had been exacerbated by the deteriorating law and order situation
o A need to ensure the privacy and anonymity of respondents
o It would probably be difficult to talk to female respondents
o A lack of trained interviewers
o No marketing research culture, meaning there would be a mistrust of interviewers
o Less than 1 per cent of the population in Pakistan has telephones and the telephone service in any case was continually breaking down. There was a lack of trained telephone interviewers to administer the survey and record responses.

Another problem to be faced was the lack of a sampling frame from which to draw an appropriate sample. The Lahore City Vehicle Registration Department held all car registrations but it was impossible to extract information regarding new car registrations over the last 5 years. Interestingly this was not because the information was seen as confidential but because the information was too difficult to access. There was no computer database and the information was not stored to enable usage of the data contained in the files.

Activity 8.2

Design a research study for this market. Given the problems outlined in the case above, you will have to be innovative whilst ensuring credibility and validity.

The case study above illustrates some of the problems associated with gathering market research data across the globe. International market research is a very complex area compounded by the number of factors we need to take into account and the number of markets we may be assessing.

Secondary research

International market research often begins with secondary data. There is generally a correlation between the stage of economic development and the availability, depth and accuracy of the information. In the developed world we have become accustomed to data overload, a plethora of cheap and accurate data in many markets. The opposite is true of less developed countries where the quality of the data is variable and its accuracy uncertain. Some countries, for example, do not carry out a population census so even estimates of population size are unreliable.

The Internet is becoming the most popular tool for gathering secondary data with many useful websites easily available, often for free. The Internet has revolutionized the ability of SMEs to carry out data searches. Another useful resource for UK companies is the Department of Trade and Industry (DTI) which provides a reasonably priced service based on a vast database and experienced staff.

There are also challenges in gathering primary data as we have seen in the car security case study above.

Primary research

Carter (2003) lists the following problems in conducting international market research.

- ○ *Costs* – These vary with the United Kingdom being one of the cheapest and Japan one of the most expensive.
- ○ *Language* – In which language should the survey be conducted? Singapore with a population of 3 million has four official languages requiring four translations and four different ethnic interviewers. Interpretation of languages (translation) can be misleading and even back-translation is not perfect. A literal translation does not always capture the respondent's cultural framework which can lead to accurate but misleading information. Some concepts are very difficult to translate and may not have an exact parallel in another culture. Levels of literacy may be a problem. Whilst pictorials may be used to overcome this, they can suffer from similar problems of translation to words. Abstract concepts such as time and leisure can be problematic.
- ○ *Sample* – Rural countries offer particular problems where respondents may be geographically scattered. There may be problems in interviewing female respondents in certain cultures.
- ○ *Geography* – Where do you conduct the study? Nigeria has a desert in the north but the south is equatorial. Responses may differ widely depending on the product category. Similarly there may be tribal differences in some countries.
- ○ *Non-response* – In some countries it may be hard to find respondents as interviewers are seen as akin to 'agents of the state'. Japanese respondents tend to be falsely positive in an attempt to please the interviewer.
- ○ *Social organization* – Family-owned businesses may value secrecy about their operations and may be unwilling to divulge information.
- ○ *Terminology* – This may differ from country to country. What do we mean by health food? Affluent? Middle age? Green?

The cultural context of the host nation will determine the level of cultural bias. Some countries such as Germany, Austria and Switzerland are seen as having low cultural context, that is their responses to questions will be straightforward. This is because understanding is based on the written and spoken word. The Japanese and the Arabs are at the other extreme where the cultural context is high. These markets require more subtlety in interpretation where the way the question is answered is at least as important as the answer itself. These cultures interpret the elements surrounding the message.

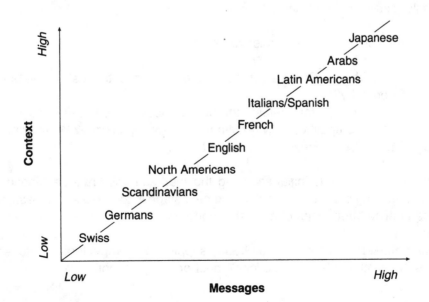

Figure 8.2 The contextual continuum of differing cultures
Source: From Usunier, adapted from Edward T. Hall

A useful way to examine other cultures is to use Lee's Self Reference Criterion (SRC). This is a four step process designed to help organizations isolate essential cultural differences.

1. Look at the situation through the eyes of the home culture.
2. Define the problem from step 1 through the eyes of the foreign culture.
3. Find the gap between the cultures in steps 1 and 2 and how this will influence the problem.
4. Bridge the gap between the cultures.

Of course this is not easy...

Scanning international markets/countries

The process of selecting an international target is often a multi-stage process as illustrated in Figure 8.3.

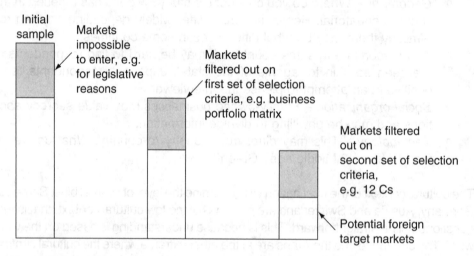

Figure 8.3 A multi-stage selection process

In the initial stage of evaluating international markets, it makes sense to scan many countries but only relatively superficially.

Three useful criteria to use at this stage are:

1. *Accessibility* – Can we get there? What is preventing us? Trade barriers? Legislation? Geography?
2. *Profitability* – What percentage of the population can afford our product? What is the level of competitive activity? What is the exchange rate? What are the payment terms?
3. *Market size* – Present and future trends.

Having undertaken this initial scanning the marketer will have developed a list of countries where marketing opportunities exist. The next stage is to make an assessment of their viability. We can define three types of market opportunity:

Existing markets – The market is already supplied by competitors. Market entry will be difficult unless the company has a superior product or new concept.

Latent markets – Potential customers exist whose needs are not being met. No competition allowing for easier market entry.

Incipient markets – Markets which may emerge in the future but do not exist at present. The nature of the product offered can be analysed in a similar way also categorizing in three ways.

We can also have three types of product:

Competitive product – Broadly similar to those already in the marketplace.

Improved product – A product which offers some improvement on existing products available but is not unique.

Breakthrough product – An innovation offering a significant competitive advantage.

We can pull these two sets of factors together to give a matrix of product/market combinations and to allow for an initial assessment of competitive advantage. This matrix allows us to evaluate the costs and risks of launching the product against the costs and risks of opening up the market (see Figure 8.4).

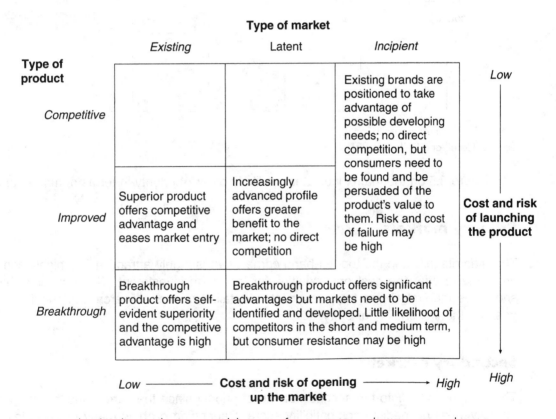

Figure 8.4 Product/market combinations and the scope for competitive advantage on market entry
Source: Gilligan and Hird (1985)

Assuming the indicators are positive after this superficial trawl, we are in a position to make a more detailed analysis of the more attractive markets.

Assessing the attractiveness of markets

Here we can use a framework similar to the directional policy matrix to map country attractiveness against corporate compatibility with each country. This is called the business portfolio matrix. Again multifactors are used and weighted to provide a composite score for attractiveness on the horizontal axis and compatibility on the vertical. The attractiveness of a country could be assessed on factors such as size, accessibility, disposable income and so on. The compatibility may be assessed on more subjective measures such as culture.

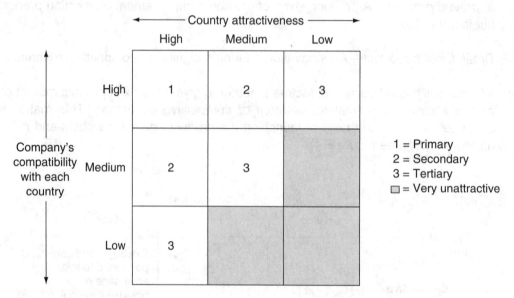

Figure 8.5 Business portfolio matrix
Source: Harell and Keifer (1993)

The Figure 8.5 on the matrix indicates the likely order of priority in terms of market entry.

Primary markets

The markets falling in the top left-hand corner, that is highly attractive and highly compatible, are likely to offer the best opportunities for long-term investment. This suggests that these should be the first choice for investment in detailed market research and should that prove positive, the first choice for entry.

Secondary markets

These markets fall into the second tranche of priority since they are hampered by a medium attractiveness or medium compatibility score. Depending on how many markets fall into the primary category, the company may decide either to undertake more detailed market research or to hold fire until the research results on the primary markets are available.

Tertiary markets

These are likely to be opportunistic markets at least in the short term.

Question 8.1

What are the problems in using this matrix?

Assuming the market passes this test we can move on to an even more detailed analysis.

The International Marketing Intelligence System

All markets passing the scanning tests above should now provide a feasible number of potential countries which require future research. A systematic method for gathering the data to allow the evaluation of candidate markets is required, that is a Marketing Intelligence System (MIS).

To be effective there must be an effective communication channel between the environment in which the company operates and the decision makers. This is always the case but the problems in international marketing research are exacerbated by geographic distance.

An effective MIS provides a solid base for strategic decisions to be made.

The 12C framework for analysis of international markets is shown in Figure 8.6 to give a structure to the data you should collect before deciding on target countries.

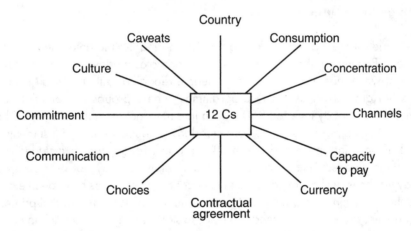

Figure 8.6 The 12 Cs
Source: Doole and Lowe (1993)

Case study

Amway expands into China

The background

China is on the verge of surpassing all known growth records. To begin with, far from being a slowly emerging economic force, it is already the world's third largest economy trailing only United States and Japan, but not for much longer. By the year 2010 it could be the world's largest. But of course the size of the economy does not equate to the standard of living. Within China itself, the major growth is taking place in the coastal regions where roughly one quarter of the population lives, a total of 300 million people, where income is set to grow at 11 per cent a year for the next ten years. To quote Lee Kuan Yew, formerly Prime Minister of Singapore, 'Never in human history have so many grown so rich so fast.'

China, with 1.2 billion people, 25 per cent of the world's population, offers the greatest single opportunity and threat for Western products.

Guadong Province, neighbouring Hong Kong, with 60 million people is China's showpiece. Since the barriers with Hong Kong ceased in 1978, its GDP has grown 13 per cent per annum and is generally proving to be the springboard for Western products. For example, Guadong is Procter & Gamble's second largest market worldwide for shampoos.

Entering the Chinese market

Patience is a virtue, creativity is a must! More open than the Japanese market, nevertheless, the careful cultivation of special relationships from influential people down to the everyday consumer is important in doing business. The word for this is guanxi – Chinese for connections. Cultivating connections is part of the culture, with word of mouth counting for more than most of the other forms of marketing communications. Whilst it is true that the market poses challenges to foreign investors, many companies are discovering the key to success is to start at the local level, learn the market, develop trust with Chinese partners, let each experience make the relationship stronger. In other words, the traditional Western approach as exemplified by the FMCG route requires serious modification – besides which the normal tools of marketing communication, that is advertising and so on, are not greatly in evidence.

Amway takes the plunge

Amway, the world's largest direct marketing firm, is gearing itself to enter the Chinese market, focusing on the Guadong Province in the short term. Amway operates worldwide via a system of personal sales people, each of whom has a number of sales people reporting to them. Much is made of door-to-door selling and what are known as 'party programmes' where groups of potential customers meet in a friend's home. It has already invested £60 million in a new factory in the province. The factory produces products for the Pacific region but these are standard products to meet consumer needs in Japan, the Philippines, Taiwan, Singapore and so on. This product range, which includes detergents, washing liquids, household cleaners and even cosmetics and vitamins, may not be appropriate for China. So whilst Amway has considerable experience in the Far East where sales have been extremely buoyant, the downside is that the Chinese market is not a mirror image of Taiwan, the Philippines and so on where capitalist economies are well established. So it has to start virtually from scratch in marketing the business in China.

Direct marketing has great potential in China. There is a history of trading stretching back hundreds of years, albeit briefly interrupted by Communist rule. The Chinese are natural entrepreneurs. With an underdeveloped retail structure, that is, few supermarkets' future – a culture of guanxi networking already established and a population with rapidly expanding disposable income – is rosy. But pitfalls abound. The market is riddled with the unscrupulous selling substandard goods with poor service, claiming to be legitimate direct marketers. The Chinese are naturally apprehensive – and they ask questions. Door-to-door cold calling is not part of the culture. But the overall portents are good. Avon, a rival direct marketer, has been in China for five years and has raked up impressive sales growth. Avon has taken the route of following the culture rather than imposing itself via heavy advertising and sales promotion. Indeed, price promotion is virtually unheard of as are discount operators.

Activity 8.3

Conduct a comprehensive macro-environmental analysis on the Chinese market, using the information in the case study and also additional secondary research. You may find the 12Cs framework useful to structure your analysis.

What are the implications for Amway's strategy?

An alternative way to assess market potential in emerging markets is offered by Cavusgil (1997).

He also uses a weighted composite score and a variety of dimensions.

Table 8.2 Dimensions, weights and measures used to assess market potential

Dimension	Weight (out of 50)	Potential measures
Market size	10	o Urban population o Electricity consumption
Market growth rate	6	o Average annual growth rate of commercial energy use o Real GDP growth rate
Market intensity	7	o GNI per capita estimates using PPP o Private consumption as a % of GDP
Market consumption capacity	5	o % share of middle class in consumption/income
Commercial infrastructure	7	o Phone lines (per 100 inhabitants) o Mobile phones (per 100 inhabitants) o Number of PCs (per 100 inhabitants) o Paved road density (km per million people) o Internet hosts (per million people) o Population per retail outlet o TVs per 1000 people
Economic freedom	5	o Economic Freedom Index o Political Freedom Index
Market receptivity	6	o Per capita imports from the United States o Trade as a percentage of GDP
Country risk	4	o Country risk rating

These market potential indicators are kept updated on the Michigan State University's globalEdge website on http://globaledge.msu.edu/ibrd/marketpot.asp.

If a country has passed all the tests in the multi-stage process, we need to determine the mode of entry.

Market entry methods

By the time an organization has to make this decision, it will already have made three others:

1. To market internationally
2. Where to market
3. What to market.

The next stage addresses how to determine the best way of entering the chosen market to optimize the potential of the chosen product range.

No way is always right. The key is to tailor the entry methods to the particular product/market situation. A mix of modes may be appropriate, and like any marketing decision we would expect it to be dynamic. There are many options to suit all types of firms. Even the size of the firm is not a useful predictor of what will work. McDonald's, for example, operates a mix of wholly owned and franchise operations; Dupont operates with wholly owned and joint venture operations.

The desired level of involvement is critical in determining the strategy with the greatest chance of success. We need to understand the firm's objectives, attitudes and commitment to successful exploitation of overseas opportunities. The choice of entry strategy is a long-term decision and needs to be made with care as it is not always possible to exit a market quickly. Any company planning to enter a foreign market should also embark on contingency planning including exit strategies.

Table 8.3 Determinants of level of involvement

Factor	Comment
Corporate objectives, ambitions, resources	Will narrow the options but not necessarily to one
Nature of the market, product category, competition	Need to know scale, number, nature and level
Nature of consumer culture	What, where, how, why and how often consumers buy
Coverage of the market	Breadth, depth and quality, dictated by consumer need
Speed of entry	Nature of product, diffusion of innovation, stage in PLC, pace of market development
Level of control	Feedback required, research information to assess effectiveness
Marketing costs	Commitment increases as these get higher
Profit payback	Paybacks tend to take longer overseas. How long will the company wait?
Investment costs	Commitment increases as these get higher
Administrative requirements	Documentation, legal requirements, foreign taxation
Personnel	Level, training, language, assimilation
Flexibility	Testing before heavy involvement, multiple entry modes, ease of exit

Market entry strategy alternatives

When we are talking about market entry strategies we essentially have two main routes. We can either:

1. Make it here and sell it there, that is export, requiring relatively little involvement or
2. Make it there and sell it there, that is overseas production, requiring a greater level of involvement.

Figure 8.7 sets out the main strategic routes with the choice of entry modes listed under each.

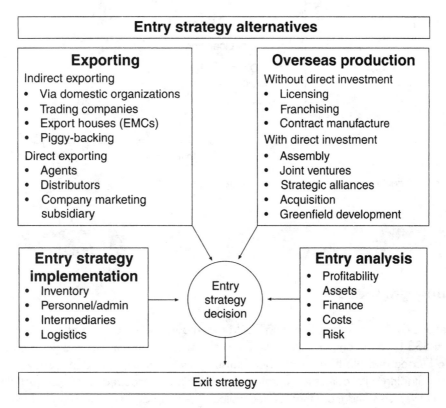

Figure 8.7 Market entry alternatives

Many texts exist on this subject so the intention here is just to give a brief overview of the issues.

To make the decision on mode of entry strategy an organization needs to address three factors.

1. What are the resources and investment necessary to enter the market?
2. To what extent does the organization want to control corporate activities in the foreign market?
3. How much knowledge can the organization gain by using this entry mode?

Figure 8.8 emphasizes the interaction between these factors on the choice of entry strategy.

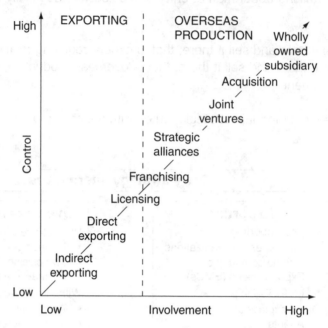

Figure 8.8 Factors in assessment of entry modes

Case study

Samsung got there

The experience of South Korea's Samsung Electronics shows how hard it can be to build brands. Today with more than $33 billion in annual sales, it is a global leader in consumer electronics: half of those sales are mainly to Europe and North America. But Samsung spends much time and money on its globalization campaign. Starting with domestic operations, the company acquired basic product development skills through joint ventures and more than 50 technology licensing agreements. Branded exports began in the early 1980s, with US prices set at a discount to those of Japanese and US competitors as a way of appealing to price-sensitive customers. Samsung also acted as a private label supplier to retailers and brands.

It slowly learned the requirements of its markets by conducting extensive consumer research and building up its overseas sales and manufacturing operations in the United States, Germany, the United Kingdom and Australia. The company invested its R&D budgets, and by the early 1990s its aspirations had led it to invest in products and technologies (for example, flat screen monitors and televisions, digital high-definition televisions and digital mobile phones) that would raise its brand profile.

Finally, in the late 1990s Samsung launched its global brand with more than $1 billion in advertising, including sponsorship of the Olympic Games. It formed alliances with high-tech partners such as US telephone company Sprint, spending more than $7 billion, or 5 per cent of sales, on R&D from 1996 to 2000 and upward of $400 million on brand advertising in 2001 alone. In the meantime, the company positioned itself as a premium brand by shifting its channel focus from mass merchants to category killers. In a 2003 survey of global brands, Interbrand, a brand strategy and design consultancy, ranked Samsung as number 25, with a brand worth $10.8 billion – a 31 per cent increase from the previous year.

Extracted from Gao, Woetzel and Wu (2003).

Activity 8.4

Read the business press to build up a folder of how different companies are entering markets. Try to understand their rationale for choosing a particular mode of entry. Also try to build a folder of exit strategies. Sometimes we can learn as much from the companies who have failed as those who have succeeded.

We have talked about how to approach international markets and implicitly mentioned culture several times but since it is such an important factor, we now look at culture as an issue in its own right.

Culture

The development of international marketing strategies is based on a sound understanding of the similarities and differences that exist in countries around the world. The whole area of culture is very complex. Here we focus on the sociocultural influences which are relevant to buyer behaviour in international markets. There are many definitions of culture. One is listed above in the key definitions section. Another widely accepted one is by Linton (1945) who describes culture as 'the configuration of learned behaviour and results of behaviour whose component elements are shared and transmitted by members of a particular society'. Or more colloquially 'the way we do things around here'. Culture is made up of many different factors which are reduced to eight cultural components in Figure 8.9.

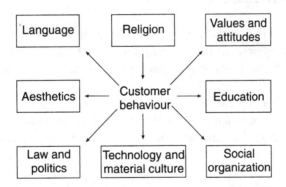

Figure 8.9 The components of culture
Source: Adapted from Terpstra and Sarathy (2000)

Activity 8.5

For each of the eight components in Figure 8.9, list five ways in which these might affect marketing within different cultures.

Role of IT

Much has been made of the role of IT and in particular the Internet in opening up the global marketplace.

According to Orlikowski (2000), companies use IT in three ways:

1. *Reinforcing the status quo* – These companies use IT to retain their existing ways of doing things. So, for example, the introduction of a new network system which allows the development of a new database to replace an old paper-based system. This type of application of IT makes little difference to organizational processes.
2. *Enhancing the status quo* – These companies use IT to augment, improve and refine their existing work processes. For example, a company might use the Internet to provide customers with more efficient communication, delivering personalized messages in real time.
3. *Transforming the status quo* – These companies treat IT as a philosophy and use IT to alter substantially their existing ways of doing business. Users tend to be more knowledgeable about technology, are motivated to use it in recasting work practices and are supported by institutional conditions and resources, including a co-operative culture. For example, an SME may use the Internet to reach new international markets in an economic way.

Case study

How e-business transformed Intel

In 1998, when Intel chairman Andy Grove first vowed to reinvent Intel as a '100 per cent e-corporation', Andy Bryant, the CFO, simply did not believe the Internet was the way to go. 'I sat there and said, "Great, we replaced fax machines with online orders. Big deal"', he recalls.

But he has become an Internet convert, making sure that every new business application within Intel is based on Internet or new commerce technologies. His early contempt for online ordering evaporated overnight when he realized that 26 per cent of orders were coming in after hours. That flexibility, he says, 'is value to our customers'.

Today, the e-transformation is practically complete. Last year, for example, 90 per cent of the company's revenue – $31.4 billion – came through e-commerce transactions. Likewise, Intel procured more than $5.5 billion in supplies over the net last year, an increase from zero in 1999. Already 70 per cent of direct and 35 per cent of indirect materials are linked to Intel via the net. This year, Bryant's goal is to move all materials transactions online.

In all, Intel has launched more than 300 e-business projects since 1998.

Bryant sees the true promise of the Internet as obscured by the attention given to web-based companies such as Amazon when Intel benefits most from internal uses of e-business.

'The Internet', he insists, 'is about how to run a company.'

Adapted from Best Practice, Intel: How e-business transformed Intel and CFO Andy Bryant, www.ebusinessforum.com.

The Internet has also affected consumer behaviour but despite all the hype estimates suggest that it only accounts for around 5 per cent of world trade. Figures are hard to verify and dynamic. Estimates are that B2B e-commerce reached $1 trillion by the end of 2003. The Department of Trade and Industry estimates that half of UK firms order goods and services online. Table 8.4 shows the numbers of active users during a month. This is obviously lower than estimates of access.

Table 8.4 Active Internet users in November 2003 (selected countries)

Country	Internet users (million)
Australia	8
Brazil	9
France	13
Germany	26
Hong Kong	2
Italy	14
Japan	29
Netherlands	8
Spain	8
Sweden	5
Switzerland	3
United Kingdom	20
United States	131
Total	279

Source: www.clickz.com

Activity 8.6

The Internet is constantly expanding. Go online and get up to date on the current situation. What can you find out about purchasing behaviour? What are the top websites?

Case study

OTITIS Elevators

Jonathan McKay was sipping a Gin & Tonic in the business class section of a Malaysian Airlines on a flight to Kuala Lumpur. Having spent the last 3 hours discussing the intricacies of international marketing strategies with François Bertrand, the Chief Recruitment Consultant of Techno Careers South East Asia on the merits of marketing, Jonathan was considering whether to pursue a potential new senior marketing at OTITIS in South East Asia, an assignment that François was currently working on.

OTITIS Elevators is an engineering company that specializes in design implementation and instillation of elevators as well as escalators in new and refurbished buildings. The company does not have a marketing orientation and is currently taking advantage of the growth opportunities in the construction industry in

South East Asia. Having spoken to Jonathan, François believes that OTITIS should attempt to become more customer focused and could learn a lot from acquiring marketing expertise from another industry.

Jonathan has spent 20 years working for Demented Fruits, a company specializing in the manufacturing, sales and marketing of tinned fruits, and was wondering whether he would be suitable for such a role.

Having arrived back from his trip a friend of his had downloaded information regarding OTITIS from the Internet and had forwarded it to him.

Strategic marketing issues requiring consideration

1. Within the context of B2B and B2C marketing – Analyse and evaluate the extent and in what way is the marketing of elevators similar to the marketing of tinned fruits?
2. How would the process of prioritizing market size and opportunity across different Asian be similar or different for OTITIS as compared to Demented?

Discussion

There are several ways to attempt the evaluation of the scenario but one could include the following in an answer plan: (Please note that this is not a full answer) One should appreciate that the buyer behaviour environments are different even though tinned fruits have a B2B segment level of involvement and complexity of products are much than the customized elevator market. Availability of secondary information in developed markets will be different in both sectors, although in lesser developed markets both organizations are likely to need to deal with information deficits making it difficult to analyse therefore increasing the risk of making risky marketing decisions, potentially affecting shareholder value. Market research activities are likely to be different and therefore require different structure. Different types of distribution strategies will also be required as more technical know-how would be needed for elevators. Intensive distribution would be a better strategy for tinned fruits as compared to a more focused concentric distribution. The use of distributors in international is a means of accessing international markets at a lower risk but the type of services required by OTITIS will be different. Communication is also likely to be different whereas OTITIS is likely to be facing different stakeholders, differentiated strategies requiring tailored word of mouth and direct selling as opposed to advertising with only slight adaptation to imagery and language would be necessary for Demented.

Summary

This unit provided an overview of how a company may select potential foreign markets. The choice of market normally occurs after a multi-stage process of filtering. Organizations need to refine their information search after successive stages. To systemize the process it is useful to set up a marketing intelligence system with a framework to collect data. The choice of export market should be based on a thorough evaluation of criteria which influence potential success abroad.

Once a potential foreign target market is selected, the organization has to determine its entry strategy. Two main routes exist: exporting and overseas production. One of the most important factors to consider is the level of involvement of the company.

If a company does not want to allocate significant resources to its overseas activities, it may opt for exporting home-produced goods into a foreign market. This is an appropriate strategy for firms in early stages of foreign activities. They may choose indirect exporting where an external partner takes over all the activities related to the foreign market, or direct exporting where the company installs direct representation in the foreign market or employs a foreign distributor.

If the organization wants to commit more fully to international marketing they may decide to produce overseas. Their choice of mode will be determined in part by the level of control they wish to exercise with the extreme being a wholly owned subsidiary.

The role of culture in this process is emphasized as well as the impact of IT on decision-making. The Internet is discussed and its part in changing business-to-business and consumer markets.

Further study

Brooke, R., Palmer, R. (2004) *The New Global Marketing Reality*, Palgrave, Macmillan.

Child, P.N. (2002) 'Taking Tesco global', *The McKinsey Quarterly*, 3, www.mckinseyquarterly.com.

Doole, I., Lowe, R. (2001) *International Marketing Strategy*, 3rd edition, Thomson Learning, London.

Hofstede, G. (1993) 'Cultural constraints in management theories', *Academy of Management Executive*, **7**(1), pp. 81–93.

Keegan, W., Schlegelmilch, B.B. (2001) *Global Marketing Management: A European Perspective*, Pearson Education Ltd.

http://globaledge.msu.edu. This is the homepage of Michigan State University's award-winning site which offers a very comprehensive compilation of information relating to international business topics.

Hints and tips

Examiners will expect you to demonstrate understanding of the global marketplace.

Try to gain a detailed understanding of a sample of other countries. Keep a folder on each of your chosen countries. It helps to take one developed country and one less developed one as a minimum. Compare and contrast your chosen countries.

Keep a file on the Internet. What are the trends? How are organizations using the Internet to market themselves. Keep examples of good and bad practices. You can learn from both of them.

Bibliography

Carter, S. (2003) *International Marketing Strategy*, Butterworth-Heinemann, Oxford.

Cavusgil, S.T. (1997) 'Measuring the Potential of Emerging Markets: An Indexing Approach', *Business Horizons*, Jan/Feb, **40**(1), pp. 87–91.

Doole, I., Lowe, R. (2001) *International Marketing Strategy*, 3rd edition, Routledge, London.

Gao, P., Woetzel, J.R., Wu, Y. (2003) 'Can Chinese brands make it abroad?' *The McKinsey Quarterly*, 4, www.mckinseyquarterly.com.

Linton, R. (1945) *The Science of Man in the World of Crisis*, New York, Columbia University Press.

Orlikowski, W.J. (2000) 'Using technology and constituting structures: A practice lens for studying technology in organizations', *Organizational Science*, **11**(4), pp. 404–428.

Porter, M.E. (1986) *Competition in Global Industries*, edited by Porter, in Research colloquium (Harvard Business School of Business Administration series), Harvard Business School Press.

Terpstra, V., Sarathy, R. (2000) *International Marketing*, 8th edition, Dryden Press.

unit 9 defining competitive advantage

Learning objectives

We come now to the final unit. The purpose of this unit is to answer the question 'So what?' We have spent all this time beavering away, collecting data, analysing it and evaluating it. Now we have to review the implications of our findings for the organization's future. In this unit you will:

o Develop an understanding of the sources of competitive advantage (see syllabus 4.3)

o Identify the implications of the external and internal analyses for the company's strategic direction (see syllabus 4.8)

o Appreciate the importance of buyer behaviour in defining competitive advantage (see syllabus 4.4, 5.2).

After completing this unit you will be able to:

o Define a source of competitive advantage for an organization

o Be able to plan scenarios effectively

o Assess the risk implicit in decision-making.

This part of the course is the link between Analysis and Evaluation and Strategic Marketing Decisions. In Strategic Marketing Decisions one will be identifying a range options that give rise to competitive advantage in order to select the appropriate ones that will maximize shareholder value. At this stage it is important to appreciate how sources of competitive advantage are analysed and evaluated.

Key definitions

Competitive advantage – is the means by which a company can outperform its competitors and earn higher than average profits.

Core competence – is something which the company does or possesses which gives it an edge over its competitors. It can be defined as the skills and technologies that enable the company to provide a particular benefit to customers. It may be a source of competitive advantage.

Scenario planning – is the identification of a diverse range of potential futures.

What is competitive advantage?

Competitive advantage is the means by which a company can outperform its competitors and earn higher than average profits.

The problem with competitive advantage is that competitors have an irritating habit of copying it. Managers need to discourage this as much as possible. Economists describe many entry barriers (economies of scale, high capital investment, patents etc.), but in fact the two most common barriers to entry are brands and core competencies based on organizational effectiveness (Doyle, 1994). These are linked. Successful brands give consumers confidence and make them reluctant to switch. The core competencies of the organization are the specific technical and marketing skills which allow it to enhance the perceived value of the brand by increasing the perceived benefits and reducing the costs of ownership.

Competitive advantages normally have the following characteristics.

Core competence

This is something which the company does or possesses which gives it an edge over its competitors. It can be defined as the skills and technologies that enable the company to provide a particular benefit to customers (Hamel and Prahalad, 1996, p. 219). But bear in mind that while all core competences are sources of competitive advantage, not all competitive advantages derive from core competences. Some may stem from history, or a particular location, or preferential access to materials or labour and so on. It is important to distinguish between what has made you successful in the past and what will make you succeed in the future.

To be a core competence, the following three criteria must be met:

1. *Customer value* – 'A core competence must make a disproportionate contribution to customer-perceived value.'

Honda's competence at making engines delivers value to customers using its cars, motorcycles or lawnmowers. They may not understand or even see the engine, but they perceive the benefits that its quality provides.

2. *Competitive differentiation* – If a competence is widely spread throughout an industry, it should not count as core unless the firm's level of competence is demonstrably superior to that of its competitors. Thus engine manufacture is a core competence for Honda, but not for Ford Motor Company.

3. *Extendibility* – The core competence must be capable of leading to a wide array of new products and services. Thus Honda's engine technology has been extended from motorcycles to cars, to lawnmowers, marine engines and portable generators. Canon's competence in imaging will find applications in any of the burgeoning range of products that use a display.

It may be a brand name – would you pay more for Gucci sunglasses than for your own label? Most people would, because they believe that higher quality is implied by the brand – and that price premium adds to higher profits.

Or it may be through distribution superiority. Viking Direct, a UK office equipment and stationery company, delivers the same or next day, which is of great benefit to its target segment of buyers – small firms and SOHOs (Small Office, Home Office).

Doing things badly – a special incompetence, perhaps, or competitive disadvantage – offers opportunities for other firms to gain a competitive advantage. So a low level of service can open the doors for a company offering a high level of service.

Creates imperfect competition

Almost by definition, competitive advantage is gained by creating imperfect competition. If all firms (and their products) were equal, then there would be no competitive advantage.

Sustainable

A successful competitive advantage is sustainable, not transitory. It should not be easily copied because the company wants to hold on to it in the long term. To some extent, the idea of a sustainable competitive advantage is an ideal for which we should strive but in reality is often hard to attain. Technological advantage, for example, is often fleeting as competitors are able to reverse engineer the product. Successful brand names, on the other hand, tend to be more long lived.

Fit with external environment

A competitive advantage derives not only from competitors' weaknesses (and therefore your strengths) but also from the market and conditions. Environmental dynamics can throw up threats and opportunities over time.

A well-thought-out SWOT analysis is invaluable here. The changes in the environment will happen anyway – there is nothing you can do to stop them. The trick is to be prepared for them and to adapt them to your advantage.

Route to above-average profits

The whole purpose of developing a competitive advantage is to earn above-average (for the industry) profits. By creating imperfect competition, attacking competitors' weaknesses and adapting to changes in the environment, the company gains an advantage in the market in which it operates.

Competitive advantage has an underlying assumption that the advantage is the result of past and present activity, and that it delivers (potentially at least) superior profits. However, competitors will be striving constantly to match and overtake the advantage, so the superior profits must be reinvested to stay ahead. The source–position–performance (SPP) model summarizes this process (Figure 9.1).

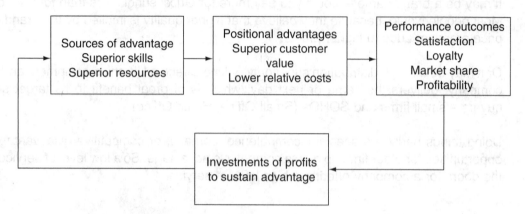

Figure 9.1 The source–position–performance (SPP) model of competitive advantage
Source: Day and Wensley (1988)

Like all models, this oversimplifies the complexity of real life, but it summarizes the structure. Let us look at the elements in turn.

Sources of advantage

The ability of a company to do things better than its direct competitors arises from superior skills or superior resources. The competitors are usually those in the strategic group in which we are competing for our served market. An alternative perspective is that we should benchmark each operation, skill or resource against the best at that particular activity, regardless of industry or market.

Superior skills

These stem from the ability of people in the firm to carry out certain tasks at a superior level. This assumes a generalized capability that does not depend on single individuals, and that can be maintained over time (though it may need support and reinvestment to do so). We can distinguish between:

- o people, that is the ability of personnel to perform certain functions at a superior level, for instance in manufacturing or the salesforce and
- o systems, that is the way the organization can deliver its products and services, or implement strategies, or respond to change.

Thus many Japanese firms have superior skills in manufacturing, such that they can produce good-quality products very efficiently. Singapore Airlines' skill at recruiting, selecting, training and managing cabin staff enables it to deliver superior personal service.

Superior resources

Resources may be financial or physical: ready availability of cash, for example, location, a state-of-the-art manufacturing plant. To a large extent, these may be regarded as interchangeable, since cash may be used to build the plant; this of course is the point of the feedback loop in the SPP model. Day and Wensley list distribution coverage and breadth of salesforce as resources, which shows the difficulty of precise definition. Is Gillette's superb ability to gain very wide and deep distribution for its products the result of resources (large salesforce) or skills (highly trained salespeople, well managed and motivated)? Perhaps it does not matter too much, as long as we can diagnose where the superiority lies, and what position of advantage it leads to. A strong brand may be a superior resource, perhaps for marketing people the major one. We may think of Sony whose name on a product immediately suggests quality and reliability; this is a competitive advantage when launching new products.

Positions of advantage

Positional advantage is delivered by the sources, and may be either superior customer value or lower relative costs. Both can be understood within the framework of the value chain popularized by Porter (1985). Porter's generic strategies of differentiation and low cost (which we will discuss soon) mirror the two categories of advantage. Lower costs are easy to understand. An example is Komatsu, which designed its cranes and earthmoving equipment so that they could be manufactured at significantly lower costs than those from the main American competitors. Superior customer value requires greater explanation, but is practised by, for example, Procter & Gamble, which aims to offer only brands that deliver superior consumer benefits.

Competitive advantage delivers to target customers an offer that they perceive as providing superior value to the offers of competitors. Customers will buy the best value as they see it. Their perception of value can be broken down into three elements, as shown in Figure 9.2.

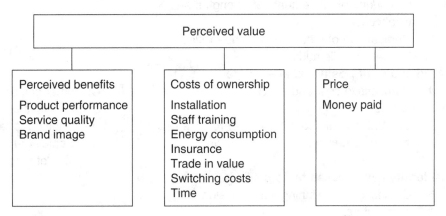

Figure 9.2 Determinants of perceived value

Since the purpose of competitive advantage is to deliver superior perceived value, companies need to work on reducing the costs of ownership and price, and increasing the customer's perception of benefits. The price paid is straightforward enough, but the other two factors require more explanation.

Basically, price and costs of ownership form barriers to purchase. Companies need to focus on reducing these as much as is realistic. Typical costs of ownership are listed above. Switching costs refer to the costs associated with changing suppliers. We may lose a loyalty bonus or have to pay a penalty charge, for example. Direct Line, a UK online insurance broker, reduces the switching costs of its new home and contents insurance customers by paying the penalty charges imposed by the previous supplier. Another financial services supplier, First Direct, a UK online bank, aims to reduce the switching costs associated with changing banks by handling much of the paperwork. There are also psychological costs associated with change – will the new product work as well as the old one?

The perceived benefits are the positive side of the equation. They give customers a reason to buy from you. The product's performance and design are usually critical, but so also are the more intangible elements of the total offering. The quality of the services augmenting the product are important, as are the staff who deliver them, since service delivery is inextricable from the people who deliver the service. Another intangible is brand image – what does ownership of that brand mean to that customer? This is probably particularly important in relation to aspirational brands, but applies in virtually every context.

The products that an organizational buyer purchases say something about them and their organization. Are they technically advanced? Are they traditional, safe but unexciting? Another example is found in the motor industry, where the image of car as an extension of self is almost a cliché. Qualitative research has revealed that owners of the same make of car often see themselves in the same way, and are attracted to similar features of the image. The exception is Saab owners, who all see the car they buy as projecting them as individual – all of them!

Methods for assessing advantage We can assess advantage from competitor-centred or customer-focused assessment, or both. It is preferable to use both, as any one method will address only a part of the total picture. Thus the views of customers do not tell us how the firm developed the advantage they value, and a superiority over competitors may not be valued by customers. We can classify methods as in Table 9.1.

Table 9.1 Methods of assessing advantage

Competitor-centred	Customer-focused
A. **Assessing sources** (distinctive competences)	
1. Management judgements of strengths and weaknesses	
2. Comparison of resource and capabilities	
3. Marketing skills audit	
B. **Indicators of positional advantage**	
4. Competitive cost and activity comparisons	5. Customer comparisons of attributes of firm versus competitors
a. Value chain comparisons of relative costs	a. Choice models
b. Cross-section experience curves	b. Conjoint analysis
	c. Market maps
C. **Identify key success factors**	
6. Comparison of winning versus losing competitors	
7. Identifying high leverage phenomena	
a. Management estimates of market share elasticities	
b. Drivers of activities in the value chain	
D. **Measure of performance**	
	8. Customer satisfaction surveys
	9. Loyalty (customer franchise)
10a. Market share	10b. Relative share of end-user segments
11. Relative profitability (return on sales and return on assets)	

Source: Day and Wensley (1988)

Let us now look at how this relates to Porter and Day's generic strategies.

Porter's generic strategies

The best-known advocate of generic strategies has been Michael Porter. Porter (1980) set out three generic strategies, although he later subdivided the third (see Figure 9.3). Porter argued that only the generic strategies – cost leadership, differentiation or focus – would lead to success. Companies that try to use a mixed strategy (e.g. cost leadership and differentiation) would be 'stuck in the middle'. This idea that a successful strategy demands a single-minded focus has been a lasting and influential one ('stick to the knitting'), although Porter has become less dogmatic on this.

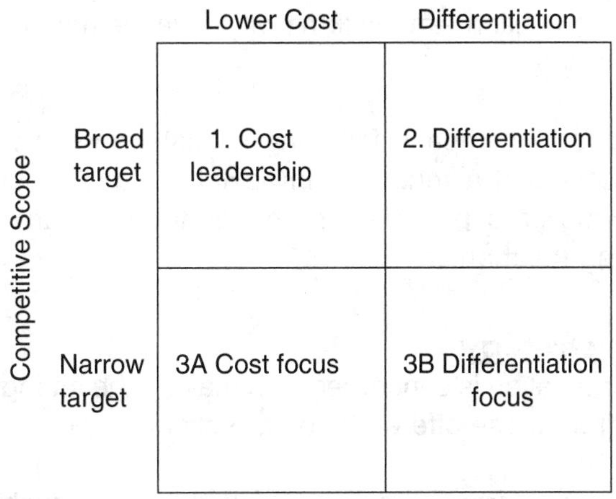

	Lower Cost	Differentiation
Broad target	1. Cost leadership	2. Differentiation
Narrow target	3A Cost focus	3B Differentiation focus

Competitive Scope (vertical axis label)

Figure 9.3 Porter's generic strategies competitive advantage
Source: Porter (1985)

As we said earlier, the search for competitive advantage is the route to above-average profits. Why would these strategies lead to higher profits? Let us look at the relationship between prices, costs and profits for both the low-cost producer and the manufacturer of the differentiated product (Figure 9.4).

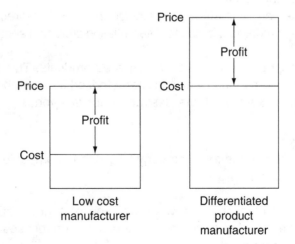

Figure 9.4 An example of competitive advantage
Source: Porter (1985)

207

Profit is obviously the differential between price and cost, so above-average profit can be earned either by charging a premium price (and accepting a higher cost for producing a differentiated product) or by keeping costs low (and often accepting a lower price for your product). These two extremes can be viewed as the two ends of a spectrum, with companies occupying positions along it.

Overall cost leadership

This strategy has the following advantages:

- o Reduced bargaining power of suppliers, as high-volume production generated by low prices will lead to your holding large accounts with the manufacturers.
- o Reduced bargaining power of customers – customers have little room to bargain against the company selling at the lowest prices.
- o Substitutes are less attractive because of lower prices.
- o Reduced competition – many firms will leave the market rather than compete with a low-cost producer.

The two dangers for a company following a cost-leadership strategy are the entry of even lower-cost producers and a reduction in flexibility. Low production costs normally mean an investment in production capabilities and hence the company is likely to become fixed in one method of servicing the market.

Differentiation strategy

A strategy of differentiation is concerned with making the intangible and/or tangible aspects of a product different from those offered by other sellers.

Firms sell unique products in the hope of building a franchise among less price-sensitive buyers. The reduced price sensitivity, and hence the higher price charged, tends to lead to higher profits. The elements of product quality, product innovation, style and image are all important factors in creating differentiation.

Differentiation as a strategy has a number of advantages:

- o Reduced bargaining power of consumers. The differences between products mean that products are not directly comparable – the consumer either has to pay the price or settle for something different.
- o Substitutes are less attractive because they are not direct substitutes.
- o Reduced competition, because differentiation creates a series of monopolistic sub-markets.

Many markets support a variety of differentiated products. This tends not to be the case with low-cost producers – a market which is characterized by a number of low-cost producers tends to suffer from price wars which are destructive for everyone.

Focus strategy

Porter's final strategy – the focus strategy – relates to companies which specialize in a certain segment of the market.

There is considerable overlap between this type of segmentation and that of differentiation strategy. The difference lies in the focus – segmentation focuses on the market and differentiation on the product differences.

A focus strategy has the following advantages:

- ○ Reduced competition, by meeting the needs of a particular segment rather than the larger market.
- ○ Reduced pressure from substitutes, by focusing on the special needs of one segment.

Its main problems occur first, by being dependent on just one segment, which is obviously risky. Second, by being successful and enlarging the segment, other, larger manufacturers may be attracted into it. Companies can either use a cost focus, aiming for cost leadership in a small market, or differentiate within the niche.

Day's matrix

Day proposed a similar model (Figure 9.5), using customer price sensitivity and real or perceived differences in the product offering as the axes. The strategies are virtually identical to Porter's, though the approach is more market oriented; that is, the axes represent customers' needs and perceptions, whereas Porter's reflect the company's viewpoint.

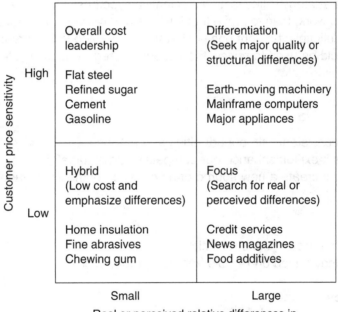

Figure 9.5 Day's matrix
Source: Day (1984)

How to use generic strategies

Generic strategies are best viewed as a framework within which to think about the strategic possibilities for your organization.

Consideration of these generic options leaves us a long way short of a specific action plan and resource deployment which will secure for us a competitive advantage. Use these generic strategies as a first step in the process of developing a strategy, but do not be tied by them. Use them creatively and adapt them to your own business and its environment.

As with all general business models, the generic strategy approach has been subject to criticism. In particular, it has been pointed out that some companies are successful while combining supposedly incompatible strategies. Increasingly, low cost has become an absolute essential rather than an option. Merely to compete at all, for instance in the global car market, companies in the mass market have to achieve cost levels similar to the leading rivals. Only then can they think about differentiation. The Japanese have shown that high quality is not only compatible with low costs, but may actually be cheaper.

Firms also need to take account of both supply and demand factors. Using the demand perspective, a firm may find one or more segments that offer profitable opportunities, but it may also have to serve less profitable segments. In many markets, the premium sector can be highly profitable, but manufacturers may also have to serve the price-sensitive standard or economy segment too, so that they can offer a complete range.

Strategy selection

Having developed a range of strategic options, they need to be evaluated before making a decision about which direction to pursue.

Evaluating a strategy is like testing a scientific hypothesis. It is far easier to prove that it is false and does not work, than to prove that it is true and will work. It is impossible to guarantee that a strategy is definitely the right one – what you want to do is to increase the odds in your favour. Criteria should be used to review the various strategic options systematically. A suggested list is given below.

Suitability

- Is it consistent with opportunities and threats?
- Does it exploit/enhance our competitive advantage?
- Does it create a new source of advantage? Is the advantage sustainable?

Validity

- Are the assumptions realistic?
- Are they based on reliable and valid information?

Consistency

- Are the elements of the strategy consistent?
- Do they meet the objectives?

Feasibility

- Do we have the resources?
- Will the operating managers be able to implement it?

Vulnerability

- Are projected outcomes based on sound data and assumptions?
- Are the risks of failure acceptable?
- Do we have contingency plans?
- Can the decision be reversed?

Potential

- ○ Rewards
- ○ Do the projected outcomes meet the objectives for the business?
- ○ Are they acceptable to the shareholders?

Once the strategy that best fits these criteria has been chosen, the means of implementing it can be examined.

Five-star web service

So what's the secret of a successful dot.com? Dean Gurden finds out how Hotelnet founder Richard Knowles hit the profitability jackpot in just 9 months.

'Try to do one thing and do it well' is the key to online prosperity, according to Hotelnet's founder Richard Knowles. It's a formula that appears to be working, judging by the continuing success of the holiday booking website he originally set up as a hobby.

Knowles was quick to spy the potential for an online hotel booking service, establishing the site hotelnet.co.uk in 1995, long before most of the travel giants weighed into the market. Self-financing the business rather than seeking venture capital backing, Hotelnet became profitable in just 9 months. Six years later, it's still making money.

'I remember taking my wife and daughter out to dinner to celebrate the first thousand hits in a week', recalls Knowles. 'Now we measure it in terms of the number of minutes before the next thousand hits. We had in excess of 16 000 people visiting the site yesterday. That's individual visitors not hits.'

Hotelnet, part of Holidaybreak, now has partnerships with hotel groups throughout the United Kingdom, Europe and North America including Superbreaks and Best Western. People can search and book 50 000 hotel rooms in more than 200 countries. Currently, more than 70 per cent of these hotels provide live online bookings, with this figure increasing to 100 per cent in 2001.

What has made Hotelnet a success is having a focused business plan and sticking to it. Rather than follow many of the other travel sites and offer extras such as flights or cars, Hotelnet's content is almost exclusively accommodation.

Many of our competitors try to be all things to all men; they offer flights, car hire, information about surroundings, booking restaurants and so on, and, to be perfectly honest, I almost don't consider them to be competitors, because they're trying to be all singing, all dancing, we-do-everything sites. As far as I'm concerned, our job is to present and sell hotel rooms.

The site has started offering some local information covering the United Kingdom, however. People looking for a hotel in Oxford, for example, can find out details about local attractions in the area. But Knowles stresses that this information is outsourced. The Superbreaks site also offers theatre breaks, where you book a theatre ticket and hotel as a package. Branching out into areas such as car hire, however, is just too far removed from Hotelnet's core business of providing hotel rooms.

For a company doing very well by new economy rules, Knowles' ideas about business are traditional. It was always his goal to set up a long-term business, rather than go for the quick sell.

I've never seen the benefit of becoming another dot.com company making another thumping great loss with a large staff. I want to run Hotelnet as a good long-term viable business, controlling the inputs and outputs. The business plan is quite simple and hasn't changed – it's a business and I want it to continue to make money.

He also looks rather different from the public perception of the dot.com entrepreneur which, coupled with his sales and marketing background, make him very persuasive to potential corporate customers.

My knowledge of what people want to hear, from my sales and marketing background, has meant that I tend to be able to talk to people in terms that they understand. I'm fifty-one years old. I'm not the popularly perceived spotty youth of dot.com culture. So many people seem surprised when I turn up to meetings in a collar, tie and suit with a normal haircut and no ponytail.

Originally, the site generated revenue by charging hotels to register. Now, by far the biggest proportion of revenue comes from commissions on bookings made.

Rather than blowing the budget on expensive marketing campaigns, Knowles has spent relatively little on advertising, opting instead to invest in search engine tags, reciprocal links with other sites and the occasional strategically placed banner advert.

The content of the site may have altered little over the past 6 years, but its design and the structure beneath it has seen some radical changes. Over the years, Knowles has brought in external designers to revitalize the site and, the company developed and built its own booking engine. But all these changes have kept to Knowles' blueprint for the company:

The principle behind the site is do your job, give the people the information they want, and make it as easy and friendly a proposition as you can.

Despite this desire for simplicity, Knowles is quick to acknowledge that websites have to keep changing to stay apace with technological advances. He is excited at the introduction of broadband and how that will help site visitors decide which hotel will best suit them.

He is also very much aware that Hotelnet will have to change and offer more alternative interfaces to cope with innovations in communication devices, such as the new G3 mobile phones.

It's simply going to be a matter of offering better facilities in a faster manner. Somebody once said to me: 'Hotelnet is one year in front of anyone else in the marketplace, but where will you be in one year's time?' I look fondly upon the person who made that comment to me, and I've always tried to make sure we're one year in front.

Knowles also credits Hotelnet's continuing success to the honesty and integrity of its approach. 'Unlike many websites, people aren't forced to register upfront. Clearly, to pay for a hotel, people need to provide personal details, but this isn't requested until after they've seen information about the hotels. *We honestly present hotels, so that people can make a good and reasonable decision*', he says. As the founder of a profitable dot.com, Knowles' enthusiasm for the business is unflagging and his advice to any fledgling start-ups out there is simple:

'Stay abreast of the technology, but don't compromise your principle of doing one job and doing it well.'

Source: Internet World (2001).

One of the ways to help you to define your strategy is to use scenario planning.

Scenario planning

Scenario planning is all about identifying a diverse range of potential futures. This can be done by the senior management group, the whole company, with external people, whatever. The important thing is that the group has alternative perspectives to offer and that all are familiar with the environmental analysis which has already been undertaken.

A simple approach involves the following four steps:

1. *Identify the critical variables* – The long-term drivers of the business should be identified and evaluated on the basis of their importance to the business and the level of certainty associated with their direction.
2. *Develop possible strings of events* – The key drivers of change are those which are important but not predictable. Important but certain variables will feature in each scenario but their impact is likely to be predictable and as such will not have a major impact on any of the scenarios. The group needs to brainstorm a number of different sequences to determine how the timing of these change agents affects the organization.
3. *Refine the scenarios* – At the end of stage 2 the group should have a range of scenarios. Some of these will be more believable than others. The group needs to assess the potential scenarios on the grounds of internal consistency, credibility and recognizability.
4. *Identify the issues arising* – Those scenarios which survive need to be reviewed. Have any critical events or outcomes been identified which would have a major impact on the organization?

Although there are many weaknesses to scenario planning, it does have strengths. It helps managers understand the critical issues in its environment. It prepares them for discontinuities and helps with crisis management. And finally it helps put fundamental strategic issues on the management agenda.

Assessing risk

All strategic options carry an element of risk as the future is uncertain. Our scenario planning carries with it an explicit or implicit prediction of the activities of many groups, but particularly those of customers and competitors. All of these have an element of unpredictability.

The Ansoff matrix can be used to allow us to determine the general level of risk. Continuing in existing markets is likely to offer the lowest level of risk since the organization is familiar both with the market and the technology. Market development and new product development each add to the risk by adding newness; the first in terms of the customer base and the second in terms of technology. The unknown always carries risk. The fourth option within the Ansoff classification is diversification, which is generally accepted as the most risky as it involves a leap in the unknown in terms of marketing and technological knowledge.

But although Ansoff offers a useful backdrop and enables an assessment of background risk, it does not drill down into the detail of individual scenarios. Since scenarios are based on assumptions, we need to think about the impact on the organization if those assumptions are flawed. It may make sense to carry out sensitivity analysis which tests the effect that changing assumptions may have on the outcome of a strategy. This sort of 'What if' analysis allows us to develop a better understanding of the risks inherent in an option should the future differ from our projections. All options are re-evaluated for each possible change and these recalculated outcomes will give us an indication of the sensitivity of the strategies to each assumption. The extensive use of spreadsheets and computer modelling means that it is relatively easy to manipulate variables to assess the implications of underlying assumptions.

Activity 9.1

We are manufacturing air conditioning units. Set up a spreadsheet with the following simple assumptions.

Sales: 3000 units

Price: $10 per unit

Variable cost: $4 per unit

Fixed costs: $100 000

Assess the effect of these on profit by changing each of these factors 10 per cent up or down, separately and then in total. Play around with potential scenarios. What are the worst possible and best possible outcomes, assuming only a 10 per cent variation in each factor?

Add another layer of complexity. Factor in some environmental variables which may affect demand. Let us say a 10 per cent increase in disposable income will lead to a 20 per cent increase in sales, a 2 °C increase in annual temperature will add 15 per cent. Add some more of your own. Again just play with the figures to assess the impact that factors beyond your control can have on outcomes.

Case study

Shell Chemicals

Companies which operate in fast moving environments or particularly unstable markets need to make scenario planning a priority. Shell Chemicals were hit by the oil crises of 1974 and 1978, and as a result developed a two-dimensional matrix linking environmental risk to business sector profitability. This allows Shell managers to focus greater attention on more attractive markets and to evaluate more closely the impact of more variables. Shell focuses on the most likely and worst case scenarios to minimize the risks to the company. This process allows the company to develop rigorous plans and has the added benefit of training managers to be objective and critical.

Aaker (1998) suggests the following responses to uncertainty dependent on the likely immediacy and potential impact.

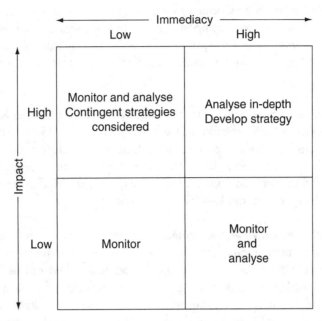

Figure 9.6 Strategic uncertainty categories
Source: Aaker (1998), p. 109

Fallen companies rarely make it back to the top

Competitive advantage is bound up with a company's history and needs to be matched to market opportunity. When it is lost or the market evolves, the consequences are generally fatal

General Douglas MacArthur, expelled from the Philippines, proclaimed 'I shall return' and arrived 3 years later as pro-consul in Tokyo. Arnold Schwarzenegger has repeatedly fulfilled his promise 'I'll be back.'

But in business, they rarely come back. The great names of global business a century ago included US Steel, International Harvester and American Tobacco. Midland Bank was once the largest financial institution in the world. ICI – Britain's biggest industrial company for most of the past century – dominated the chemical industry across the empire. Pan American and Eastern were America's leading airlines, when Sears was as dominant a retailer as Wal-Mart is today. These market leaders not only lost pre-eminence but ceased to be significant players in their industries.

In the 1980s, the management of AT&T believed that if the company freed itself from regulatory restriction by relinquishing local telephone monopolies it could reinvent itself for the world in which computers and telecommunications were emerging. Their vision of the evolution of the industry was right: the hope that their company could play a big role in it was wrong. When a company loses the top slot, it rarely regains it.

So the apparent renaissance of Marks and Spencer, which last week reported strong recovery in sales and profits, may be an exception to the rule. There are others. IBM was humbled when the personal computer it had itself pioneered took away much of the mainframe market it had dominated. But, the company restructured. Never to recapture its former glory, but again to be one of the best regarded companies in its industry. BMW is also a remarkable comeback story. The company was twice on its knees. Once in 1945, when to be Germany's leading aircraft engine producer was an unenviable and unviable position. Its troubles were compounded by Soviet seizure of its main plant. Again in 1959, when unsuccessful diversification brought it to the edge of bankruptcy. In the following decade, the company would establish a seemingly durable position as one of the world's best regarded automobile businesses.

Competitive advantage is bound up with a company's history and needs to be matched to market opportunity. Loss of competitive advantage is generally fatal. The US Steel declined in part because of complacency, but more because competitive advantage in steel production no longer rested on owning large plants in the United States. American Tobacco failed to sustain its marketing capabilities in the face of innovative competition from companies such as Philip Morris. AT&T's strength rested on its monopoly and there were nimbler rivals in markets it aspired to enter.

Other businesses begin to fail when their competitive advantages remain intact but markets evolve in a way that makes these advantages less relevant. There is more hope here, as IBM illustrates: the reconfigured business recognized that its strength had rested less on the technical excellence of its hardware than the quality of its customer support. Sears, however, failed to reassert its reputation with customers and strengths in the supply chain when the shoppers of middle America began to drive to out-of-town malls. Under Herbert Quandt's leadership, BMW established a new market segment – the high-performance saloon – which utilized its capacity to use a German workforce to achieve precision engineering in mass production.

M&S is an intermediate case. In failing to adapt to changing retail trends in the 1990s, the company eroded but did not altogether destroy its customer relationships and supply chain strengths. Not quite Eastern Airlines – whose competitive advantage had vanished, though its market grew – nor yet a BMW, whose competitive advantage remained intact as its market vanished.

But the prognosis for M&S is better than for many other businesses facing market turbulence. If Europe's energy companies lose the protection of vertical integration, can they find new roles? Can telecom giants reinvent themselves where control of the last mile of wire is no longer decisive? When the historic sources of underlying competitive advantage have gone, businesses rarely return.

Source: John Kay, *Financial Times* 16 January 2007

Summary

Strategy is defined as the set of decisions taken to determine how an organization allocates its resources and achieves sustainable competitive advantage in those markets. Its sources are superior skills and superior resources, which deliver the positional advantages of superior customer value and lower relative costs. These link to Porter's generic strategies of differentiation and cost leadership. The performance outcomes of these advantages are of enhanced market share and profitability.

We examined how to use scenario planning and how to assess risk using sensitivity analysis to allow the organization to make sound strategic marketing decisions.

Further study

Aaker, D.A. (1998) *Strategic Market Management*, 5th edition, Wiley.

Tenaglia, M., Noõonan, P. (1992) 'Scenario based strategic planning: A process for building top management consensus', *Planning Review*, March–April, pp. 3–18.

Hints and tips

Examiners are interested in your ability to see the strategic implications of your analysis. Since we cannot change the past, the future is important. Practise your ability to plan alternative future scenarios which are logically based on your analysis. Include a sensitivity analysis which allows the company to make strategic decisions effectively.

Return to the learning outcomes listed in Unit 1. Remember that the examiners will be assessing you on these. Make sure that you feel comfortable with your ability to demonstrate each of these. Look at the syllabus in Appendix 4. Work through each of these, checking your understanding.

Bibliography

Ansoff, I. (1988) *Corporate Strategy*, Penguin Books, Harmondsworth.

Day, G.S. (1984) *Strategic Market Planning: The Pursuit of Competitive Advantage*, West Publishing, Minneapolis.

Day, G.S., Wensley, R. (1988) 'Assessing advantage: A framework published by American Marketing Association for Diagnosing Competitive Superiority', *Journal of Marketing*, **52**, April, pp. 1–20.

Doyle, P. (1994) *Marketing Management and Strategy*, Prentice-Hall International, Hemel Hempstead.

Gurden, D. (2001) *In Internet World,* Mecklermedia Corporation, Westport, Conn.

Hamel, G., Prahalad, C.K. (1996) *Competing for the Future*, Harvard Business School Press, Boston, MA.

Johnson, G., Scholes, K. (1997) *Exploring Corporate Strategy*, Prentice-Hall International, Hemel Hempstead.

Porter, M.E. (1980) *Competitive Strategy: Techniques for Analysing Industries and Competitors*, New York: The Free Press.

Porter, M.E. (1985) *Competitive Advantage:* Creating and Sustaining Superior Performance, New York: The Free Press.

appendix 1
guidance on examination preparation

You are now nearing the final phase of your studies and it is time to start the hard work of exam preparation.

During your period of study you will have become used to absorbing large amounts of information. You will have tried to understand and apply aspects of knowledge that may have been very new to you, while some of the information provided may have been more familiar. You may even have undertaken many of the activities that are positioned frequently throughout your coursebook, which will have enabled you to apply your learning in practical situations. But whatever the state of your knowledge and understanding, do not allow yourself to fall into the trap of thinking that you know enough, understand enough or, even worse, that you can just take it as it comes on the day.

Never underestimate the pressure of the CIM examination.

The whole point of preparing this text for you is to ensure that you never take the examination for granted, and that you do not go into the exam unprepared for what might come your way for three hours at a time.

One thing is sure: there is no quick fix, no easy route, no waving a magic wand and finding you know it all.

Whether you have studied alone, in a CIM study centre or through distance learning, you now need to ensure that this final phase of your learning process is tightly managed, highly structured and objective.

As a candidate in the examination, your role will be to convince the Senior Examiner for this subject that you have credibility. You need to demonstrate to the examiner that you can be trusted to undertake a range of challenges in the context of marketing and that you are able to capitalize on opportunities and manage your way through threats.

You should prove to the Senior Examiner that you will be able to apply knowledge, make decisions, respond to situations and solve problems. Essentially you will be expected to demonstrate an ability to:

- Analyse
- Critically evaluate
- Understand models and techniques
- Draw implications
- Develop scenarios
- Develop implementation plans.

Very shortly we are going to look at a range of revision and exam preparation techniques and time management issues, and encourage you towards developing and implementing your own revision plan, but before that let us look at the role of the Senior Examiner.

A bit about the Senior Examiners!

You might be quite shocked to read this, but while it might appear that the examiners are 'relentless question masters' they actually want you to be able to answer the questions and pass the exams! In fact, they would derive no satisfaction or benefits from failing candidates; quite the contrary, they develop the syllabus and exam papers in order that you can learn and then apply that learning effectively so as to pass your examinations. Many of the examiners have said in the past that it is indeed psychologically more difficult to fail students than pass them.

Many of the hints and tips you find within this Appendix have been suggested by the Senior Examiners and authors of the coursebook series. Therefore you should consider them carefully and resolve to undertake as many of the elements suggested as possible.

The Chartered Institute of Marketing has a range of processes and systems in place within the Examinations Division to ensure that fairness and consistency prevail across the team of examiners, and that the academic and vocational standards that are set and defined are indeed maintained. In doing this, CIM ensures that those who gain the CIM Certificate, Professional Diploma and Postgraduate Diploma are worthy of the qualification and perceived as such in the view of employers, actual and potential.

Part of what you will need to do within the examination is be 'examiner friendly' – that means you have to make sure they get what they ask for. This will make life easier for you and for them.

Hints and tips for 'examiner friendly' actions are as follows:

- Show them that you understand the basis of the question, by answering *precisely* the question asked, and not including just about everything you can remember about the subject area.
- Read their needs – how many points is the question asking you to address?
- Respond to the question appropriately. Is the question asking you to take on a role? If so, take on the role and answer the question in respect of the role. For example, you could be positioned as follows:

  'You are working as a Marketing Assistant at Nike UK' or 'You are a Marketing Manager for an Engineering Company' or 'As Marketing Manager, write a report to the Managing Partner.'

These examples of role-playing requirements are taken from questions in past papers:

o Deliver the answer in the format requested. If the examiner asks for a memo, then provide a memo; likewise, if the examiner asks for a report, then write a report. If you do not do this, in some instances you will fail to gain the necessary marks required to pass.

o Take a business-like approach to your answers. This enhances your credibility. Badly ordered work, untidy work, lack of structure, headings and subheadings can be off-putting. This would be unacceptable in the work situation, likewise it will be unacceptable in the eyes of the Senior Examiners and their marking teams.

o Ensure the examiner has something to mark: give them substance, relevance, definitions, illustration and demonstration of your knowledge and understanding of the subject area.

o See the examiner as your potential employer or ultimate consumer/customer. The whole purpose and culture of marketing is about meeting customers' needs. Try this approach – it works wonders.

o Provide a strong sense of enthusiasm and professionalism in your answers; support it with relevant up-to-date examples and apply them where appropriate.

o Try to do something that will make your exam paper a little bit different – make it stand out in the crowd.

All of these points might seem quite logical to you, but often in the panic of the examination they 'go out of the window'. Therefore it is beneficial to remind ourselves of the importance of the examiner. He/she is the 'ultimate customer' – and we all know customers hate to be disappointed.

As we move on, some of these points will be revisited and developed further.

About the examination

In all examinations, with the exception of Marketing in Practice at Professional Certificate level, Marketing Management in Practice at Professional Diploma level and Strategic Marketing in Practice at Professional Postgraduate Diploma level, the paper is divided into two parts:

1. Part A – Mini-case study = 50 per cent of the marks
2. Part B – Option choice questions (choice of two questions from four) = 50 per cent of the marks.

Let us look at the basis of each element.

Part A – Mini-case study

This is based on a mini-case or scenario with one question, possibly subdivided into between two and four points, but totalling 50 per cent of marks overall.

In essence you, the candidate, are placed in a problem-solving role through the medium of a short scenario. On occasions, the scenario may consist of an article from a journal in relation to a well-known organization: for example, in the past Interflora, easyJet and Philips, among others, have been used as the basis of the mini-case.

Alternatively, it will be based upon a fictional company, and the examiner will have prepared it in order that the right balance of knowledge, understanding, application and skills is used.

Approaches to the mini-case study

When undertaking the mini-case study there are a number of key areas you should consider.

Structure/content

The mini-case that you will be presented with will vary slightly from paper to paper, and of course from one examination to the next. Normally the scenario presented will be 400–500 words long and will centre on a particular organization and its problems or may even relate to a specific industry.

The length of the mini-case study means that usually only a brief outline is provided of the situation, the organization and its marketing problems, and you must therefore learn to cope with analysing information and preparing your answer on the basis of a very limited amount of detail.

Time management

There are many differing views on time management and the approaches you can take to managing your time within the examination. You must find an approach to suit your way of working, but always remember, whatever you do, you must ensure that you allow enough time to complete the examination. Unfinished exams mean lost marks.

A typical example of managing time is as follows.

Your paper is designed to assess you over a three-hour period. With 50 per cent of the marks being allocated to the mini-case, it means that you should dedicate somewhere around half of your time to both read and write-up the answer on this mini-case.

Do not forget that while there is only one question within the mini-case, it can have a number of components. You must answer all the components in that question, which is where the balance of times comes into play.

Knowledge/skills tested

Throughout all the CIM papers, your knowledge, skills and ability to apply those skills will be tested. However, the mini-cases are used particularly to test application, that is your ability to take your knowledge and apply it in a structured way to a given scenario. The examiners will be looking at your decision-making ability, your analytical and communication skills and, depending on the level, your ability as a manager to solve particular marketing problems.

When the examiner is marking your paper, he/she will be looking to see how you differentiate yourself, looking at your own individual 'unique selling points'. The examiner will also want to see if you can personally apply the knowledge or whether you are only able to repeat the textbook materials.

Format of answers

On many occasions, and within all examinations, you will most likely be given a particular communication method to use. If this is the case, you must ensure that you adhere to the requirements of the examiner. This is all part of meeting customer needs.

The likely communication tools you will be expected to use are as follows:

- Memorandum
- Memorandum/report
- Report
- Briefing notes
- Presentation
- Press release
- Advertisement
- Plan.

Make sure that you familiarize yourself with these particular communication tools and practise using them to ensure that, on the day, you will be able to respond confidently to the communication requests of the examiner. Look back at the Customer Communications text at Certificate level to familiarize yourself with the potential requirements of these methods.

By the same token, while communication methods are important, so is meeting the specific requirements of the question. This means you must understand what is meant by the precise instruction given. *Note the following terms carefully*:

- *Identify* – Select key issues, point out key learning points, establish clearly what the examiner expects you to identify.
- *Illustrate* – The examiner expects you to provide examples, scenarios and key concepts that illustrate your learning.
- *Compare and contrast* – Look at the range of similarities between the two situations, contexts or even organizations. Then compare them, that is ascertain and list how activities, features and so on agree or disagree. Contrasting means highlighting the differences between the two.
- *Discuss* – Questions that have 'discuss' in them offer a tremendous opportunity for you to debate, argue, justify your approach or understanding of the subject area – *caution*, it is not an opportunity to waffle.
- *Briefly explain* – This means being succinct, structured and concise in your explanation, within the answer. Make your points clear, transparent and relevant.
- *State* – Present in a clear, brief format.
- *Interpret* – Expound the meaning of, make clear and explicit what it is you see and understand within the data provided.
- *Outline* – Provide the examiner with the main concepts and features being asked for and avoid minor technical details. Structure will be critical here, or else you could find it difficult to contain your answer.
- *Relate* – Show how different aspects of the syllabus connect together.
- *Critically evaluate* – Review and reflect upon an area of the syllabus, a particular practice, an article and so on, and consider its overall worth in respect of its use as a tool or a model and its overall effectiveness in the role it plays.

Source: Worsam, Mike, *How to Pass Marketing*, Croner (1989).

Your approach to mini-cases

There is no one right way to approach and tackle a mini-case study, indeed it will be down to each individual to use their own creativity in tackling the tasks presented. You will have to use your initiative and discretion about how best to approach the mini-case. Having said this, however, there are some basic steps you can take.

o   Ensure that you read through the case study at least twice before making any judge-ments, starting to analyse the information provided or, indeed, writing the answers.

o   On the third occasion read through the mini-case and, using a highlighter, start marking the essential and relevant information critical to the content and context. Then turn your attention to the question again, this time reading slowly and carefully to assess what it is you are expected to do. Note any instructions that the examiner gives you, and then start to plan how you might answer the question. Whatever the question, ensure the answer has a structure: a beginning, a structured central part of the answer and, finally, always a conclusion.

o   Keep the context of the question continually in mind: that is, the specifics of the case and the role which you might be performing.

o   Because there is limited material available, you will sometimes need to make assump-tions. Do not be afraid to do this, it will show initiative on your part. Assumptions are an important part of dealing with case studies and can help you to be quite creative with your answer. However, do explain the basis of your assumptions within your answer so that the examiner understands the nature of them, and why you have arrived at your particular outcome. *Always ensure that your assumptions are realistic.*

o   Only now are you approaching the stage where it is time to start writing your answer to the question, tackling the problems, making decisions and recommendations on the case scenario set before you. As mentioned previously, your points will often be best set out in a report or memo-type format, particularly if the examiner does not specify a communication method.

o   Ensure that your writing is succinct, avoids waffle and responds directly to the questions asked.

Part B – Option choice questions

Part B is worth 50 per cent of the marks also. You will be asked to answer two questions from four, each of the two being worth 25 marks each.

Realistically, the same principles apply for these questions as in the case study. Communication formats, reading through the questions, structure, role-play, context and so on – everything is the same.

Part B will cover a number of broader issues from within the syllabus and will be taken from any element of it. The examiner makes the choice, and no prior direction is given to students or tutors on what that might be. Something you should consider is that each of these questions will not singularly assess one area of the syllabus, but will be more complex and assess a number of different areas from within the syllabus, namely two or more.

As regards time management in this area, you should have used half your time for the mini-case and you should have around half the time remaining. This provides you with around 45 minutes to plan and write a question review and revise your answers. Keep practising – use a cooker timer, alarm clock or mobile phone alarm as your timer and work hard at answering questions within the timeframe given.

Specimen examination papers and answers

To help you prepare and understand the nature of the paper, go to www.cim.co.uk/learning zone to access Specimen Answers and Senior Examiner's advice for these exam questions. During your study, the author of your coursebook may have on occasions asked you to refer to these papers and answer the questions. You should undertake these exercises and utilize every opportunity to practise meeting examination requirements.

The specimen answers are vital learning tools. They are not always perfect, as they are answers written by students and annotated by the Senior Examiners, but they will give you a good indication of the approaches you could take, and the examiners' annotations suggest how these answers might be improved. Please use them.

The CIM learning zone website provides you with links to many useful case studies which will help you to put your learning into context when you are revising.

Key elements of preparation

One Senior Examiner suggests the three elements involved in preparing for your examination can be summarized thus:

- o Learning
- o Memory
- o Revision.

Let us look at each point in turn.

Learning

Quite often students find it difficult to learn properly. You can passively read books, look at some of the materials, perhaps revise a little, and regurgitate it all in the examination. In the main, however, this is rather an unsatisfactory method of learning. It is meaningless, shallow and ultimately of little use in practice. Additionally, it leads to likely problems in the examination.

For learning to be truly effective it must be active and applied. You must involve yourself in the learning process by thinking about what you have read, testing it against your experience by reflecting on how you use particular aspects of marketing, and how you could perhaps improve your own performance by implementing particular aspects of your learning into your everyday life. You should adopt the old adage of 'learning by doing'. If you do, you will find that passive learning has no place in your study life.

Below are some suggestions that have been prepared to assist you with the learning pathway throughout your revision:

- o Always make your own notes, in words you understand, and ensure that you combine all the sources of information and activities within them.
- o Always try to relate your learning back to your own organization.
- o Make sure you define key terms concisely, wherever possible.
- o Do not try to memorize your ideas, but work on the basis of understanding and, most important, applying them.

- o Think about the relevant and topical questions that might be set – use the questions and answers in your coursebooks to identify typical questions that might be asked in the future.
- o Attempt all of the questions within each of your coursebooks since these are vital tests of your active learning and understanding.

Memory

If you are prepared to undertake an active learning programme then your knowledge will be considerably enhanced, as understanding and application of knowledge does tend to stay in your 'long-term' memory. It is likely that passive learning will stay only in your 'short-term' memory.

Do not try to memorize parrot-fashion; it is not helpful and, even more important, examiners are experienced in identifying various memorizing techniques and therefore will spot them as such.

Having said this, it is quite useful to memorize various acronyms such as SWOT, PEST, PESTLE, STEEPLE or, indeed, various models such as Ansoff, GE matrix, Shell directional and so on, as in some of the questions you may be required to use illustrations of these to assist your answer.

Additionally, with the new syllabus there is also a requirement not just to use the models and acronyms but also to show you understand how to use the models and various techniques. Therefore ensure your understanding is very thorough and developed.

Revision

The third and final stage to consider is 'revision', which is what we will concentrate on in detail below. Here just a few key tips are offered.

Revision should be an ongoing process rather than a panic measure that you decide to undertake just before the examination. You should be preparing notes *throughout* your course, with the view to using them as part of your revision process. Therefore ensure that your notes are sufficiently comprehensive that you can reuse them successfully.

For each concept you learn about, you should identify, through your reading and your own personal experience, at least two or three examples that you could use; this then gives you some scope to broaden your perspective during the examination. It will, of course, help you gain some points for initiative with the examiners.

Knowledge is not something you will gain overnight – as we saw earlier, it is not a quick fix; it involves a process of learning that enables you to lay solid foundations upon which to build your long-term understanding and application. This will benefit you significantly in the future, not just in the examination.

In essence, you should ensure that you do the following in the period before the real intensive revision process begins.

- o Keep your study file well organized, updated and full of newspaper and journal cuttings that may help you formulate examples in your mind for use during the examination.
- o Practise defining key terms and acronyms from memory.

- o Prepare topic outlines and draft answers, perhaps in report format as opposed to essay style questions. Even think about developing discussion documents and so on to enhance your approach.
- o When you start your intensive revision, ensure it is planned and structured in the way described below. And then finally, read your concentrated notes the night before the examination.

Revision planning

You are now on a critical path – although hopefully not too critical at this time – with somewhere in the region of between four and six weeks to go to the examination. The following hints and tips will help you plan out your revision study.

- o You will, as already explained, need to be very organized. Therefore, before doing anything else, put your files, examples, reading material and so on in good order, so that you are able to work with them in the future and, of course, make sense of them.
- o Ensure that you have a quiet area within which to work. It is very easy to get distracted when preparing for an examination.
- o Take out your file along with your syllabus and make a list of key topic areas that you have studied and which you now need to revise. You could use the basis of this book to do that, by taking each unit a step at a time.
- o Plan the use of your time carefully. Ideally you should start your revision at least six weeks prior to the exam, so therefore work out how many spare hours you could give to the revision process and then start to allocate time in your diary, and do not double-book with anything else.
- o Give up your social life for a short period of time. As the saying goes 'no pain – no gain'.
- o Looking at each of the subject areas in turn, identify which are your strengths and which are your weaknesses. Which areas have you grasped and understood, and which are the areas that you have really struggled with? Split your page into two and make a list on each side. For example:

Analysis and Evaluation	
Strengths	**Weaknesses**
Audit – PEST, SWOT, models	Ratio analysis
Portfolio analysis	Market sensing
	Productivity analysis
	Trend extrapolation
	Forecasting

- o Break down your list again and divide the points of weakness, giving priority in the first instance to your weakest areas and even prioritizing them by giving them a number. This will enable you to master the more difficult areas. Up to 60 per cent of your remaining revision time should be given over to that, as you may find you have to undertake a range of additional reading and also perhaps seeking tutor support if you are studying at a CIM Accredited Study Centre.
- o The rest of the time should be spent reinforcing your knowledge and understanding of the stronger areas, spending time testing yourself on how much you really know.
- o Should you be taking two examinations or more at any one time, then the breakdown and managing of your time will be critical.

o Taking a subject at a time, work through your notes and start breaking them down into subsections of learning, and ultimately into key learning points, items that you can refer to time and time again, which are meaningful and that your mind will absorb. You yourself will know how you best remember key points. Some people try to develop acronyms, or flowcharts or matrices, mind maps, fishbone diagrams and so on, or various connection diagrams that help them recall certain aspects of models. You could also develop processes that enable you to remember approaches to various options. (But do remember what we said earlier about regurgitating stuff, parrot-fashion.)

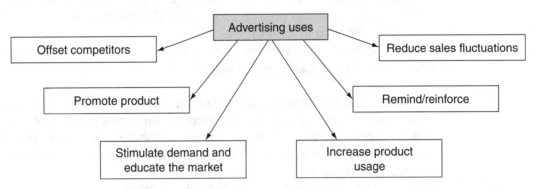

Figure A1.1 Use of a diagram to summarize key components of a concept
Source: Adapted from Dibb, Simkin, Pride and Ferrell, *Marketing Concepts and Strategies*, 4th edition, Houghton Mifflin (2001)

Figure A1.1 is just a brief example of how you could use a 'bomb-burst' diagram (which, in this case, highlights the uses of advertising) as a very helpful approach to memorizing key elements of learning.

o Eventually you should reduce your key learning to bullet points. For example, imagine you were looking at the concept of Time Management – you could eventually reduce your key learning to a bullet list containing the following points in relation to 'Effective Prioritization':

    – Organize
    – Take time
    – Delegate
    – Review.

Each of these headings would then remind you of the elements you need to discuss associated with the subject area.

Time management has been highlighted as a key issue with the new examinations, and the new Senior Examiners are keen that students understand the limitations of the examination and the depth of answers required. Therefore getting as much practice as possible would be extremely valuable to your examination success.

o Avoid getting involved in reading too many textbooks at this stage, as you may start to find that you are getting confused overall.
o Look at examination questions on previous papers, and start to observe closely the various roles and tasks they expect you to undertake and, importantly, the context in which they are set.
o *Use the specimen exam papers and specimen answers* to support your learning and see how you could actually improve upon them.

o Without exception, find an associated examination question for the areas that you have studied and revised, and undertake it (more than once if necessary).

o Without referring to notes or books, try to draft an answer plan with the key concepts, knowledge, models and information that are needed to successfully complete the answer. Then refer to the specimen answer to see how close you are to the actual outline presented. Planning your answer, and ensuring that key components are included, and that the question has a meaningful structure, is one of the most beneficial activities that you can undertake.

o Now write the answer out in full, within the time-constrain, without the use of computers. (At this stage, you are still expected to be the scribe for the examination and present handwritten work. Many of us find this increasingly difficult as we spend more and more time using our computers to present information. Do your best to be neat. Bad handwriting is often offputting to the examiner.)

o When writing answers as part of your revision process, also be sure to practise the following essential examination techniques:

- Identify and use the communication method – requested by the examiner.
- Always have three key parts to the answer – an introduction, middle section that develops your answer in full and a conclusion. Where appropriate, ensure that you have an introduction, main section, summary/conclusion and, if requested or helpful, recommendations.
- Always answer the question in the context or role set
- Always comply with the nature and terms of the question
- Leave white space – do not overcrowd your page. Leave space between paragraphs, and make sure your sentences do not merge into one blur. (Do not worry – there is always plenty of paper available to use in the examination.)
- Count – how many actions the question asks you to undertake and double-check at the end that you have met the full range of demands of the question.
- Use examples – to demonstrate your knowledge and understanding of the particular syllabus area. These can be from journals, the Internet, the press or your own experience.
- Display your vigour and enthusiasm for marketing

o Remember to think of the Senior Examiner as your customer, or future employer, and do your best to deliver what is wanted to satisfy their needs. Impress them and show them how you are a 'cut above the rest'.

o Review all your practice answers critically, with the above points in mind.

Practical actions

The critical path is becoming even more critical now as the examination looms. The following are vital points:

o Have you registered with CIM?

o Do you know where you are taking your examination? CIM should let you know approximately one month in advance.

o Do you know where your examination centre is? If not find out, take a drive, time it – whatever you do, do not be late!

o Make sure you have all the tools of the examination ready. A dictionary, calculator, pens, pencils, ruler and so on. Try not to use multiple shades of pens, but at the same time make your work look professional. *Avoid using red and green as these are the colours that will be used for marking.*

In the words of one Senior Examiner, this is how you should pass brilliantly:

- Show you can critically analyse and evaluate a range of information and situations
- Be creative and innovative in providing marketing solutions
- Present your work in a professional style
- Ensure your recommendations are well argued and justified.

Summary

Above all you must remember that you personally have invested a tremendous amount of time, effort and money in studying for this programme and it is therefore imperative that you consider the suggestions given here as they will help to maximize your return on your investment.

Many of the hints and tips offered here are generic and will work across most of the CIM courses. We have tried to select those that will help you most in taking a sensible, planned approach to your study and revision.

The key to your success is being prepared to put in the time and effort required, planning your revision and, equally important, planning and answering your questions in a way that will ensure that you pass your examination on the day.

The advice offered here aims to guide you from a practical perspective. Guidance on syllabus content and developments associated with your learning will become clear to you as you work through this coursebook. The authors of each coursebook have given subject-specific guidance on the approach to the examination and on how to ensure that you meet the content requirements of the kind of question you will face. These considerations are in addition to the structuring issues we have been discussing throughout this Appendix.

Each of the authors and Senior Examiners will guide you on their preferred approach to questions and answers as they go. Therefore where you are presented with an opportunity to be involved in some activity, or undertake an examination question either during or at the end of your study units, do take it. It not only prepares you for the examination, but helps you learn in the applied way we discussed above.

Here, then, is a last reminder:

- Ensure you make the most of your learning process throughout.
- Keep structured and orderly notes from which to revise.
- Plan your revision – do not let it just happen.
- Provide examples to enhance your answers.
- Practise your writing skills in order that you present your work well and your writing is readable.
- Take as many opportunities to test your knowledge and measure your progress as possible.
- Plan and structure your answers.
- Always do as the question asks you, especially with regard to context and communication method.
- *Do not leave it until the last minute!*

The writers would like to take this opportunity to wish you every success in your endeavours to study, revise and pass your examinations.

Karen Beamish
Academic Development Advisor

answers and debriefings

Unit 1

Debriefing Question 1.1

Outline solution – please read the proposed only after having considered your own answer

It is interesting to note that although all three companies are competing within the same industry, each company, due to their possessing different resources and capabilities, would need to position the same product differently within their companies. The first company, having large financial resources and technical ability but no brand image or corporate reputation in the cancer market, need to establish their reputation and because of having no history they would have no qualms about taking on any competitor present in their particular disease segment in order to establish themselves. The third company on the other hand has similar resources and technical capability but additionally they have an established heritage in the cancer segments. This heritage has an advantage as well as a disadvantage as the company is likely to need to position the new product alongside its existing older products, as they may not be able to afford to cannibalize their existing business. The second company is too small and has limited sales and marketing capability; they are an effective product development company but would need to partner with a bigger player to effectively compete. In conclusion the same product in the same market is likely to be positioned differently by different companies in the same industry due to capability constraints.

Debriefing Question 1.2

Your answers should vary because the motivations and requirements of the different product categories are individual. But, for example, the benefit of going to a grocery retailer may be for convenience, value for money and so on. The retailer gains enhanced profit and increased shareholder value. A professional qualification will offer you increased knowledge and hence self-confidence as well as greater professional standing. The awarding body makes some profit but also safeguards the quality of the profession and its long-term reputation.

So the philosophy of marketing is that of mutually beneficial exchange; everyone is happy. A very positive picture but how do we go about achieving this?

Debriefing Activity 1.3

Different stakeholders have different perceptions of value. Shareholders are interested in the economic benefit they gain. Customers are interested in the perceived value of the proposition to them. Employees value the perceived worth of their efforts compared to their rewards and so on.

Unit 2

Debriefing Question 2.1

Market share

%		2000	2001	2002	2003	2004
Stokes Services	Value	40	40	41	37	31
	Volume	25	29	32	29	28
Woods for Work	Value	32	40	41	42	44
	Volume	20	24	18	21	16
Edwards Enterprises	Value	20	13	13	11	9
	Volume	50	48	50	50	56

1. In 2004, Woods for Work has a dominant value share of 44 per cent with its nearest competitor Stokes Services at 31 per cent, giving it a relative market share of 1.4. Edwards Enterprises trails with only 9 per cent in value terms. In volume terms the reverse is true. Edwards Enterprises are clearly winning the most contracts with 56 per cent of the market, followed by Stokes Services at 28 per cent and Woods for Work at 16 per cent.

2. Trends over time show Edwards Enterprises as gaining the volume of contracts but only relatively small ones. Hence their volume share has increased but value share has suffered (50–56 per cent and 20–9 per cent, respectively). By contrast, Woods for Work have won a lower percentage of contracts over time, down from 20 to 16 per cent but managed to improve their value share position to 44 from 32 per cent over the 5 years. In value terms they took over the No.1 slot from Stokes Services in 2003. Stokes Services were No. 1 in value (40 per cent) in 2000.

3. Market size trends

	2000	2001	%	2002	%	2003	%	2004	%	Cum % 2000–2004
Revenue in Euros (m)	25	30	+20	32	+7	38	+19	45	+18	+80
Number of contracts	20	21	+1	22	+1	24	+9	25	+4	+25

The overall picture is of growth although value has grown ahead of volume. Value growth has been steady and high; volume growth steady but low. This and the evidence from the previous tables suggests an increasing divide in the market with a few large orders and a lot of small contracts, an effect that has possibly intensified over the five-year period.

4. Woods for Work appear to have increasingly focused on a few but large contracts, possibly reflecting an increased focus on Customer Relationship Management and a move towards a partnership/preferred supplier approach. Edwards Enterprises have spread their risk far more and aimed for many but small contracts. Stokes Services cover the middle ground spreading risk to some extent but not with such a fragmented base as Edwards Enterprises. The average value of a Woods for Work contract in 2004 is €500 000, for Stokes Services €200 000 and for Edwards Enterprises €29 000.

5. It is hard to tell which has been the most successful on the basis of this information. My initial response would be Woods for Work. They have appeared to have captured the premium end of the market and have minimized their set up costs by narrowing down their negotiations. But there is much information that we do not have, such as profit,

client base and so on the downside of the Woods for Work strategy is that they are quite exposed if they lose one contract. The opposite is true of Edwards Enterprises who can afford to lose a contract with negligible impact but possibly have high set up costs and do not appear to be charging a premium. Stokes Services may, by occupying the middle ground, have the best of both worlds.

Debriefing Activity 2.2

This exercise should help you think of your organization in a more holistic way rather than just focusing on the marketing perspective. You may find that your organization has set objectives that it cannot measure. Or that objectives are inconsistent, for example improve quality whilst reducing costs, cut staff costs while increasing service expectations.

As with any framework, there are advantages and disadvantages. Kaplan and Norton were keen to move away from relying on financial measures in isolation since they regarded accounting figures as unreliable and subject to manipulation. In addition, changes in the business environment do not show up in financial results and hence the opportunity for early warning could be missed if we were to rely entirely on financial results. But there is a danger that the balanced scorecard could become part of a political process. The four perspectives each focus on a different stakeholder group (shareholders, customers, managers and employees). There is a danger that each of these interest groups may use the scorecard to apply pressure to have a greater regard for their interests, hence unbalancing the scorecard.

Debriefing Activity 2.4

In terms of structuring an answer you need to include an overview of the reasons for why performance measures would be important for the New Zealand Tourist Board, they are not a profit-making organization but they are a government agency competing for budget with other agencies and have a need to justify their existence. They therefore have a need to show the funding bodies the returns they are likely to get for their investment. Ultimately the need for the government funding bodies is to make themselves look good to the electorate and maximize their votes so they will seek funding opportunities that will ultimately gain the support of their voters. The Tourist Board will need to develop an additional communication campaign targeting the government bodies (lobbying) and showing why their cause at that particular point in time is far more justified than any other and performance measures are part of the communication objectives showing what they are likely to achieve with the external communication campaign.

What performance measures would you choose? You will need to develop a rationale and justification for each performance measure you develop and have a good mix of both financial and non-financial measures.

Debriefing Activity 2.5

You need to appreciate that performance measures form part of your marketing plan with an objective of gaining funding through the relevant stakeholders buying – in and adopting your ideas/concepts. You should highlight that in this case as it is a small business the marketing plan is likely to be equivalent to a business plan emphasizing the overall strategic plan of the business. The investors will need to be confident that your operations will be efficient and that costs will be adequately controlled. They are also likely to be interested in the timings of when the business will start generating a positive cash flow. Therefore a number of financial and non-financial measures need to be developed.

Debriefing Activity 2.6

Although the question is not specifically asking about performance measures it is implicit within the question as you are expected in the CIM syllabus to show the skills required of a senior strategic marketing executive by demonstrating that you need to justify to shareholders, in this case, the benefits of this growth opportunity (opportunity costs) compared to other opportunities available. You therefore need the tools to evaluate the benefits which are in fact performance measures. In terms of identifying the costs involved you need to demonstrate your knowledge of assessing the size of the market and your method of market entry. Now the question is how readily is the information available in the country you wish to launch? What are the implications for your company and to what extent does it increase the risk of potentially making a poor decision? What will you do to overcome this? These are all points that you need to consider when structuring your answer.

Unit 3

Debriefing Activity 3.1

When Interbrand applied their formula to global brands the following ten emerged as the top ranking brands.

The world's ten most valuable brands:

Rank	Brand	2002 brand value ($ billion)
1	Coca-Cola	69.6
2	Microsoft	64.1
3	IBM	51.2
4	GE	41.3
5	Intel	30.9
6	Nokia	30.0
7	Disney	29.3
8	McDonald's	26.4
9	Marlboro	24.2
10	Mercedes	21.0

Debriefing Activity 3.2

You have developed a picture of your life, your past, present and future.

An organization is the same, but more complex with many more variables. So is a brand. Some of the changes in your life will have been certain (you have got older), some could have been predictable (grandparents die, children get more independent) but some not (friends leave the country, marry people you do not like) and so on.

The same happens with a brand. We know that brands age, but if it is a good brand still meeting its promise then longevity can be positive. Most of the top brands have been around for a long time. Some brands are successful because they meet a need in the short term but then disappear.

When a company capitalizes a brand, that is includes its equity on the balance sheet, it reduces the goodwill write-off to reserves. This makes the balance sheet appear much stronger and hence more attractive to banks if a company requires a loan. It also helps the company to meet the stock market rules on trading.

The most obvious effect of adding brand equity is a reduction of the gearing ratio, which is the company's borrowings expressed as a percentage of its net assets. When we add brands to the list of assets we make borrowings look smaller in comparison. As a result, a bank is more likely to offer larger loans since they perceive them to be more secure.

Another area where adding brands to the asset portfolio may help is in mergers and acquisitions. It helps companies to borrow more if they want to acquire a company as we have already discussed. But it can also help defensively by raising the value of a company so that fewer predators can afford to buy them.

But there are problems here. A balance sheet is intended to allow comparison between companies so that, for example, potential investors can make informed decisions. But if we want to make direct comparisons we need consistency. And there is not yet a consistent approach to how companies value brands and whether they value them at all. The rules on brand valuation with regard to the balance sheet vary from country to country. In Britain, brands can only be added to the balance sheet if they are acquired in a takeover, and even then they must be depreciated over 20 years.

Debriefing Activity 3.4

With almost every market there will have been significant changes in the recent past. These may have been as the result of macro-trends such as demography or micro-trends such as new competitors or a change in the balance of power between retailers and manufacturers. If we merely extrapolated past trends we would not have accurately predicted future performance.

Secondly, the future value of the brand may be dependent on the people managing it. So unless there is effective sales and marketing and infrastructure underpinning the brand, the future earnings might be overestimated (or underestimated).

And finally, there is the problem of separability. How can we separate the cash flows from one brand from others in the portfolio? If they use the same production, marketing and distribution system, how can we allocate the costs between the brands?

Unit 4

Debriefing Question 4.1

Obviously the answer to this question will depend on the product category in which you operate.

But the important issue is that you answer this question in terms of the need met, that is that you do not fall into the trap of marketing myopia.

So although your product may be a mop, its purpose is to provide a clean floor. If it is a pension scheme, its purpose is to provide financial security for the old. If it is a textbook, its purpose is to transfer knowledge. Without wishing to belabour this point, it is essential to specify need so that we can determine the appropriate competitive set.

So mops are competing with cloths as well as other mops, pensions with equities and so on.

Debriefing Activity 4.2

There are many and varied reasons for these gaps. Managers may think they know what they want but do not. Customers do not articulate their service requirements in a way that is easily translated into an operational service specification. The willingness and ability of employees to perform to specification may be a factor. There could be a promise gap where the external communications are promising more than the organization can deliver.

Debriefing Activity 4.4

Since the matrix specifies relative price and relative quality, it makes sense to index the figures using 100 as the break point on each axis.

The use of composite scores always blurs the picture. McGill Enterprises, for example, scores 5.3 but is only really let down by its efficiency rating. Also the use of average price per holiday may cover a whole range. Perhaps one company specializes in expensive weekend breaks and another in more cost-effective fortnights.

The problem of market definition rears its head as we need to decide who our competitors are. The travel market is a good example of one which has niches. Perception of high and low price and high and low quality will vary dramatically according to the consumer. A single mother of four living on benefit may see one holiday as high priced (for her) but reasonable quality; the same holiday may be seen as incredibly cheap but appalling quality for an affluent merchant banker. Similarly definitions of exclusivity are very personal. What might be exclusive to me probably would not seem so for Michael Douglas and Catherine Zeta Jones. Not all customers have the same needs. It is important to look at the differences between segment and to shape their needs accordingly. Also the weighting of the criteria may vary between different members of the DMU. In B2B markets, for example, you might expect the financial director to be more price sensitive but technical staff to focus on quality.

Debriefing Activity 4.5

It is always important to monitor your competitive price position as your customers will. You also need to check whether the same price is being offered through alternative distribution channels. Since all intermediaries will have a margin and add their own mark-up, the prices to the customer may well vary.

To analyse the value you are adding to the process you need to see how your cost structure works.

Debriefing Activity 4.6

Organizations need to look at each component and see how it can be manipulated to increase profit. One often neglected way is to review dealer margin. Increasing rate of sale can compensate for a reduced percentage.

Note: Make sure that you are familiar with the difference between manufacturer margin and retailer mark-up. Although both are often expressed as a percentage, they are calculated on a different base. If a product costs €60 to make and is sold to a retailer for €100, it makes a manufacturer margin of 40 per cent (calculated as a percentage of selling-on price). The retailer then sells it to the consumer for €120, making a mark-up of 20 per cent (calculated as a percentage of the buying-in price). These calculations represent the convention in most industries, though these may vary. Make sure that you understand how the margin and mark-up are calculated in your industry, for example sometimes margin is calculated on cost, in this case giving a margin of 67 per cent.

Debriefing Question 4.2

As we have already said, PR is very difficult to measure. At best any assessment will be subjective. The first step is to determine your objectives and then develop relevant measures against which to assess them. In the article above, both parties get mixed press and much will depend on the mindset of the reader. If the reader is already a consumer of bottled water, they may be convinced by Coca-Cola's claim of additional purity. A more cynical consumer may have their view reinforced by the reporting of Thames tap water being bottled and sold at a premium. Although the coverage is broadly critical of Coca-Cola in tone, the company is given a chance to respond and several inches are given to their explanation of the purifying process. Although there is no direct criticism of Thames Water, it is implied by the necessity of additional purification. The UK Water are therefore left in the position of defending an implied accusation which has no real foundation.

Unit 5

Debriefing Question 5.1

Managers use financial statements to manage effectively, to calculate their remuneration if their bonus is dependent on it and to forecast future performance based on historic trends.

Shareholders, as the legal owners of the company, can use them to hold the directors accountable for their performance.

Stock market investors and financial advisors use them to assess whether the company is likely to be a good or bad investment.

Banks will be interested in the company's published financial statements when deciding whether to agree a loan. They may also ask for financial forecasts before agreeing any substantial loan.

Trade suppliers may examine financial statements when determining how much credit to give a company and on what terms.

Customers may want to understand the financial position of the company before placing a major order.

Employees may be interested in seeing how well their organization is faring. In particular they may be concerned about its financial stability and profitability. Trade unions may use them to claim for higher wages for their members.

Competitors will want to know how their rival is performing financially.

Debriefing Activity 5.2

1. Fixed assets plus current net assets = £27 800 + £5400 = £33 200
2. Total assets minus current liabilities = £27 800 + £13 200 − £7800 = £33 200
3. Share capital plus reserves plus long-term creditors and provisions for liabilities and charges = £32 850 + £300 + £50 = £33 200.

It works! The capital employed in Diploma plc is £33 200 whichever method you choose.

Debriefing Activity 5.3

12 100

33 000 × 100 = 36.6 per cent

Debriefing Activity 5.4

The dividend cover is 8.1/4.6 = 1.77. This shows that the company is distributing nearly half its profit to its shareholders but retaining the other half for reinvestment in the company.

Unit 6

Debriefing Question 6.2

The Internet is probably changing your life both as a consumer and as a manager. Here are some examples but there are many more.

Many products and services are available online now. Consumers have high expectations of customer service. Comparison shopping is easier. Response times are expected to be rapid. We live in an era of instant gratification. Consumers shop internationally. Research can be done online.

Debriefing Question 6.3

The samples are different. The websites were probably different. The choice of product category may well affect the order of priority. The research objectives were probably different, one study was commissioned by a client with their own agenda, the other carried out by an agency with the likely aim of generating publicity.

Debriefing Question 6.4

Organizations such as ASH, health care professionals, medical associations, consumer groups.

Unit 7

Debriefing Activity 7.1

Most metaphors about organizations focus on organizational practices. These might be:

- Managerial skills
- Organizational structure
- Operations
- Organizational life cycle
- Strategic orientation
- People orientation
- Power orientation.

Taking this approach allows us to gain a better picture of the organization and its climate.

Debriefing Question 7.1

The company are launching far more products (up from 15 to 25) but they are being less successful (success rates are down from 67 to only 12 per cent). The percentage of sales from new products is declining (hardly surprising!). Those new products which are successful tend to be smaller. And process innovations are less dramatic leading only to marginal cost reduction. The payback period has also increased, probably as a result of the lower sales per new product and lower success rate.

So what does this mean? The company may be launching more but they are not succeeding. Perhaps the innovations are not needed by the customer, perhaps the screening process is not sufficiently rigorous. Sales per new product are low which may reflect the growing maturity of the market and increasing fragmentation. Maybe the new products are line extensions which would probably only add incremental volume anyway. Process cost savings are down. This could be because the previous cost savings made a big difference and any subsequent cost saving would be likely to seem small by comparison.

So what should the company do? A more rigorous screening process seems obvious since the product failure rate is high. A review of the market and customer needs would help. Perhaps also benchmarking against competitors to see if the market response is consistent. It may be that the organization is being reactive and launching me-too products rather than focusing on pioneer products which would add more value and generate a higher level of profit.

Unit 9

Debriefing Activity 9.1

You will notice how it is important to see how your assumptions affect your planning. The activity asks you to look at the effect of 10 per cent changes which are in themselves quite small but cumulatively have a huge impact. It also makes sense to factor in macro-environmental variables. You cannot alter these, but they may have a huge impact on your business. Integrate your PEST analysis into your scenario planning.

appendix 3

past examination papers and examiners' reports

The Chartered
Institute of Marketing

Professional Postgraduate Diploma in Marketing

61 – Analysis and Evaluation

Time: 14:00 – 17:00
Date: 6th December 2005

3 Hours Duration

This examination is in **TWO** sections.

PART A - Is compulsory and worth **50%** of total marks

PART B - Has **FOUR** questions; select **TWO**. Each answer will be worth **25%** of the total marks

DO NOT repeat the question in your answer, but show clearly the number of the questions attempted on the appropriate pages of the answer book.

Rough work and notes must be written into the answer book or on supplementary sheets and must be clearly identified.

Professional Postgraduate Diploma in Marketing

61 - Analysis and Evaluation

PART A

Protecting Money

There are three main competitors offering security services for banks within a certain geographic area. Business is won by contract which is normally put out for tender on an annual basis, although this varies depending on the financial services organisation. Once the tender has been won, the winning organisation offers security services such as money transfer protection between branches, and night watchmen and dogs etc. It also acts as consultants if a branch of the bank wishes to install a new alarm system.

The Big Three have very different profiles. Dennisons are an old established family firm, founded in 1935, run by the grandson of its founder and benefiting from years of experience in the marketplace, passed on from father to son. Impact Limited, by contrast, are relatively new in the market, but have recruited strongly, offering high incentive packages to experienced staff. Frost Finance are part of a larger group which offers security to a number of different sectors, each division being named after the sector it serves.

Table 1 below shows how the Big Three in this market (Frost Finance, Impact Limited and Dennisons) are performing.

Table 1 Market information

		2001	2002	2003	2004	2005
Frost Finance	Revenue euros (m)	10	12	13	14	14
	No. of contracts	5	6	7	7	7
Impact Limited	Revenue euros (m)	8	12	13	16	20
	No. of contracts	4	5	4	5	4
Dennisons	Revenue euros (m)	5	4	4	4	4
	No. of contracts	10	10	11	12	14
TOTAL MARKET	Revenue euros (m)	25	30	32	38	45
	No. of contracts	20	23	25	27	27

The above data has been based on a fictitious situation drawing on a variety of events and do not reflect management practices of any particular organisation.

PART A - Compulsory

Question One

As a consultant employed by a large multinational security business looking to enter the financial services sector, you have been asked to assist in measuring marketing attractiveness.

Using the information above, assess and comment on the following:

a. the relative share positions in 2005

(5 marks)

b. volume and value trends over time

(5 marks)

c. market size trends and structure

(5 marks)

d. strategies which appear to have been employed in the period 2001–2005, and their relative effectiveness

(10 marks)

e. the process you might follow to assess the possible benefits of entering this market.

(25 marks)

(Total 50 marks)

243

Part B - Answer TWO questions only

Question Two

How would you assess the capability of a biscuit manufacturer in a country of your choice to expand in international markets?

(Total 25 marks)

Question Three

"Not-for-profit organisations face different challenges to more traditional businesses but can benefit from the experience of the profit sector."

Critically evaluate this statement, illustrating your answer with examples of the transferability (or otherwise) of analytical models and processes developed for the profit sector.

(Total 25 marks)

Question Four

Evaluate the main challenges in collecting international market research, and advise a food retailer on how to minimise these when dealing with a less developed country.

(Total 25 Marks)

Question Five

Critically evaluate how a gaps model of service quality might help a car dealership (i.e. a firm that sells, services and repairs a particular manufacturer's vehicles) to develop its strategy.

(Total 25 Marks)

The Chartered
Institute of Marketing

Moor Hall, Cookham
Maidenhead
Berkshire, SL6 9QH, UK
Telephone: 01628 427120
Facsimile: 01628 427158
www.cim.co.uk

The Chartered
Institute of Marketing

Professional Postgraduate Diploma in Marketing

Analysis & Evaluation

SENIOR EXAMINER'S REPORT FOR STUDENTS AND TUTORS

DECEMBER 2005

SENIOR EXAMINER'S REPORT
FOR STUDENTS AND TUTORS

MODULE NAME: Analysis and Evaluation

AWARD NAME: Postgraduate Professional Diploma

---

1. General Strengths and Weaknesses of Candidates

The performance of the cohort was in line with previous cohorts on this module. However there continue to be very few A grades. This is disappointing since there continues to be a repetition of the problems with previous students.

On the whole students need to focus on:

- time management
- critical evaluation
- application of theory, particularly to the specific context given, rather then theory dump

More minor criticisms are the use of formatting inappropriate at this level eg the continuing use of the memo format and active voice.

2. Strengths and Weaknesses by Question

Question 1

The better students allocated their time appropriately, answered all sections of the question and used both qualitative and quantitative data to reach a coherent data. Some used graphs well to illustrate trends

However a significant proportion ignored the quantitative data completely (approx a quarter) and a similar proportion made inaccurate calculations. There was some confusion about the concept of relative market share although it would be expected that students at this level would be familiar with the concept from BCG at least.

There was also a tendency merely to repeat the information from the case rather than to integrate it or analyse it.

Apart from the problems illustrated above, the main contributor to poor performance was the answer to part (e). A significant number of students allocated insufficient time to this and wrote extremely brief answers to a part which accounted for 25 marks and should have therefore taken 25% of their time.

Some students also chose to answer Q1 holistically which made it more difficult for examiners to judge which part was being answered in which section of the report. Students should be encouraged to use the sections indicated in the question in their answer format to maximise their potential mark.

Question 2

This was a popular question with most students attaining a pass mark although with few excellent answers. The main problems here have already been referred to in the general comments but relate to students describing theories rather evaluating and applying. Some answers never mentioned the word "biscuit" and others only as a superficial attempt at context without demonstrating thoughtfulness about the specific challenges.

Question 3

Although this was not as popular a question, those who attempted this tended to fare better. They showed a greater appreciation of context, and also made more attempt at critical evaluation. There was clear evidence in many answers of the specific context of NFP, which may be the result of a self-selecting sample. A few however only used one model.

Question 4

This was also a commonly answered question. Marks were on the whole reasonable. The main criticism here of the weaker answers was that they did not answer the specific question set. Some focused on how to conduct an IMR study rather than the challenges and how to minimise them. Also some showed little knowledge of other countries.

Question 5

This was answered adequately by most students. There was considerable variation however in their knowledge of gaps models with many showing competent knowledge of a model (normally SERVQUAL-related), but others clearly confused. The best answers did a very thorough job of applying their model to the context of car dealerships

3.   Future Themes

The module will continue to reinforce the previous themes. Examiners will be looking for the students' ability to synthesise qualitative and quantitative data and reach relevant conclusions. Students need to be more focused on critical evaluation and application. More attention should be paid to higher level concepts such as shareholder value and brand equity.

The Chartered
Institute of Marketing

Professional Postgraduate Diploma in Marketing

Analysis and Evaluation

Time: 14.00 – 17.00

Date: 6th June 2006

3 Hours Duration

This examination is in **TWO** sections.

PART A – Is compulsory and worth **50%** of total marks

PART B – Has **FOUR** questions; select **TWO**. Each answer will be worth **25%** of the total marks

DO NOT repeat the question in your answer, but show clearly the number of the questions attempted on the appropriate pages of the answer book.

Rough work and notes must be written into the answer book or on supplementary sheets and must be clearly identified.

Professional Postgraduate Diploma in Marketing

Analysis and Evaluation

PART A

Niche Book Publishing

Niche Book Publishing (NBP) is a small independent publishing firm which was founded in 1910 by the current chairman's great grandfather. They have a restricted portfolio of 47 titles, written by their few authors (19). The company focuses on specialist books, such as the 'Guide to Freshwater Amphibians in Northern France', 'Classification of Lichen in Eastern Europe', 'South East Asian Proteans' and 'British Algae'. Their focus on specialist natural history has earned them a loyal, but restricted audience. The titles attract a price premium of around 50%. However, given their low print runs and high colour content, there are limited economies of scale, and therefore low profit margins, despite the relatively high prices.

NBP have a number of competitors, many of whom are far larger, such as Dorling Kindersley, Butterworth-Heinemann, Prentice Hall and Pearson. Some of their competitors are very similar in profile to themselves, being smaller niche players in family ownership. However, there are pressures in the industry for consolidation, as the competitive environment favours larger companies with attractive economies of scale.

The company employs 10 people, 8 of whom are young and inexperienced although enthusiastic. The company has a turnover of 5 million euros, against the industry average of 20 million euros, but this average masks the huge variation within the industry.

Other publishers have tended to target the broader educational markets of children and young adults whereas NBP's buyers tend to be academics or specialist groups. This allows them to gain a comprehensive understanding of their target market, even knowing some of their most loyal readers by name.

Depending on how the market is defined, NBP has a value market share of 25% (specialist natural history titles to academics), 0.5% (general natural history) or 0.001% (the total non-fiction market).

The geographic spread of NBP's sales is wide, covering Europe, South East Asia and Africa. Sales in Europe are predominantly UK; South East Asian sales come from Singapore, Colombo and Hong Kong, and African sales from Ghana. It could be argued that this reflects the fact that all titles are only available in English. NBP are considering whether to translate their existing titles into other languages, but are unsure whether the rewards will justify their investment. They are also undecided as to which language to launch first, if they take this step.

The above data has been based on a fictitious situation drawing on a variety of events and do not reflect management practices of any particular organisation.

PART A – Compulsory

Question One

a. Use a multi-dimensional portfolio matrix to show how NBP might evaluate their portfolio of titles and authors. What are the advantages and shortcomings of such a model? What are the strategic implications of the different boxes in the matrix?

(20 marks)

b. How might Value Chain Analysis be used to add value to NBP's offering? Critically evaluate the use of this technique.

(20 marks)

c. Explain how NBP could approach making the decision on whether or not to translate their titles into other languages, and if so which to choose.

(10 marks)

(Total 50 marks)

PART B – Answer **TWO** questions only

Question Two

Explain how an office equipment supplier can improve customer satisfaction levels with particular reference to complaints that are received. Evaluate how this might aid strategic decision-making.

(Total 25 marks)

Question Three

Advise a snack foods company on whether or not to measure brand equity and how this should be undertaken. In doing so, discuss the benefits and disadvantages of valuing brands.

(Total 25 marks)

Question Four

When advising a construction company dealing with a lesser developed country, explain the main challenges in undertaking international market research. In this context, evaluate the available research methods.

(Total 25 marks)

Question Five

Using an organisation of your choice, explain how to undertake a competitor analysis. Outline the content and structure of such an analysis and illustrate how each aspect can be used to inform strategic decision-making.

(Total 25 marks)

The Chartered
Institute of Marketing

Moor Hall, Cookham
Maidenhead
Berkshire, SL6 9QH, UK
Telephone: 01628 427120
Facsimile: 01628 427158
www.cim.co.uk

The Chartered
Institute of Marketing

Professional
Postgraduate Diploma
in Marketing

Analysis & Evaluation

**SENIOR EXAMINER'S REPORT FOR STUDENTS AND TUTORS
JUNE 2006**

**SENIOR EXAMINER'S REPORT
FOR STUDENTS AND TUTORS**

MODULE NAME: ANALYSIS & EVALUATION

AWARD NAME: PROFESSIONAL POSTGRADUATE DIPLOMA IN
MARKETING

DATE: JUNE 2006

1.   General Strengths and Weaknesses of Candidates

The performance of the cohort was in line with previous cohorts on this module. However there continues to be very few A grades. This is disappointing since there continues to be a repetition of the problems with previous students.

On the whole students still need to focus on:

1. Time management – students appear to be spending a disproportionate amount of time on the case as compared to the Part B questions. Students need to be aware that they are likely to maximise their marks by starting and completing a new question rather than over allocating time to completing an existing one.

2. Answer plans – there is evidence to suggest that students are writing plans for their answers. At this level it is difficult to see how students can successfully analyse and evaluate marketing issues without developing answer plans.

3. Critical evaluation as opposed to creating bullet point laundry lists

4. Application of theory, particularly to the specific context given, rather than theory dump – very little information regarding the context is provided by students in the executive summary

More minor criticisms are the use of formatting inappropriate at this level eg the continuing use of the memo format and active voice.

No particular questions proved unpopular. Overseas students this year also did particularly well.

PART A – Compulsory

Question 1

The main problems – as anticipated by the marking meeting – were the phenomenal amount of BCGs – which limited the max mark that could be given for 1a. The BCGs were generally adequately covered. I would estimate that less than ¼ of candidates discussed a DPM – and only a few of them did it well. The better candidates tended to score about 15 or so marks. Many candidates did not understand the concept of multi-dimensions. Few used the data in the case.

In terms of the value chain – the main problems seemed to be in not applying it – at least half the candidates described it well but failed to apply it to NBP. The critical evaluation was also very sketchy.

The third part of the question was addressed either very cursorily or very well – with little middle ground.

Question 2

This was the question with the widest variation. This question was also the third most popular question having been selected by almost half of the students.

There were a lot of poorly applied SERVQUAL models and very few seemed to tackle how customer satisfaction can aid SDM in anything other than a trite way. There was very little evidence of high marks for this question. Many ignored the focus on complaints.

Question 3

Half of the candidates selected this question making it the second most popular one selected by the candidates.

There were some good answers to this question with lots of keen understanding of equity, many methods of carrying it out and their advantages and disadvantages.

Question 4

This was the most popular and the best question tackled by all students. Some examiners noted that overseas students from LDCs were better at applying theory – much better than UK based students. This was a well answered question generally, although some students struggled with the detail of an LDC.

Question 5
This was the least popular question chosen by students. The better candidates answered this very well and strategically – the poorer ones just did a very cursory Porter's 5 forces – or no theory at all, unfortunately there was a higher number of poorer students who demonstrated very superficial understanding of a competitive environment. Students are appear to be more reliant on memorizing the model or theory without showing any understanding of the rationale or issues behind the models that would provide useful insights into marketing issues, a necessary skill required in senior marketing managers.

2.   Future Themes

The module will continue to reinforce the previous themes. Examiners will be looking for the students' ability to synthesize qualitative and quantitative data and reach relevant conclusions. Students need to be more focused on critical evaluation and application. More attention should be paid to higher level concepts such as shareholder value and brand equity. Marketing metrics including measures are an important component of this module.

appendix 4

curriculum information and reading list

Aim

The Analysis and Evaluation module covers the first part of strategic marketing in a strategic and global context. It aims to provide participants with the knowledge and skills required to undertake strategic analysis and evaluation of the organization's current situation as a foundation for making strategic marketing decisions. It sets strategic marketing in context as a key creator of stakeholder value and deals with strategic insights into the organization, its customers and the challenges it faces.

Related CIM Professional Marketing Standards

- ○ Define intelligence requirements and lead the intelligence gathering process.
- ○ Develop a detailed understanding of the organization and its environment.

Learning outcomes

Participants will be able to:

1. Explain the concept of business orientation and critically appraise the different orientations in management and planning and the roles of marketing used by organizations.
2. Identify the business intelligence required to inform the organization's strategy-making activities in domestic and international markets.
3. Assess the impact of the major trends in the strategic and global context on the strategy-making process.
4. Conduct and synthesize a detailed strategic audit of the organization's internal and external environments, including an evaluation of business performance, using appropriate tools and models and analysis of numerical data and management information to support decisions on key strategic issues.
5. Appraise the nature of culture in organizations and the importance of its 'fit' with strategy and operations across different cultures.
6. Synthesize a coherent and concise assessment of the situation facing an organization, and develop alternative scenarios.

Knowledge and skill requirements

Element 1: Strategic management and the role of marketing (10 per cent)

1. Demonstrate an understanding of the role of marketing in creating exceptional value for customers and shareholders.
2. Demonstrate an understanding of the role of marketing in organizations that are driven by performance measures other than shareholder value, for example not-for-profit organizations.
3. Critically evaluate the characteristics of the marketing models and criteria for success used in organizations with a strong market orientation.
4. Critically evaluate the characteristics of marketing models used by, and the challenges facing marketing in, organizations with a weak market orientation.
5. Give examples of the strategic planning process used in organizations and evaluate marketing's role within it.

Element 2: Evaluation of business and marketing performance (30 per cent)

1. Critically evaluate and use quantitative techniques for evaluating business and marketing performance over current and historic business cycles. Techniques to be covered should include:

   o Balanced scorecard, with an emphasis on customer and innovation measures.
   o Evaluation of marketing performance including the audit of marketing activities and valuation of marketing assets, such as brands.
   o Financial techniques such as shareholder value analysis (using total shareholder return and economic profit), financial ratio analysis, trend analysis, benchmarking and evaluation of historical financial decisions.

Element 3: Analysis of the internal environment (20 per cent)

1. Use and appraise the available techniques and processes for the objective assessment of the internal environment of an organization, including portfolio analysis, value chain, innovation audit and cultural web.
2. Critically evaluate the resource-based and asset-based views of the organization.
3. Demonstrate the ability to use appropriate information and tools to evaluate the core competencies, assets, culture and weaknesses of an organization.
4. Assess the 'fit' between an organization's culture and its current strategy.
5. Summarize the salient factors and insights emerging from the internal analysis.

Element 4: Analysis of the external environment (20 per cent)

1. Use and appraise the available techniques and processes for the objective assessment of the external environment covering the macro-environment, competitive environment, customers, channels and evaluation of the organization's offers against customer needs.
2. Define the organization's intelligence needs, research needs and resources required to support an analysis of the external environment.
3. Acquire and use appropriate information and tools to evaluate the organization's current competitive position, position within the value chain and sources of competitive advantage.

4. Develop customer insights by analysing potential and current customer bases and developing an understanding of their needs, preferences and buying behaviours (as a prelude to segmentation).
5. Use relevant techniques such as forecasting to quantify the opportunities available to an organization and any threats to its position.
6. Summarize the salient factors and insights emerging from the external analysis.
7. Consolidate, synthesize and distil the analysis of the internal and external environments to provide an insightful summary of the organization's market position and performance.
8. Identify the implications for the organization's future and strategic decisions to be made using conclusions drawn from the internal and external analysis.

Element 5: Characteristics of the global and international marketplace (20 per cent)

1. Assess the variances in key factors influencing customer buying behaviours and competition in global and international markets.
2. Identify the specific challenges in collecting and interpreting information to develop a detailed understanding of customers and markets in a foreign market and explain how they may be overcome.
3. Identify and assess the processes, techniques and factors to be used in assessing the attractiveness of international markets (e.g. assessing rate of development of economic development, cultures, consumer profiles etc.).
4. Assess the position of an organization working in an international or global marketplace.
5. Critically assess the capability of an organization to expand in international markets taking into account factors such as its cultural expertise, organizational structure issues, current strategic objectives (defending home market from attack, operating in foreign market etc.) and so on.
6. Critically evaluate the effectiveness and value of ICT in cross-border marketing.

Assessment

CIM will offer a single form of assessment based on the learning outcomes for this module. It will take the form of an invigilated, time-constrained assessment throughout the delivery network. Candidates' assessments will be marked centrally by CIM.

Analysis and Evaluation

Core texts

Collier, P.M. (2006) *Accounting for Managers: Interpreting Accounting Information for Decision-making*, 2nd edition, Chichester: John Wiley and Sons.

Doole, I., Lowe, R. (2005) *Strategic Marketing Decisions in Global Markets*, London: Thomson.

Gilligan, C., Wilson, R. (2004) *Strategic Marketing Management: Planning, Implementation and Control*, 3rd edition, Oxford: Butterworth-Heinemann.

Syllabus guides/Workbooks

BPP (2006) *Analysis and Evaluation*, London: BPP Publishing.

Lomax, W., Raman, A. (2006) *Analysis and Evaluation*, Oxford: BH/Elsevier.

Supplementary readings

Aaker, D. (2005) *Strategic Market Management*, 7th edition, US: Wiley.

BH (2006) *CIM Revision Cards: Analysis and Evaluation*, Oxford: BH/Elsevier.

Bradley, F. (2003) *Strategic Marketing*, Chichester: John Wiley and Sons.

Doole, I., Lowe, R. (2004) *International Marketing Strategy: Analysis, Development and Implementation*, 4th edition, London: Thomson Learning.

Doyle, P. (2000) *Value Based Marketing: Marketing Strategies for Corporate Growth and Shareholder Value*, Chichester: John Wiley and Sons.

Doyle, P. (2001) *Marketing Management and Strategy*, 3rd edition, Harlow: Pearson.

Hooley, G.J., Saunders, J.A., Piercy, N.F. (2003) *Marketing Strategy and Competitive Positioning*, 3rd edition, Harlow: Prentice-Hall.

Johansson, J.K. (2005) *Global Marketing: Foreign Entry, Local Marketing and Global Management*, 4th edition, Maidenhead: McGraw-Hill.

Johnson, G., Scholes, K. (2004) *Exploring Corporate Strategy: Text and Cases*, 7th edition, Harlow: Prentice-Hall.

Rugimbana, R., Nwankwo, S. (2003) *Cross-cultural Marketing*, London: Thomson.

Overview and rationale

Approach

This module has been developed to provide the knowledge and skills for analysis and evaluation of performance required by strategic marketers. It is based on the statements of marketing practice to ensure that it prepares participants for practice at a strategic marketing level. Participants and tutors will note that the module is integrated both horizontally and vertically across the range of CIM syllabus modules.

Participants with appropriate experience should find that they are able to apply the knowledge learned immediately within their organization and therefore add value quickly to themselves and their employer.

Syllabus content

The balance of weighting allocated to each of the five elements reflects the importance of the area to the achievement of learning and performance outcomes, and the depth and breadth of the material to be covered. Although each area may be regarded as a discrete element, there are clear progressions and overlaps in the knowledge, and skills requirements have important implications for the delivery of the module.

Element 1: Strategic management and the role of marketing (10 per cent)
This element focuses on the role of marketing within organizations, and in particular the differences in its role in organizations with varying degrees of market orientation and contexts. It is important that participants understand how marketing creates value for customers, shareholders and other stakeholders and how the role can alter in different contexts. Within this, the different criteria used to define and assess success should be explored.

Element 2: Evaluation of business performance (30 per cent)
Organizations need to evaluate their past and current performance to make informed decisions about future activity. This element looks at the processes and techniques available to do this, acknowledging their strengths and limitations. In particular participants should be aware of the measures and quantitative techniques used, both financial and marketing-based. Emphasis is placed on sources of data and potential bias.

Element 3: Analysis of the internal environment (20 per cent)
The first stage in objectively analysing an organization's position is to review its internal capabilities and environment. This element examines the available techniques and processes, emphasizing the need for objectivity. Participants should understand corporate capabilities, identify core competencies, and itemize and evaluate marketing assets. The relationship between culture and strategy is also important, particularly the degree of market orientation. There is a clear expectation that participants will be able to demonstrate effective use of a variety of techniques for analysis and evaluation such as Porter's value chain and portfolio analysis.

Element 4: Analysis of the external environment (20 per cent)
This element builds on the internal environmental analysis, turning to the organization's position in the external environment. Again the available techniques and processes are examined. Participants should be familiar with and be able to conduct an analysis of and draw conclusions from both the macro level and the micro level, paying particular attention to the quantification of trends. Participants are expected to demonstrate knowledge of and an ability to use the relevant frameworks and models such as PEST/SLEPT and Porter's Five Forces. At the end of this element, participants should be able to draw together the results from their internal and external analyses to provide an objective summary of an organization's competitive position and performance. In addition they should be able to review the implications for the organization's future.

Element 5: Characteristics of the global marketplace (20 per cent)
As organizations increasingly operate in a global marketplace, there is a need to appreciate the difference in approaching foreign markets and dealing with foreign competitors. Participants should be aware of and be able to evaluate the available frameworks and their appropriateness. This module covers entry evaluation procedures for candidate countries as well as the role of the Internet in developing the global village.

Delivery approach

Although it is expected that the learning outcomes should be achieved as discrete goals of attainment, it is assumed that tutors will also recognize and impart an understanding of the integrated nature of the syllabus content. Practical exercises, such as data gathering and the application of models and frameworks, are critical to the development of skills required in the module. Particular emphasis should be placed on the critical and objective evaluation of data, being aware of potential bias. It is important that the projects or case studies illustrate the integration of analysis and evaluation within the process of strategy formulation.

Additional resources

Introduction

Texts to support the individual modules are listed in the syllabus for each module. This Appendix shows a list of marketing journals, press and websites that tutors and participants may find useful in supporting their studies at stage 3.

Marketing journals

Participants can keep abreast of developments in the academic field of marketing by reference to the main marketing journals.

- *Corporate Reputation Review*
- *European Journal of Marketing*
- *Harvard Business Review*
- *International Journal of Advertising*
- *International Journal of Consumer Behaviour*
- *International Journal of Corporate Communications*
- *International Journal of Market Research*
- *Journal of the Academy of Marketing Science*
- *Journal of the Market Research Society*
- *Journal of Marketing*
- *Journal of Marketing Communications*
- *Journal of Marketing Management*
- *Journal of Product and Brand Management*
- *Journal of Services Marketing*
- *Marketing Review.*

Press

Participants will be expected to have access to current examples of marketing campaigns and so should be sure to keep up to date with the appropriate marketing and quality daily press, including:

- *Campaign*
- *Internet Business*
- *Marketing*
- *The Marketer*
- *Marketing Week*
- *Revolution*
- *The Economist.*

265

Websites

The Chartered Institute of Marketing

www.cim.co.uk	CIM website containing case studies, reports and reviews
www.connectedinmarketing.com	A CIM site providing information on current marketing issues and applications
www.cim.co.uk/learningzone.com	Website for CIM students and tutors containing study information, past exam papers and case study examples. Also access to 'the marketer' articles online.

Publications online

www.revolution.haynet.com	*Revolution* magazine
www.brandpublic.com	*Marketing* magazine.
www.FT.com	A wealth of information for cases (now charging)
www.IPA.co.uk	Need to register – communication resources
www.booksites.net	*Financial Times*/Prentice-Hall text websites

Sources of useful information

www.acnielsen.co.uk	AC Nielsen – excellent for research
http://advertising.utexas.edu/world/	Resources for advertising and marketing professionals, participants and tutors
www.bized.com	Case studies
www.esomar.nl	European body representing research organizations – useful for guidelines on research ethics and approaches
www.dma.org.uk	The Direct Marketing Association
www.eiu.com	The Economist Intelligence Unit.
www.euromonitor.com	Euromonitor consumer markets
www.europa.eu.int	The European Commission extensive range of statistics and reports relating to EU and member countries
www.managementhelp.org/research/research.htm	Part of the 'Free Management Library' – explaining research methods
www.marketresearch.org.uk	The MRS site with information and access to learning support for participants – useful links on ethics and code of conduct
www.oecd.org	OECD statistics and other information relating to member nations including main economic indicators
www.quirks.com	An American source of information on marketing research issues and projects
www.un.org	United Nations publish statistics on member nations
www.worldbank.org	World bank economic, social and natural resource indicators for over 200 countries. Includes over 600 indicators covering GNP per capita, growth, economic statistics and so on.

Case sites

www.bluelagoon.co.uk	Case – SME website address
www.ebay.com	Online auction – buyer behaviour
www.glenfiddich.com	Interesting site for case and branding
www.interflora.co.uk	e-Commerce direct ordering
www.moorcroft.co.uk	Good for relationship marketing
www.ribena.co.uk	Excellent targeting and history of comms

© CIM 2007

Index

6 Cs framework, 154

Acquisition cost, 48
Advertising, 95–7
Asset utilization ratios, 116
Assets, 110
Audit of marketing activities, 78
  complaining, 85
  product, 80
  SERVQUAL, 83

B2B model, 3
  see also Capital projects
Balanced scorecard, 41, 51
Base profit, 48
BCG growth–share matrix, 161
  market growth, 163
  market share, 161
Brand, 62
  current or replacement cost, 67
  future earnings potential, 67
  incremental value added, 67
  interbrand model, 68
Brand equity, 62
  brand valuation, 66
Breakeven volume, 89

Capital, 110
  employed, 110
  projects, 3
  structure ratios, 118
Cash cows, 164, 166
Competitive advantage, 201–17
Competitor orientation, 8
Core competence, 202
Corporate strategy, 20
  determining competitive
    positioning, 21
  identification of customer
    requirements, 20
  implementing the marketing
    strategy, 21
  role of marketing in, 20
Cost of sales, 110
Creditors, 110
Culture, 179, 195
Current assets, 110

Customer orientation, 8
Customer satisfaction and service
  quality, 81
  services, 82

Day's matrix, 209
Debtors, 110
Direct marketing, 93
Directional policy matrix (DPM), 167
Distribution audit, 97
Dogs, 165

Economic value added, 122
Environmental monitoring, 135
Environmental scanning, 134

Fast moving consumer goods
  (FMCG), 3
Financial ratio analysis, 114
Financial statements, 111
  costs, 113
  profit, 113
Fixed assets, 110

Generic strategies, 209
  assessing risk, 213
  scenario planning, 213
  strategy selection, 210

Incremental value added, 67
Innovation audit, 173
  cognitive styles of the senior management
    team, 176
  measures of innovation orientation, 175
  organizational climate, 174
  policies and practices to support
    innovation, 175
Interbrand model, 68
Interfunctional co-ordination, 8
Internal environment, 157–7
International market intelligence
  gathering, 181
  primary research, 185
  scanning international markets/countries, 186
  secondary research, 184
Investor ratios, 119
Issue analysis, 154

Liabilities, 110
Liquidity ratios, 117
Loyalty, 47

Macro-environment, 134, 138
  demographic factors, 138
  economic factors, 139
  legal and political factors, 140
  physical factors, 141
  social and cultural factors, 139
  technological factors, 142
Management accounts, 114
  asset utilization ratios, 116
  capital structure ratios, 118
  financial ratio analysis, 114
  liquidity ratios, 117
  profitability ratios, 115
Market attractiveness, 167–8
Market definition, 43
Market entry methods, 192
Market entry strategy alternatives, 193
Market orientation, 8, 12
Market share, 43
  and profitability, 46
Marketing activities, audit of, 75–102
Marketing and value, 20
Marketing audits, 77
Marketing environment, 134–5
Marketing Intelligence System,
      179, 189
Marketing metrics, 38–57
Marketing philosophy, 12
Marketing planning, 21
Marketing stakeholders, 19
Micro-environment, 134, 144
  competition, 148
  customers, 144
  intermediaries, 151
  publics, 151
  suppliers, 150

Net operating profit, 110
New Product Development (NPD),
      61, 80, 140
New Service Development
      (NSD), 80
Not-for-profit, organization, 3

Objectives, 41, 42
Operating costs, 48

Organizational climate, 174
  attitude survey, 174
  metaphors, 174
Outsourcing, 124

PBIT, 110
Performance outcomes, 42
  market definition, 43
  market share, 43
  timescale, 44
  volume and value, 44
Porter's Five Forces, 152
Portfolio analysis models, 161
  BCG growth-share matrix, 161
  directional policy matrix (DPM), 167
Portfolio analysis, 160
Price premium, 48
Pricing strategy, 86
Problem children, 165
Profitability ratios, 115
Profitability, 46
Public, 151
  consumer action groups, 152
  financial community, 151
  government–central and local, 152
  media, 152
  organization itself, 152
Public relations, 92

Ratio analysis, 120, 121
Referrals, 48
Resource-based view (RBV), 160, 161
Revenue growth, 48
Risk, assessing, 213
ROCE, 41

Sales promotion, 91
Scenario planning, 55, 202, 213
SERVQUAL, 83
Shareholder value analysis, 121
SMEs, 41
Stars, 165
Stock, 110
Strategic market management process, 23
SWOT analysis, 153

Target return on sales, 89
Timescale, 44

Value chain analysis, 160, 172